INTUITIVE LIVING:

A PRACTICAL GUIDE FOR WOMEN

WHO WANT TO DEEPLY TRUST THEMSELVES

Hille House
PUBLISHING

Concept: Krystal Hille
Editor: Vanessa Frazon-Nelson
Cover Design: Stephanie Wicker-Campbell (Muse Design)
Formatting: Shahid Aziz
Publishing: Hille House Publishing

Disclaimer:
The authors in this book do not dispense medical advice or prescribe the use of any technique as a form of treatment for physical, emotional, or medical problems without the advice of a physician, either directly or indirectly. The intent of the authors is only to offer information of general nature to help you in your quest for emotional, physical, and spiritual well-being. In the event you use any of the information in this book for yourself, the authors and the publisher assume no responsibility for your actions.

Copyright © 2022 by Hille House Publishing

All rights reserved.

Apart from any fair dealing for the purposes of research or private study, or criticism or review, as permitted under the Copyright, Designs, and Patents Act 1988, this publication may only be reproduced, stored, or transmitted, in any form or by any means, with the prior permission in writing of the copyright owner, or in the case of the reprographic reproduction in accordance with the terms of licensees issued by the Copyright Licensing Agency. Enquiries concerning reproduction outside those terms should be sent to the publisher.

CONTENTS

Introduction by Krystal Hille iii

PART-I - TEACHINGS ON INTUITION

Dr. John Demartini : Voids, Values, Instincts, Impulses And Intuition 3

James M. Powell : Intuition Hacks 15

Cindy D Cerecer : Living Intuitively Through Connection With Source 24

Katerina Lenarcic : Your Greatest Gift To Humanity 35

Farrah Miller : Intuition Is Our Guiding Light 44

Tracy Jenkins : Embrace Your Intuition And Trust Your Path 54

Daniel Werner : Don't Figure It Out – Feel 63

PART-II - THE FEMININE AND INTUITION

Brenda K. Johnson : Strength Plus Sisterhood Equals Success 75

Randa Sultan : Banging My Head Against The Wall 84

Christiane Ameya : Womb Awakening 94

Justina Casuarina : Your Blood Is Sacred 103

Eva Arissani : She Phoenix: The Rise 113

PART-III - INTUITION IN PERSONAL DEVELOPMENT

Isabelle Tierney : Your Intuition's Greatest Obstacle 125

Jules Schroeder : Intuitive Action 135

Niki Woods : The Lies I Told Myself 144

Sophia Harvey : Embodied Remembrance 153

Stacey Hollowood : Feel It And Heal It 163

Irma Vargas : The Magic Of Seeing Around Corners 171

PARTT-IV - INTUITIVE PRINCIPLES OF ART, NATURE & EMBODIMENT

Kelly Boucher : Radical Trust: Attending And Attuning To The World 181

Rivka Worth : The Stories We Tell Ourselves 192

Kate Lionis : Sitting With It... 201

Bianca de Reus : Loving Whispers Of A Furry Kind 210

Kate Gardner : The Courage To Cleanse And Connect................................. 221

Joanne Makas : Embodied Awareness 230

About Hille House Publishing 239

INTRODUCTION

*I*ntuitive awareness is becoming an increasingly important skill to master as we are moving into the Aquarian Age, where old ways of living from the mind alone, simply don't work any more. If you're reading this, you've heard the call. Congratulations for paying attention.

Living intuitively means that we can come into deeper alignment with our soul essence and co-create our lives with a higher power, instead of co-creating it with fear. If we want to maintain, or rather regain, even discover our sanity and that feeling of ease and flow, then it is of utmost importance to stop prostituting ourselves to the expectations of others, or to social and political pressures.

It's time to stop selling ourselves out to other people's values, ideas of who we should be or what we should do.

Have you ever gotten sucked into the reality of your family after some time away? Have you ever been swept away by certain mainstream narratives? Have you ever submitted to the expectations of your friends, or to the beliefs of your partner? Have you ever noticed yourself shapeshifting based on who others want you to be? I know I have.

As a teenager, I was the perfect diplomat and could easily understand everyone else's perspective. I was also a chameleon and often didn't have access to my own feelings or opinions for fear of conflict and abandonment. They were frozen and locked away deep within my unconscious mind. As an adult, I have always made a stand in the world, but after the recent dissolution of my 11-year marriage, I had to re-define who I am beyond the projections of another. Was it even my mission that I was standing for? Hille House Publishing was born in response to this question.

What are you taking a stand for? Is it really yours? Or is it that of your fears, your family, your partner, your friends, or society? And why?

Are you still allowing fear to make important life choices?

Are you still allowing the frightened inner four-year-old to hold you back?

Are you still concerned about what others think of you?

There are many archetypes that are born out of the need to belong, to be loved and to be safe, such as the pleaser, the martyr and the victim. These archetypes belong to the wounded feminine within all of us, especially those of us who identify as women.

They often come out of our natural desire to nurture. But when that natural mother-archetype impulse becomes enmeshed with our fears and feelings of lack, it becomes dysfunctional and out of alignment with our soul. That's when we do anything to stay safe and loved, often to our own detriment. That's when we fall into someone else's reality.

We've all done it, because we are human and hold duality within us. But our intuition can guide us back into equilibrium if we allow ourselves to listen. Global thought leader and human behaviour expert Dr. John Demartini expands on this concept in his chapter. When we release the shame around our human weaknesses and accept them as 'well-meaning' parts of ourselves, instead of enemies, we can claim our wholeness. We can then seek love, safety and belonging in a healthy way instead of abandoning ourselves in the process.

When we come from the fear to fulfil our needs, we literally can't access our intuition. It's physiologically impossible. Impossible! Isabelle Tierney explores how she discovered this phenomena in her chapter.

To recognise our intuition we must get into a calm, relaxed state. Katerina Lenarcic, Kate Lionis and Kelly Boucher, in particular, share tools that have worked for them on this journey.

Once we begin to hear our intuition, we also hear the even louder voice of the ego that screams at us to stay in our safe and familiar environment. The mind doesn't want us to leave that dysfunctional relationship or quit that soul-draining job. Because we are wired to do more to avoid pain than to seek pleasure, our intuition has to get louder too. If we ignore it, it will send us messages in the form of accidents, illness, or loss. This book is full of examples of the universal journey that ultimately leads us into the embodiment of our true essence. Randa Sultan, Sophia Harvey and Rivka Worth share powerful examples of this process.

Are you ready to find the courage to dissolve the inner conflict of clashing values? Are you prepared to trust intuition despite your logical mind? James M Powell, Jules Schroeder, and Cindy Cerecer offer tools to take the first steps towards that intention.

The dysfunctionality of the outer world is reflected in our inner self. In order to change the world, we must first heal our own dysfunctionality. Every awakening soul goes on a hero's journey to overcome the inner chaos and contradiction of head-heart, intuition-impulse dualities before they arrive in their zone of flow where they can express the yin-yang nature of their being. When we learn to embrace and accept our light *and* our darkness, the darkness loses power *over* us and instead contributes its power *towards* our dreams and desires.

It is evident in the lives of many that magic unfolds when we do our inner work and learn to embrace our shadows. Niki Woods, Tracy Jenkins, Kate Gardner, Farrah Miller, Daniel Werner and Stacey Hollowood dive into this in their chapters.

Decisions, decisions...

Over the years, I've had many conversations with coaching clients and friends who were in conflict about large life decisions. Should I leave my partner? Should I move overseas to chase my dream job? Should I follow my passion and leave a workplace that no longer lights my fire? Can I afford to stay true to myself in the face of losing job security? What about safety?

In these moments, we are all confronted with the different parts of our being: the five-year-old that is yearning for safety, belonging and love; the mind that is trying to keep us safe; the heart wishing to fly free and follow passion, joy, and adventure. Decisions can be agonising. Unless we address the underlying fears, unless we can bring all the different aspects within our being into wholeness, we can't step into our zone of flow or find the magic life wants to gift us.

Making this shift is not easy, but absolutely possible. To live a fulfilled life, means to step into the courage to follow our inner knowing against the odds, trust in our ability to land on our feet, and have faith that the universe has our back.

Until we have taken enough small, courageous steps to develop our faith, we can borrow it from the stories of others. This book is full of examples where contributors have followed their inner voice which has led them exactly where they needed to be. Not always the first time, mind you.

I was no different.

One night in bed, I felt sick to my stomach. I thought I was about to throw up, because his naked skin repulsed me. This was the moment I realised I had to act on what I had known for a rather long time. At age 31, I had to end my marriage. My mind had delayed this decision for months. Home renovations aren't finished. It's not convenient. I am not ready.

Well, are we ever ready? Are we ever ready to become pregnant, lose a loved one, have cancer, or get fired from a secure job? I don't think so. Our human mind is too attached to security, safety and belonging. But our soul has its own timeline *and* its own means.

After the divorce, everything stalled. I started asking myself what was keeping me in England and turned to the universe to ask where I was meant to be? Back to my home country Germany? Back in the USA? Another English speaking country?

The universe responded. Suddenly, friends were travelling to Australia and I met Australians at a new temp job. Then, a dream: I was in a plane and just as the plane was about to land, I heard the words: "Welcome to Australia!". In that exact moment, my alarm went off as if the universe was saying: "Haven't you got it yet?"

Yes, I got it. But I was still hesitant, because it was such a big decision! Still, I asked the question and the universe responded so powerfully through synchronicities and the dream. I had promised myself that I would never ever ignore my intuition again just because it wasn't 'convenient'.

It wasn't convenient to initiate a divorce and it wasn't convenient to relocate continents. I didn't even know how I would stay in Australia beyond my tourist visa. All of my credit cards were maxed out except one that had just enough money on it to book a flight to Australia. I had put that money aside to pay my taxes. But since there were such strong signs (and I like to think that I learn from my mistakes) I found my courage, took a leap of faith and bought that flight. A week later, the *exact* amount I had spent to make my dream a reality, came back to me in the form of a translating job I had applied for ages ago. You see, the universe has its own means. All we have to do is allow ourselves to stay in inspired action, be courageous and trust.

The parachute doesn't open until we jump out of the plane. There is always a period of free fall where we can't hold onto anything visible or tangible, where we must hold onto faith.

But what about the everyday decisions?

Despite this trust and faith in my inner guidance, regarding big decisions, I still wasn't determined, powerful, or strong in everyday choices. It's almost as if the focused attention on co-creation with intuition needs to be trained separately in everyday life because the fear of lack of safety is so strong it creates interference patterns.

Have you ever ended up in a relationship or a job, waking up one day wondering how you got there? This usually happens when we go on autopilot, allowing our patterns to take the driver's seat.

It's as if patterns prevent awareness and allow out-of-alignment situations to take place. Ultimately, we grow through the struggles these misaligned situations create. Just like the emerging butterfly must strengthen the muscles of its wings by freeing itself from the cocoon, we must develop our strength in relationship with the world. We can be guided, but if we want to take flight like the butterfly, we must walk our path without crutches, or we will not develop our full potential. We must let go of codependency and learn to deeply trust ourselves and our intuitive guidance.

How to read this book

Do what feels best for you. Feel free to start at the beginning and work through the entire book or read in a mosaic fashion, jumping to the section or title that speaks to your soul in the moment.

Regardless of your chosen method, all the experts provide tools that have helped them embody their wholeness and walk their walk guided by intuition. In some chapters you will learn through stories, in others, through scientific and/or spiritual principles, or both.

There are four sections in this book that focus on the different aspects of intuition. The first section, *Teachings on Intuition*, explores intuitive principles and tools.

The Feminine and Intuition, touches on the special relationship the feminine body, the womb, and the female cycle have to intuition. If you are curious about this dynamic, you will find the chapters by Christiane Ameya and Justina Casuarina enlightening. Brenda K. Johnson and Eva Arrisani celebrate feminine power, female strength and sisterhood.

In the section on *Intuition in Personal Development*, you will learn from the voices of experts specialising in this field including Irma Vargas, whose chapter focuses on lessons in trust.

The final section, *Intuitive Principles of Art, Nature and Embodiment*, focusses on qualities that assist us to access our intuitive knowing, including Bianca Reus' chapter that guides us to intuitively connect to our furry friends, and Joanne Makas' chapter on embodied awareness.

It is my intention that this book will bring inspiration, provide hope and share tools to help you deepen into aligned living.

It is my prayer that from this place, we can create a world of sovereign, empowered humans who celebrate their unique essence and trust their inner guidance.

It is my vision to create a future where humans are profoundly connected to themselves, know and enact their values, and follow their inner compass to embody intuitive living as a natural way of being.

With love,

Krystal

PART I

TEACHINGS ON INTUITION

DR. JOHN DEMARTINI

VOIDS, VALUES, INSTINCTS, IMPULSES AND INTUITION

There are moments in life that change the trajectory of who we become. I remember two of those moments vividly.

The first one was when I turned 17 and met Paul C. Bragg. After a childhood of learning difficulties, the message he presented that night inspired me to think that maybe I could overcome my learning problems and go on to become verbally intelligent. I had never thought this could be possible before. I thought I was going to be a surfer, not that surfers are not intelligent, but it's a different form of intelligence.

Being a highschool dropout, I decided to go back to school and try to take a General Education Degree (G.E.D.) test, which was equivalent to a high school degree.

When I enrolled in my first college-level course I failed the class. I received a grade of 27 instead of the 72 I needed to pass, and I was really distraught. I thought maybe this dream about being academically intelligent was just a delusion.

That's when my mom found me crying in the living room under this Bible stand that she had, which sits in my office today. She asked me, "What happened, son?"

I said, "Well, I blew the test. I needed a 72 to pass and I got a 27."

She sat there quietly for a moment. Then she put her hand on my shoulder and said, "Son, whether you become a great teacher and philosopher and travel the world, like you say you want to do now, or whether you return to Hawaii to ride giant waves like you've done, or whether you return to the streets and panhandle as a bum, I just want to let you know that your father and I are going to love you no matter what you do."

In that moment, her presence and her unconditional love made me put my hand into a fist and look upward. I saw the same vision I had the night that I met Paul Bragg, of me standing in front of a million people speaking. Probably a dissociated illusion at the time, but that's what I saw. In that moment, I reclaimed that vision.

I promised myself that I'm going to master these things called reading and studying and learning, that I'm going to master these things called teaching, healing and philosophy. That I'm going to do whatever it takes, travel whatever distance and pay whatever price, to share my service of love across the planet. I'm not going to let any human being on the face of the Earth stop me, not even myself! And I had this moment of determination, there was no turning back.

I got up to hug my mom, then walked into my room. I got a Funk and Wagnalls Dictionary out. If you bought $20 worth of food at Kroger's supermarket, you were given an encyclopedia or dictionary. I got the dictionary, and I made a commitment that I was going to read, study and learn 30 words a day. I was going to spell them, pronounce them and understand the meaning of them as best I could. Every day, my mom would test me on 30 words until my vocabulary was strong enough that I could go to school and eventually pass that test.

Soon my vocabulary grew beyond the essential and I ended up not only passing but I started to excel. I never stopped reading from that day forward.

My mom's intuition of what to say at that moment was powerful. Something probably only a mom could say. Something that I needed to hear at that moment. Her intuition led her to say the right thing at the right time in the right place and it made a meaningful trajectory change, and that confidence changed my life.

Being in my mom's presence when I faced my biggest obstacle was significant to me. So was my meeting with Paul Bragg. Those two events together created a massive change in the course of my life. One was my mom's centered and intuitive state that enabled her to know exactly what to say in that moment. The other was an inspirational epiphany about what I wanted to do with my life, when I was in meditation with Paul Bragg.

Our Voids determine our Values

I sometimes wonder if I would have become who I am today, traveling the world and teaching millions of people, if I hadn't found it so difficult to learn as a child. My learning disability created a void that was aching to be filled. This void created a significant value.

Whatever we perceive to be most missing can become that which becomes most important. I did not only have learning difficulties as a child, but was also born with a speech impediment and with an arm and leg that turned inward. Until I was four years old, I had to wear braces on my arm and leg and I had to use strings and buttons in my mouth to properly use the muscles in my mouth.

The void of the restriction on speech and movement made me want to be free, unrestricted and to speak out. So now I travel the world. My internal affirmation is that the universe is my playground, the world is my home, every country is a room in my house, and every city is a platform to share my heart and soul. The movement constraint made me want to be global and the speech impediment created a desire to be heard.

Because of my learning problems, my first-grade teacher said that I would never amount to anything. They thought that I would never be able to read or write, probably never communicate effectively. That void, later, when I realized I could overcome it, pushed me to want to learn how to read, speak properly, travel the world, be of service, amount to something and make some sort of memorable difference.

There is a sort of a polarity in a perception of something missing and the perception of wanting to fulfill it.

The hierarchy of your values is derived from the hierarchy of the voids that you perceive. And, as stated before, whatever is perceived to be most missing can become most important. If you perceive you don't have a relationship, you'll search for a relationship. If you perceive you don't have business or income, you'll perceive a way to strive for a way of solving that. So in my case, those deep core voids, once I realized I could overcome and overpower them, became very important to me.

Today, when I read my mission statement, I can see that all those voids have culminated in a highly focused objective to transcend them. I am grateful for those voids. If I hadn't had that teacher saying that I wouldn't amount to anything and if I hadn't had learning problems, I wouldn't be who I am today. I am grateful for them.

> *Anything you can't say 'thank you' for is baggage*
>
> *and anything you can say 'thank you' for is fuel*

I'm a firm believer that yes, you have voids, but those are often the greatest drivers. I know a gentleman who had health problems when younger and he became one of the greatest, most driven doctors. I became a neurologist specializing as a chiropractor for spinal concerns because my mom had Lou Gehrig's disease, my dad had Parkinson's disease, and I had strychnine cyanide poisoning when I was a teenager. All of those illnesses affect the neuromuscular conditions. So those voids helped initiate some of those values. They are all gifts and there is nothing in life that is not a gift. And if you look carefully, everything that happens in your life is 'on the way' not 'in the way'.

Overcoming Victimhood and Self-doubt

It can take time to shift our perspective to see the opportunity instead of the obstacle. Until we do, we can be riddled with self-doubt, especially when we allow ourselves to fall into other people's realities and try to take on other people's values in order to be loved. To me, this self-doubt is not failure, it's feedback that we are not living in alignment with our own true highest values.

Every human being has a set of priorities, a set of values, things that are most to least important to them. These sets of values are as unique as our fingerprints and whatever is highest on that list of values, we are spontaneously inspired to fulfill. But whatever is lower on that list, requires external extrinsic motivation to accomplish.

Anytime you're attempting to do something that is lower on your list of values, you're going to be frustrated, you're going to procrastinate and hesitate, instead of being disciplined, reliable and focused.

So often, people compare themselves to other people they put on pedestals. They go into a mall and see somebody they think is more intelligent, more successful, more attractive, physically fitter, spiritually more advanced, socially more connected, has more wealth, or a more stable relationship. The moment they compare themselves to others, instead of comparing their daily actions to what they value most, they automatically inject the values of these other people and attempt to live these other people's values and lives.

Einstein said, if you're a cat trying to swim like a fish, you'll beat yourself up. But if you honor yourself as a cat, you'll climb like a master. So focus on your own highest values and live by priority in alignment with that.

Every time you're not feeling grateful, inspired or enthused towards an objective, it's usually a sign that you're trying to live by lower values, either those injected from others where you are trying to be something you are not, or those just lower on your value list.

The symptomatology of self-depreciation, low self-esteem and procrastination, something people have called 'limited beliefs' or 'sabotage', are not real. They are just feedback mechanisms, here to guide you back to what *is* your true highest priority and lead you back to what *is* authentic.

Your ontological identity revolves around whatever is highest on your list of values. This means that your most authentic self is whatever is most meaningful, inspiring, and fulfilling to you. So all of those symptoms of trying to live by lower values are there to create a refinement of your path to get you back to what is most authentic, most true, most meaningful, most inspiring and real for you.

Everything is on the way, not in the way

When you finally quit comparing yourself to others or to the fantasy of trying to live in other people's values, you free yourself from the nightmares of not being true to yourself. Life continuously gives you feedback and your own physiological and psychological homeostatic mechanisms are guiding you back to what's true and inspiring to you.

If you prioritize your life, and ask yourself: what is the highest priority action I can take today, that fulfills the highest priority in my life, that is most meaningful and serves the greatest number of people with the resources I have? If you do that and delegate the rest, you transform any self-esteem issue into something that you become enthused by and you will be on fire.

I delegate everything and all I do is research, write, travel, and teach. It liberates me from uninspiring, unproductive, less meaningful activities. It is wise to surround yourself with people that are doing what you want to delegate and let them do something that inspires them. You give job opportunities, you help the economy, and liberate yourself to do what's most meaningful and in service for you. You produce more income and exemplify what's possible as a path of mastery, instead of living in misery, trying to be somebody you're not. Anytime you are doing low priority things, you devalue yourself. Anytime you do the highest priority thing, you are inspired by your life, you are grateful and you tend to contribute and exemplify what's possible as a human being.

Intuition as a neutralizer of emotions

Intuition is not necessarily what people think it is. Let me explain. If I am infatuated with someone, or infatuated with an idea, or an object, I am conscious of the upsides and I am unconscious of their downsides.

If I am resentful to someone, I am conscious of the downsides, but unconscious of their upsides.

If I am fully conscious and mindful of both sides simultaneously, I feel love for someone.

Now, when we are infatuated with someone, our intuition is trying to point out and whisper to us to ask questions to see the downside and bring us back into mindfulness, so that we can be fully conscious. When we are resentful on the other hand, our intuition tries to bring up the upside to bring us back up to full consciousness.

For example, let's say you have a young lady that is infatuated with a guy. When she's highly infatuated and googly-eyed, and just absolutely elated with him, her intuition is saying, "It's too good to be true. Be careful. Watch out, there's got to be a downside." She knows that and her intuition is pointing it out, trying to bring her back into full consciousness. Because if she doesn't, she'll tend to inject his values, and try to be somebody she's not just to be with him. But she still wants to be loved for who she is and wonders why he can't do that.

If she is minimizing herself to him and is too humble to admit that what she sees in him is actually inside her, she will play small, which doesn't serve the relationship and becomes a mismatch. So her intuition is trying to ask about the downsides overlooked in him in order to level the playing field so there can be a sustainable match.

On the other hand, if someone has done something that she's resentful over, her intuition will attempt to point out the upsides of that behavior and say,

"There's got to be meaning to this. There's got to be a reason why this happened." In this way, her intuition is trying to point out the opposite to level the playing field. Intuition helps her to realize there is a purpose and some form of meaning to it all. Intuition is constantly trying to take partial awareness, subjectively biased information, and bring it back to objectivity and wholeness.

If you are infatuated with someone, you minimize yourself in relationship to them and become inauthentic. If you're resentful, you exaggerate yourself and that's inauthentic as well. In either case, you are either too proud to admit, or too humble to admit, that what you see in them is inside of you. But the moment you have pure reflective awareness, and you're not too humble or proud to admit what you see in others, is inside of you, you have true intimacy and an unconditional, mindful state of love.

The homeostatic mechanisms of our brain, literally our neurotransmitters and the electricity of our brains, have mechanisms that try to bring us back into homeostasis, so that we can live by our highest value in the most authentic, most inspired state.

Intuition is a negative feedback system guiding our subcortical amygdala's* subjectively biased misinterpretations of reality, back into wholeness, so we can be grateful for the magnificence of who we are and the people that we're caring about and life in general.

The amygdalae are part of the limbic brain and responsible for processing our memories, decisions and emotional responses.

In my own life, I've had many of those whisperings and feedbacks, when I've been infatuated or resentful to any human being or situation. It's attempting to whisper inside of me to bring me back into balance. When I apply my own Demartini Method of internal and external conflict resolution, it makes me accountable to balance the equation between infatuation and resentment, and pride and shame.

Life is like a mathematical equation, as Galileo and others have said. If you ask the right questions you become liberated from the bondage of what occupies space and time in your mind when you're not balanced. People who are really infatuated or really resentful can't sleep at night because they're not mindful. They are mindlessly distracted by these misinterpretations of their reality.

Your intuition is there to hold you accountable, to love yourself, to love others, and to do something that is inspiring and authentic. This makes intuition one of the most powerful homeostatic mechanisms.

How intuition has been misunderstood

Many people have confused gut instinct with intuition because they occur simultaneously. Whilst intuition is an equalizer of emotions, gut instinct is an avoidance response from subconsciously stored information of the past, and impulses activate our pleasure center.

When external stimuli remind us of something that we previously perceived to have drawbacks, our gut instinct, or gut brain, will be initiated to protect us from such associated stimuli. However, if we listen to intuition, our perception becomes balanced, opens our heart and allows our heart brain to function, not our 'gut brain'.

There is an easy way to distinguish between the heart brain and the gut brain, between intuition and instinct / impulse. Your gut instinct makes you perceive more drawbacks than benefits. It can activate phobias and you may say, "Get the hell out of there". It's a survival response activated by the septum in the amygdala, which is an instinct to avoid things or people.

The Nucleus Accumbens in the amygdala on the other hand, is the reward or pleasure center. It activates a philia and you will assume that there are more benefits than drawbacks, seeking mechanisms for pleasure, such as food or the impulse towards someone we are infatuated by. In both cases, you are blinded and not seeing both sides.

Whenever you're subconsciously biased, blinded and not seeing the whole, you can't thrive. Your gut instincts and impulses kick in as a survival mechanism, to avoid a predator and/or seek a prey. Here, we create the fear of loss.

Intuition is trying to bring you back into homeostasis by allowing you to see the benefits to the animal that's chasing you, and the drawbacks to eating. Maximum fitness and development occurs at the border of the two.

If you had nothing but prey, and no predator, you'd end up gluttonous, fat and unfit. If you had predator without prey, you'd end up emaciated, starved and unfit. But if you put the two together support-challenge, prey-predators, positives-negatives, and put the polarities together into perfect equilibrium, you get fitness, because you eat just the right amount to maintain your own physiology, at the same time making sure that you're not overeating so you can run and keep yourself in fitness. Nature with its supportive and challenging events, is there to ensure that we are not too dependent or precariously independent. It creates a perfect balance so we can have a social interaction for love and intimacy in our life.

The moment you're living by the highest priority, your blood glucose and oxygen goes into your forebrain, which affects the hypothalamus, controls the autonomics and literally creates a perfect synchronicity in the heart because the intracardiac complex of our heart, the network that causes auto rhythmicity, is correlated with the hypothalamus, the autonomics, and the forebrain. This allows, in a sense, a resilient adaptability and heart rate variability that's maximal, to allow us to actually be able to adapt with unconditional love.

Our intuition is trying to lead us back in our heart

Our gut instinct and impulse is trying to make us run for food or avoid predators. Both occur simultaneously. So when we're judging something, if we're highly charged, our lower amygdala is going to run and the gut instincts are going to say "get the hell out" or "run after it". It needs that acceleration and geometrically progressive release of adrenaline in order to avoid the predator or catch the prey.

But our intuition is working at the same time and trying to say, if the prey gets away, there's still a benefit. And if you get almost eaten, you're still going to win from it. You are going to grow more resilient from it. There's a thrival mechanism to transcend that survival polarity. And that's the difference between human beings and the other animals. The animals have that survival mechanism, but the human being has the capacity to find objectivity and to transcend with its transcendent mind, as Emmanuel Kant would describe it – we can transcend our survival impulses and instincts. We have the capacity to love, to have reason and intuition and do something inspiring. And when we do, we create amazing accomplishments and feats. Our sciences, religions, philosophies and arts emerge from the transcendence of our survival nature, by our intuitions and inspirations, as Einstein said, those are the two that give rise to genius.

True intuition is thus a homeostatic mechanism guiding us to the most fulfilling state of inspiration in our life. This state of inspiration is a confirmation that we have listened to intuition. It guides us back to mindfulness and authenticity, where we can live by our highest value-inspired fashion.

Our Potential for Self-Actualisation

We all have the potential for self-actualisation and tap into our genius, which we can access when we live in alignment with our true highest values.

I teach people to determine what they really value. I've been studying values for 44 years now and I've asked people by the millions, "What do you value in life? What's your priority?" Most people are unclear.

But it simply comes down to what you spontaneously do on a daily basis that you love doing that makes a difference and inspires you. This reflects what you value most.

People will tell you what they value according to what they think it should be from mothers and fathers to preachers and teachers and conventions, traditions and more. I have no interest in that. I'm only interested in what your life demonstrates, not what you think it should be. To determine what your life actually demonstrates ask the following questions:

1. What exactly is your life demonstrating?
2. How do you fill your personal or intimate space most?
3. How do you spend your time most?
4. What is it that energizes you most?
5. What is it that you spend your money on most?
6. What is it you are most organized and most disciplined in?
7. What are you thinking about visualizing and affirming to yourself about how you would love your life to be that shows evidence of coming through?
8. What do you converse with other people about most that inspires you?
9. What inspires you with tears in your eyes? And what is common to those that inspire you?
10. What are the most consistent, persistent goals you have that show evidence of coming true?
11. What can't you wait to get up for and learn about most consistently?

You will discover a pattern and find what that is and structuring your life and living by priority and filling your day with that, that liberates you from any mediocrity in life, and any survival mentality. It gives you permission to shine, not shrink, and do something extraordinary, not ordinary. It gives you permission to lead the way, spontaneously, instead of following. Why follow a culture when you can lead a culture? Everybody has that capacity to do that if they start prioritizing their life, and living by authenticity.

For the full questionnaire to determine your values for free go to https://drdemartini.com.

ABOUT THE AUTHOR

DR. JOHN DEMARTINI

DR. JOHN DEMARTINI is a world-renowned specialist in human behavior, a researcher, author, and global educator. He was recently selected for the prestigious Lifetime Achievement Award for 2021 by the International Association of Top Professionals (IAOTP).

He has over 4 decades of research across multiple disciplines and his work has been described by students as the "most comprehensive body of work", "an extensive library of wisdom" and "wisdom of the highest and most valuable order"

Dr. Demartini's mission and vision is to share knowledge and wisdom that empowers you to become a master of your own life and destiny.

He's an internationally published author, a global educator and the founder of the Demartini Method, a revolutionary tool in modern psychology.

His education curriculum ranges from personal growth seminars to corporate empowerment programs. He shares life, business, financial, relationship and leadership empowerment strategies and empowerment tools that have stood the test of time.

Connect with John here:

https://drdemartini.com/

JAMES M POWELL

INTUITION HACKS

YOUR ULTIMATE GUIDE TO BECOMING A WORLD CLASS DECISION MAKER

*I*ntuition is THE No.1 skill that the world's highest achieving entrepreneurs use when making their most impactful decisions in both life and business. As a person who wants to deeply trust yourself in making your most successful decisions, even when everyone and everything else is telling you to do the exact opposite, you need to learn how to properly unleash the limitless but untapped potential of your mind's natural intuition.

> *"I've trusted the still, small voice of intuition my entire life. And the only time I've made mistakes is when I didn't listen." - Oprah Winfrey*

In my experience the main reason why a shocking 50% of people fail in business within the first five years is because they never learn how to (or even that they need to) develop their intuitive skill set.

The world's highest achieving entrepreneurs, whom we can learn from because success leaves clues, such as award-winning actress Kim Basinger, or CEO of Fortune 500 companies Maggie Wilderotter, and countless others, each say that they've made their most successful decisions in both life and business always with heart, intuition and gut, never with data or analysis.

Intuition has enabled me to work with global brands such as Hilton helping them launch a one-million euro project, as well as win an international competition. By discovering how to properly implement intuition to make highly successful decisions, I've been able to become No.1 for sales nationally within just six weeks of working with the second largest UK company in its industry, while breaking all but one sales record in its history.

By being able to properly leverage intuition, I've now interviewed some of the highest-achieving and most successful people on the planet on my podcast. My guests include, among others, co-author of the No.1 best-selling personal finance book of all time and financial advisor to two U.S. presidents, Sharon Lechter, world-renowned human behavior expert and featured media celebrity in the hit movie 'The Secret', Dr. John Demartini, as well as corporate trainer and philanthropist, Darren Jacklin, who has helped grow a company from startup to one-billion dollars publicly trading on the NASDAQ in under five years. And I've been able to do this before even launching my very first episode or having any listeners or downloads. The experiences and life changing insights my amazing guests share via my podcast are truly incredible!

On a more personal note, in 2012 I attended a scheduled six-month health checkup a full two months in advance based solely on specific and actionable insights I experienced intuitively. Even though the clinic staff advised me that I didn't need to come yet for another two months, following my intuition I asked them to test me anyway. After doing so, the oncologists confirmed I had cancer and said that if I had waited until the time of my appointment it would have been too late to treat me and I would already be dead. They then said that the fastest they'd seen cancer grow was doubling per week but mine was tripling, and told me that if I don't do chemotherapy within the next two weeks I wouldn't have long left to live.

But considering the fact that I had attended my appointment a full two months early based uniquely on the specific and actionable insights I'd experienced intuitively, I consulted my intuition again and made yet another life changing decision. I said 'No' to chemotherapy and instead found my own way to healing. Upon returning to the oncologists two months later, at the time of my original appointment when they said I would already be dead, they were astonished with my healing and said I don't need to do the chemo anymore.

Recognizing intuition as my core competency and the skill by which high achievers make their most successful decisions in both life and business, I've received endless requests over the years to teach how to be able to make life changing decisions using intuition. As a result, I've packaged up my experience and insights into a training and development opportunity that includes, among others, two strategies to help you get specific and actionable intuitive insights without even needing to train or develop your intuition. The feedback I receive from just these two strategies alone is incredible because they eliminate the learning stage which means you can jump directly into implementing.

Being A Highly Successful Decision Maker Using Intuition

As a child my intuition was proven accurate and reliable in clinical settings by three psychologists when I was just ten years old. My parents, who desperately wanted to better understand their rather unusual son, couldn't easily grasp how I was able to know things without learning it first from someone or somewhere else, like people or books. They wanted to know what made me different and why it was that after the psychologists discontinued their analysis of my siblings they continued studying me.

While my parents walked into the room where one of the sessions was being held, I remained standing in the entrance of the doorway and refused to come in any further. With a feeling that I was being watched emanating from the mirror on the left wall, I doubted that my parents and the couple of psychologists sitting at the table with them were being honest about why we were there. Rather than joining them, I remained by the door and stared at the mirror. Several minutes passed, then one of the psychologists slowly walked over to me and put his left hand on my right shoulder, and asked: *"James, Do you want to see what's behind the mirror?"* Surprised, yet curious, I silently nodded, 'Yes'.

He then escorted me along the corridor and into an adjacent darkened room, inside which stood a suited woman with a clipboard and pen taking notes, looking through the mirror into the other room where I had been previously. In front of her were two men operating a couple of large camcorders on metal tripods. They were filming the counseling session through what I could now see was secretly a one-way mirror in the wall.

That psychologist's decision to show me into the room behind the mirror where my intuition was guiding me to see had a majorly significant impact on me trusting my intuition since a very early age. This pivotal experience early on in my life helped me realize that the intuitive insights I experience are real and with further training I understood there's a way to interpret intuitive feelings into specific and detailed information that can be used to accomplish goals.

"You must train your intuition. You must trust the small voice inside you which tells you exactly what to say and what to decide." - Ingrid Bergman

At age fourteen I left home to explore my unique human potential and, in avoiding the typical societal conditioning, grew more into my intuition rather than out of it as most people unfortunately do. Through my teens and into my early twenties I engaged in relentless self-study of the 'ologies' such as ontology, anthropology, psychology and molecular biology, as well as quantum field theory in addition to topics including the laws of causality and reciprocity while using, at the core, retrodictive logic and reasoning by first principles.

At any one time my floor would be carpeted by twenty or more academic and non-fiction books that I would study non-linearly. Time and again I was amazed at how it's humanly possible to compose a question and be able to discover relevant facets of the answer using intuition to select particular books and then pages and sentences within those books without having to read the entire book. The more specific and nuanced your question, the better will be the answer you find in terms of its quality, accuracy and relevancy.

When through study you realize that the information you're seeking is not in that which you've previously consumed, you can then perform a search function using intuition on remaining known or unknown sources of information to gain new knowledge as insights. If your sincerity is 100% as demonstrated in your commitment to discover the truth yourself without help, then typically the search function you perform using intuition will yield significant results quickly and reliably.

Your investment of sincerity required in both your studies and performing the search function will depend on how impactful the outcome of your discovery will be for humanity. The greater the purpose or result, the greater a challenge you will face. In my experience, I have found it most effective to saturate myself with relevant knowledge until, analogously, I feel full. Then I rest mentally and allow the information to settle into its own shape. Any missing pieces in that shape will become apparent to me as either a glaring obviosity resulting from passive mental calculation or in the form of a specific intuitive insight. True intuitive magic happens when you're able to achieve this final step without exposing yourself to relevant knowledge through study beforehand.

Information is plentiful. However, experience is key to transformation. At every opportunity you must practise what you study to gain experience. I researched the findings of scientific experiments conducted on monks who, while meditating on the edge of an ice lake high up in the snowy Himalayan mountains, wore only thin robes while the scientists, who were measuring the monk's biorhythms and brain waves, wore heavy duty winter jackets with scarves, hats and gloves, yet were still shivering.

Without having the tech to measure my body's vitals I instead experimented using the monks' descriptions of what it felt like to perform, and discovered many incredible realities that helped me realize the human potential is truly limitless. After years of training with lots of experimental trial and error, for six months I meditated between seven and eleven hours per day in a single sitting while fasting on only rice and water while listening to uncomfortably loud music until my sensory perceptions shifted and I entered a totally new realm of experience consisting solely of light with infinite vanishing points in all directions. Time dilation is at its maximum and only your experience as projected by your heart geometrically differentiates now from then and here from there. This is a state that can be entered into consistently and reliably.

During my late teens and into my early twenties I toured the UK by invitation for several months, spoke from stages and took every opportunity to be trained and developed, mentored and coached by elders from a diverse array of spiritual cultures and traditions. Since then I've been invited to share my experience and insights to help others level up. I've done so at multi-day action seminars in beautiful places like the Black Forest of Germany, Colorado in the U.S., London in the UK, Amsterdam in the Netherlands, Vienna in Austria, and more locations around the world. I've also been featured as an invited guest speaker and author on leading national and global media publications and platforms including the world's largest coaching organization, the ICF - International Coach Federation, Brainz Magazine, Fox, NBC, CBS, and Dublin FM's 'Inspirational People, Inspirational Stories' that looks into the mindset of inspiring high performers in their field and their mindful nature of giving back to help others.

How To Make Your Most Successful Decisions Using Intuition

You'll find that the common teaching on intuition is that of it simply being a feeling or at best a hunch which can't be logically explained. But it's so much more than that. I've had highly successful people tell me that my clear definitions on the structure and function of intuition is the best they've ever heard. That's because my unique insights into the 'ologies combined with my unusually extreme experiences in making highly successful decisions using intuition have resulted in my understanding of intuition being one which makes so much sense that it seems like it should already be known.

There are many factors affecting how you feel, and there are many things that can feel good when you do them but which actually aren't such as certain mental and physical behaviours or habits. Though there are situations where how you feel is contextually relevant, a fleeting feeling is not the best indicator to base an important decision on. When making high priority decisions where there's a lot more at risk, emotions and feelings should not be the deciding factor or even involved at all. Intuition then becomes about you being able to properly access new knowledge or relevant information that can help you make informed decisions successfully.

> *"James helped me learn how to properly use my intuition and I'm so grateful for the fact that he was able to answer any question I put to him!" - Alan Becker, YouTube Animator, 12 Million Subscribers*

Before I tell you where you can access my £1000 intuition training for free, let me give you an insight of just how powerful intuition can be even when using it to make seemingly insignificant yes or no decisions. When fundraising as a volunteer in South Korea, I traveled by subway to a nearby city for the day but missed the last train back. Not wanting to spend team money on a taxi over such a long distance, I decided to walk. I didn't know where I was going. I only knew the general direction because of the destination signposts attached to the subway station. However, after walking for over two hours using only my intuition, I found myself exactly where I wanted to be.

At each junction where I had the choice of walking right or left, I used my intuition to ask the questions 'shall I go right here, yes or no?' and 'shall I go left here, yes or no?'. I asked the appropriate question for the direction and then made my decision and took action based on the very first response I experienced. When doing this it's key to remind yourself that the first response is truth, and the second is you thinking about what you intuited. Intuition precedes intellect as I'll explain in just a moment.

The time it takes for you to receive feedback on whether or not a decision was correct is usually minimal with smaller yes or no decisions because the time delay between asking the question, intuiting the answer, making the decision, taking the action, and the result being achieved is much shorter. However, as I was making countless smaller decisions over a longer period of time, I didn't know if I had cumulatively made all those right decisions until I found myself actually at my destination. This required 100% trust in the process and my ability to follow it.

Just like the brain, every organ, including the heart, emits an electromagnetic field that can be measured technologically. Similarly, the heart, brain, and gut each contain many thousands of neurons and together form an interconnected three part system that exchanges electrical information via their neural network. The heart is predominant. The flow of information from your heart to your brain to your gut is the order in which your intuition (heart), intellect (brain) and instinct (gut) takes place, which you can leverage to help you make your most successful decisions.

After responding to stimuli, your heart sends electrical information pertaining to its state via neurons to your brain. Using your intellect you can then reason and rationalize about the intuitive information your brain has received from your heart. This information which has been processed by you using your intellect is then sent from your brain to your gut which is where your instinct is, and you get that gut response to put the information into appropriate action. Because the heart is predominant in this flow of information, intuition is the highest sense.

The very first step to take in honing your intuition further is to develop a dataset of experience which you can use as a reference for making higher level decisions later on. You do this through making countless small yes or no decisions continuously each day, decisions that don't have any significant long term impact but which provide you with feedback in the shortest amount of time possible, allowing you to develop your dataset of experience quickly.

Remind yourself that the first response is your intuition and the second is your intellect. You want to act on the very first response you receive. If you're not sure if it's your intuition or you thinking about it, then it's already too late and you're overthinking. In my complete training I show you not only how to access increasingly specific and actionable insights using intuition and intellect, but also how you can get specific intuitive insights without even needing to develop your intuition. This part of my curriculum is one that gets a lot of attention.

"James is the 'Yoda for entrepreneurs' who can help take your business to the next level of where you want it to be!" - Akbar Sheikh, 7-Figure Coach & TEDx Speaker

The shortest route to success that I've personally experienced and which any high achiever will also tell you is to learn directly from others with the success you want. As the saying goes, a single conversation with a wise person is far greater than ten years of study. That's why in my program I bring in guests from my podcast and network, that includes some of the most successful people on the planet, to spend time with the valuable and valued members of my community.

Having personally spent time interviewing high achieving entrepreneurs on my podcast I can vouch for how powerful and transformational even a single conversation with any one of them has been. And in financial terms, if you were to request a one-on-one directly, you can expect to spend upwards of tens of thousands of dollars for even a single hour of their time. So the value of my community, in more ways than one, is off the charts.

The reason I'm bringing them in is because, in addition to my program, which I've been told by highly successful entrepreneurs is the best training on intuition they've seen, I want to provide the best possible environment for you to level up your intuition to make your most successful decisions in both life and business, just the world's highest achieving entrepreneurs, who do so using intuition in every case.

To get full and immediate access to my £1000 intuition training for free, and to get a taste of my full program where you can learn how to properly unleash the limitless but untapped potential of your mind's natural intuition and be able to make your most successful decisions in both life and business just like the world's highest achieving entrepreneurs, simply go to my podcast website and subscribe. Once you subscribe, the course is yours completely free.

Go to The Spirituality Podcast to subscribe:
https://www.thespiritualitypodcast.com

ABOUT THE AUTHOR

JAMES M POWELL

Entrepreneurs, business owners and CEOs come to JAMES M POWELL to get the specific insights and actionable strategies they need to properly unleash the limitless but untapped potential of their mind's natural intuition, so they can make their most successful decisions in both life and business just like the world's highest achieving entrepreneurs.

Using his intuition, James M Powell (Fox, NBC, CBS, ICF, Brainz) became No.1 for sales in the UK, helped Hilton launch a one-million euro project, and created The Spirituality Podcast where he explores spirituality and self development with high achieving entrepreneurs including a financial advisor to U.S. presidents, a serial Inc.500 entrepreneur, and a corporate trainer who has helped grow a company from startup to one-billion dollars publicly trading on the NASDAQ in under five years.

Through his program, Intuition Hacks, James trains entrepreneurs to make their most successful decisions in life and business using his 'intuition hacks' while also bringing into his community guests from his podcast and network to spend time with his clients. Because the best way to level up both personally and professionally is by learning directly from the best.

Connect with James here:

Website: https://www.thespiritualitypodcast.com

CINDY D CERECER

LIVING INTUITIVELY THROUGH CONNECTION WITH SOURCE

Intuition is the ability to understand something instantly without the need for conscious reasoning. It's an innate knowledge that does not explain or justify - it only points the way.

It's a soft whisper, easily drowned out by noise of the mind, but when the mind is calm it can be heard crystal clear. It is an inner knowing without doubt, but also often without reasoning. This is because the mind is responsible for reasoning, but intuition comes from the neurotransmitters inside of our heart brain and gut brain. The heart knows long before the mind does and a "gut feeling" is rarely wrong. Intuition is information from a higher perspective - it sees the bigger picture.

Intuition is the communication from your soul or higher self to your human body. Without it, we wouldn't have known to take our first breath as we left the womb. It is a pathway to connect with our dreams and life purpose.

***

I feel like I was born with a very strong sense of intuition. As I grew and started to go through the motions of the regular world, I started to lose that beautiful connection to Source that I was born with, like many of us do.

Life became hard, and scary. Life felt like trying to cram a square into a circular hole. Impossible and frustrating. I just couldn't understand why things were the way that they were. I always knew that something was not quite right, but like most teenagers, I thought it was just me. I thought that the best way to fit in was to buffer myself down into a more acceptable, agreeable, and likeable version of myself. This seems to be the adolescence experience in a nutshell for so many and I always imagine what life would be like for young people if school taught them that there was no other option but trusting and honoring themselves - rather than intellectualizing the bejeezus out of everything.

I'll never forget a conversation I had once with a close friend in high school. I was about 16, still very caught up in confusion and self-doubt - but he somehow saw something very different within me. He saw an inner connection that I had no idea that I was longing to reclaim, and spoke to me as if I had already found it - a truly transformational friendship and one that I am eternally grateful for.

He said to me one day, super excited like he had somehow figured out a way to fix everything, "What if we got everyone in the whole world to hold hands, then we electrocuted them, then they would all just wake up, all at the same time. Wouldn't that be amazing?" I honestly had no idea what he was talking about, but I was excited by his excitement and impressed by his creativity and enthusiasm. In hindsight, now I can see that he was referring to me as if I was somehow already awake enough to help him wake up the rest of the planet. It took me years to fully understand what he meant but he intuitively saw something within me before I could even see it within myself.

Perhaps this was a moment that sparked my own awakening and growth, or perhaps it was something that was always destined to unfold. Nevertheless, my journey of self discovery and reconnection with my inner knowledge and guidance has been the most fulfilling adventure I have ever embarked on.

Learning to let go of what others thought of me, or at least what I thought that others were thinking about me, developing a deep acceptance of who I was and trust in my own ability to guide myself through life has been the greatest gift I could have ever allowed myself to accept. For me it wasn't as simple as flipping the switch from unsure and insecure to connected and trusting myself, but a constant practice of reminding myself that I am capable and protected. That my connection with source and my higher self is all that I would ever need to guide myself through the most precarious of situations. It's a daily practice of embodiment and conscious action. Trusting that my mistakes are important lessons that my soul came here to learn, that my supposed breakdowns are actually just a micro-step before my next breakthrough and that my frustrations and challenges are simply my higher self pushing me closer to self awareness and alignment.

I wanted to make this chapter different. I didn't just want it just to be me looking back and sharing with you a story of challenges I have been through and all the wonderful insight I gained by going through that experience. I wanted it to be practical, creative and colourful. I wanted it to ignite your right hemisphere and inspire you to spill your creative juices all over your life.

***

For too long we have lived in a world where our intuition and self-trust have been shut down. We are taught that we are simply a result of biological processes. Are hearts merely pumps for blood, our gut only a pipe to release waste. "Science" is king and intuition is something for superstitious hippies. Spirituality is for the weak and ignorant, brainwashed by cult leaders and gurus. Imagination is for lazy people, and any pursuit that doesn't make a heap of money is for dreamers and stoners.

It's exciting for me to write about intuition as an expert on gut health because over 12 years in practice has taught me a lot about the connection between people's personalities and how they poop.

I know this sounds crazy, but I'm serious.

Highly anxious people that put others before themselves are chronically constipated.

People who are exhausted, fed up and just want to make their problems disappear will be prone to bouts of diarrhea.

Highly organised people who like to follow the rules will poop once a day, at the same time.

People who often get triggered by others and angry or upset at others' behaviour will suffer from IBS.

Your gut is connected to your brain via the vagus nerve, so your brain is in constant communication with your gut. Any emotional trigger is immediately relayed to the rest of your body. Without a calm and centered mind it's impossible to have a balanced and aligned connection to the rest of our body. In other words, stress will block intuition.

As a science graduate I studied all the apparently "really important stuff" that would help me understand life. Unfortunately, the more knowledge I acquired, the more I realised just how little science really understood.

In chemistry I learnt that both diamonds and graphite are made up of exactly the same thing.

In physics I found out that electrons behave differently when observed, that nothing ever really touches anything, and the perception of touch or closeness is actually just two atoms repelling each other.

In biology, I realised that one archeological discovery could completely disprove everything that we thought we knew about evolution, and that we have just as many neurotransmitters in our heart and gut as we do in our brain.

In psychology we were shown how scientific studies are so subjective that under the right conditions you could essentially prove anything you like if you had enough money to fund the research.

BOOM! The matrix had started to crack! There had to be more to it than just the big bang, and the possibility that humans got lucky and somehow just ended up here.

In all my years in the colonic clinic, what I have realized is that there is an exception to every rule. You can expose 3 people to the same chemical and they will all react differently. You can ask 3 people what colour something is and you can get 3 different answers.

So what is true?

This leads me back to a word I used earlier in this chapter, "Source". God, Spirit, The Universe, call it what you like, but it's that extra thing that makes life so magical. It's the reason why seeds sprout, sometimes in the harshest of conditions. It's the reason why you run into someone you haven't seen in years at the bank when you were literally only thinking about them the night before. It's that little voice deep down inside yourself that despite the world looking like a complete and utter mess, it tells you that everything is going to be ok.

It's the voice that tells you that you were meant to be here. That your life isn't accidental and you have the ability to spread large amounts of love and light and leave a positive impact on the world.

Intuition is connection to Source. Without it you would never have been able to be born, that's because you are Source. Every hydrogen atom in your body is likely 13.5 billion years old because they were created at the birth of the universe, literally the same force that birthed the Universe is inside of YOU.

How can you connect more to the source and become more in touch with your intuition? By connecting more with yourself.

Sometimes you just have to let go. No more second guessing, doubting, putting everyone else first, getting sucked into spirals of limiting beliefs, illusions, fear and projections of others. Once we can let go of the noise from the external world, aka the illusion, we are met with silence, inner peace and deeper connection and trust with our higher self, with who or what we truly are, and in that silence we can hear the whispers of our own intuition.

***

OK, so let's do this! Let's get down to the nitty gritty. I wanted to fill this chapter with practical steps that will help you connect to your intuition and harness aspects of it into your daily life.

Daily embodiment of connection with one's own intuition is what intuitive living means to me. But how does one achieve this? ¶ ¶In this section I have listed some daily rituals that you can do to connect with your intuition and at the end I have included an activity called "Rapid Fire Free Flow". This is a great way to help you reflect deeper and connect more profoundly to find answers, direction and guidance from within.

Daily Rituals for Intuitive Living

1. Permission to Remember

When you wake up in the morning, start your day by giving yourself permission to be intuitive. Remember, intuition is your natural state, therefore, you do not need to work at it, but rather allow it to express itself through you as You.

Remind yourself that you are magical. That you have powers beyond your 5 senses and that you are connected to and part of the great spirit that resides inside of everything. Remind yourself that you do not need to look outwards for answers because you have all the answers you need inside of you.

2. A prayer for Intuition

Aho, Great Spirit

Thank you for the memory of who I truly am and where I come from.

As a sovereign spiritual being, I connect with my heart and trust its guidance. I am guided by my own inner wisdom and have the courage and clarity to take action.

Thank you for the peace and calmness I feel when I connect with certainty to the source of divine inspiration that constantly flows through me.

As I grow spiritually, emotionally and physically in perfect alignment, Spirit flows through me delivering divine inspiration, guidance and healing. I release with love any fear or doubt. I trust my intuition even when I might not fully understand it.

I am grateful for this healing that is my life and for the perfect unfoldment of my being. I give thanks for the way life is perfectly expressed through me today.

AHO!

3. Daily Gratitude

Take time daily to reflect on all the things that you have manifested that you are grateful for. Focusing on things that you are grateful for is an incredible way to focus your mind and bring yourself back into your heart's consciousness.

Some people like to do this at night before they fall asleep. I like to do it every morning as I am drinking a cup of tea. You can list things quietly in your head, write them down, say them allow or share them with those around you. All are equally as powerful and transformative.

4. Deep Breathing

Our first Language is breath, so it's super important to make sure we are engaging the biology that created our life. No matter where you are, you always have time to do this.

Deep breathing should be slow and gentle. Remember to fill the abdomen, not just the chest. A simple way to make sure you are doing this is to place one hand on your stomach and one on your chest. Breath deeply and make sure your hand on your stomach is rising. Try to be aware of your breath, heartbeat and to release tension from your body.

There are so many amazing benefits of deep breathing for our mind and body but when the mind is calm and the body is relaxed this is when you will be most likely to tap into your intuition.

5. Move Your Body

Your intuition will never speak to you through your mind - it will speak through your body. If your body is stagnant, so will your flow of thoughts and inspiration. So it's important to move your body daily to connect with our intuition.

6. Inquiry and Self Reflection

Don't be afraid to talk to yourself. Asking yourself questions will enable you to open your heart to new answers and perspectives that come through your intuition.

Think of someone you look up to or admire. They are actually a reflection of you. A reflection of something that exists within you - or else you wouldn't be able to see it. Sometimes when I am trying to explore a situation I imagine myself in conversation with a person I admire. What would this person say about this situation? What advice would they have for you? - This person you admire is actually a reflection of your higher self, so will always lead you in the right direction.

7. Be Mindful of Your Frequency

It's called your "higher self" for a reason. - The reason is that it is not connected to any lower frequencies or vibrations.

Emotional states create a strong frequency or vibration. The whole concept of someone giving you "bad vibes" comes from them having a lower emotional state or frequency than you.

Think about it - on a scale of 1 - 10 (1 being low and 10 being high) how good do you feel when you think about these emotional states?

Fear
Hate
Frustration
Anger
Understanding
Gratitude
Love
Excitement
Appreciation
Connection

Different emotions will move you up and down the frequency scale. This doesn't mean that it is a bad thing to experience an emotion with lower frequency - it just means it's not a good idea to stay there.

Negative emotions can often be a slippery slope of feeling shitty, so make sure you have ways to shift your vibration and frequency if you're feeling low. Putting on some music that makes you feel good and having a bit of a dance is a great way to shift your vibration in seconds. Making yourself smile or laugh with a funny joke or memory will also do the trick. Giving someone a hug or connecting with nature will shift your frequency within seconds.

8. Seek Beauty

It's so important for us to surround ourselves with beautiful things. This reminds us of the magic of creation and the beauty of life itself. By beautiful I don't mean expensive or extravagant possessions, but simple things like plants, flowers, nature, art, poetry, pictures of people you love, anything that ignites your heart with joy.

9. Meditate Daily

Ok, I know this might sound impossible - but it's really non-negotiable. Setting aside 5 minutes every morning to meditate can truly change your life.

Some people get caught up in a "I don't know how to meditate" - "What do I have to do?" - "How do I do it?" - "I don't think I'm doing it properly" cycle. But really it's simple. You don't have to *do* anything. You just stop and do nothing, nothing at all. You can listen to some meditation music, focus on your breath, whatever feels right, but just do it. There is no right or wrong, but the practice of making time and space to meditate often opens up an incredible portal for intuitive living.

As a busy mum of 4, Active Meditation was an absolute game changer for me. When I realised that I could meditate whilst doing menial tasks like folding clothes or doing the dishes, I knew I had cracked the code. You can do it whilst walking, stretching, gardening and even cleaning. You allow yourself to get lost in the task, quiet the mind and move the focus down to the heart and the belly. When your mind wanders, just keep coming back to the simple sensorial experience that is happening in the present.

10. Rapid Free Flow

This is a really fun way to get yourself connected with your intuition. It will only take about 10-15 minutes.

Make sure you are settled in a quiet place with a pen and paper and minimise all distractions. Turn your phone off or leave it in the other room. You might want to do a little meditation before you start, light a candle, prepare some ceremonial cacao, set your intention of connecting with your inner wisdom - whatever you need to do to get yourself into a space of reflection.

As you read the questions, the goal is to answer in rapid fire. Literally write down the first things that come to your head. Don't try to make sense of it until you have finished. When you have completed all the questions you can then go back and read over them. The idea is to let your subconscious take over and let your spirit answer instead of your mind.

The questions that I have written are a guide. You can add questions to your rapid fire list and allow your subconscious to answer when you are in free flow. It can be surprising and very insightful what your inner world has to say.

Approach the activity with an open mind and light heart, allow yourself to freely express without judgement or consequence.

1. Who are you?

2. What are your 5 main values? What are the 5 things that are most important to you?

3. How do you know that you are an intuitive being?

4. What are you holding on to that you need to let go of?

5. What is the one thing that you would do if you literally didn't give a f%*^ what anyone else thought?

6. Where are you holding pain in your body?

7. What do you need to do to release it?

8. What does your heart want?

9. What is your intuition saying?

10. What decision feels good/right?

11. What makes your soul happy?

Thank you so much for sharing this chapter with me. My hope is that you enjoyed it and found some insights and tools to bring you closer to your intuition and guide you on your journey. It is always such a pleasure to participate in these collaborations. If you are wanting to connect with me, I have included my points of contact below.

Big Love to all you enlightened beings walking the talk and committed to growth. oxox

Cindy D Cerecer

ABOUT THE AUTHOR

CINDY D CERECER

CINDY D CERECER is a mum of four and a leader in the Wholistic Wellness Community. A veteran Colon Hydrotherapist, is the owner of Colonic Care in Melbourne Australia and has led the way for many as a Colon Hydrotherapy Trainer and Mentor.

Cindy has also been a Certified Holistic Nutritionist, Life Coach and Theta Healer for more than a decade. She is the Principal of ICHTA (International Colon Hydrotherapy Training Academy) and the President of ICHA (International Colon Hydrotherapy Association).

Currently she is completing 4 PHD Programs in Holistic Health, Healing and Medicine at the University of Natural Health in Indianapolis.

Intuitive Living is something that Cindy is very passionate about - often known for her unconventional approach to EVERYTHING - marching to the beat of her heart and dancing to the rhythm of her soul is a non negotiable agreement that Cindy has made with her higher self to live a life of love, learning and happiness.

Connect with Cindy here:

Website: https://coloniccare.com.au/

Email: cindy@coloniccare.com.au

Linktree: https://linktr.ee/CindyDCerecer

KATERINA LENARCIC

YOUR GREATEST GIFT TO HUMANITY

*M*oving through our lives we have one certainty and that is our intuition. No matter what is occurring and how we are feeling on the outside, it guides us along, even if we do not fully understand it. Our outside world is full of distractions, and the sound of words that are spoken is getting louder and sometimes these distractions occur to keep us from listening to our intuition. But the unspoken word, within the quietness of our soul, is also getting louder. We can no longer ignore what our inner voice wants to tell us.

How do we maneuver all that is happening within us? How do we know what is correct or not when there is so much in our world telling us how we should move from one space of our lives to another? Even when we are asleep the deepest part of our consciousness is very clear and speaks to us all the time. Every single person has the ability to tap into the inner voice that guides us along in our everyday lives. The inner voice that carries us to know which way to go, or which way not to go, gives us sudden warnings, or feelings of love and hope when we have accomplished something wonderful. The question is, do we listen or do we doubt it? Our greatest gift to each other is the ability to know that our intuition is natural and organic and that no matter what is going on, we are all guided.

How I Discovered My Inner GPS

My intuition is my greatest asset, no matter what is occurring in my life and how it looks, my inner voice always knows how to get me to a certain place where a significant change will occur. My intuition is a strong frequency of knowing and there are many moments where I just know and cannot explain it. I am sure you have had that experience. My intuition has led me to my higher self. It has taken me down many dark rabbit holes and great places of light where I had to learn that everything I am feeling takes me to my bigger picture that unfolds every hour of my life. My journey is about trusting my process and knowing this is my greatest gift to humanity.

I grew up in an environment where my intuition was not encouraged, where I had to live up to expectations to fit into what the world wanted me to do. I intuitively rebelled because I knew in my heart how I was supposed to live. This rebellion led me into my dark night of the soul which taught me how to trust my own deep knowing. No matter what I did, my intuition always helped me to feel that I was supported even if I didn't understand it. Every moment of my dark night of the soul I had always just suddenly known what to do. When I quieted down and took myself within my heart center, I would always feel a lightness that was very comforting and a strong knowing that my next step was going to lead me to something much more rewarding. This would manifest as a person who came into my life to show me how to understand that I am worthy of anything in my life. This gave me the courage to move through feelings of anxiety that wanted to keep me stuck in my fears because I did not feel I belonged to this world.

My intuition is my nature that moves me from one place to another. It guides me to have everything I require to ensure I am fulfilling my purpose. It is my nature that ensures I create balance and synchronicities, to ensure I stay on my life path. My purpose is to help you raise your awareness into your own higher self so you can embody your full potential as a human being. I connect you to your spiritual families so you are able to receive love and support and understanding of who you are. I connect you to your humanity so you can feel how worthy you are of all you have come here to be.

From my spiritual awakening at the age of 14, I had this deep knowing that I had to learn about my intuition and how that would work for me to create a wonderful future. After a car accident at twenty-five, I said yes when Archangel Gabriel asked me to enter my "Cave" to face my own darkness and to learn how to move through it with my full attention.

Leading up to this point, my life truly felt like an emotional rollercoaster. Wrong decisions were made and I connected myself to people and substance abuse that kept me on a dark path. During this time I was fully aware of my own intuitive nature and my psychic abilities and how I just knew about the hidden world our physical world did not speak about (1980's). When I reached 29 years old (1992), I was exhausted and traumatized by my physical life. Not only was I dealing with dysfunctional people and behaviors, but I was also fighting demons in the invisible dimensions while I slept. I knew in my heart that I was in a dark place and I had to find ways to get out of it, but I really had no idea how. So I thought ending my life was the answer. I just knew I had enough.

When I fell to the floor and cried out for help my inner self knew that my guidance was reaching out for me, all I had to say was 'yes' to my healing. So God sent me help. I answered a newspaper advert to visit a medium that could help with life struggles. I did not want to see a doctor because I knew intuitively they would not be able to help me but give me pharmaceutical drugs and this was not my path. I just knew I had to go to the medium because I knew there was nothing wrong with me. I had a deep feeling inside of me that was tapping me on the shoulder and my energy saying very loudly, "listen to me and don't be afraid".

It's like a feeling that never goes away and something you cannot hide from or avoid. So I listened, and off I went to visit her. She was a beautiful soul who had the ability to reconnect me to my higher self and to my authentic intuition. This is where I was given the tools to learn how to listen to my inner GPS. I was afraid, but with her guidance, Navaro, a celestial galactic being, taught me how to do automatic writing, so I could communicate with my higher self and listen to my own energetics. By listening, I had learned that the reason I was being moved into the darkness was to understand how the darkness operates. I discovered that this was how I learned to listen to my intuition. While I was in this place of darkness, there was no light, only shadows. I had to find my own light from within so I could create the mastery that my future demanded. So spending a year with this lady showed me how my intuition was pulling me out of my darkness and into my own mastery of light. This was a significant turning point in my life because now I teach and hold space for others to do the same.

Moving forward to 2007. I had intuitively been guided to connect with another beautiful soul who was very much connected to her spiritual guidance, she became my mentor for 10 years. She held space for me to go deeper into my own intuition. Navaro returned to tell me that he would be my celestial mentor and family. This started my deeper journey of self-discovery and remembering who I am, even though this was the most challenging time of my life, I would not change a thing.

Learning to be still and quiet

I created a sacred room/space in my home where I would sit for hours and hours with Navaro and learn how to be still and quiet. Navaro and I developed a relationship where automatic writing and telepathic abilities were my tools to communicate with him. He was my gatekeeper who oversaw my training from the galactic community, to ensure I was safe during this part of my journey.

I would sit down, breathe in very deeply until my mind and body were relaxed and then Navaro would say, "please sit quietly and remove all that chatter from your mind." Then I would feel into my own heart and visualize holding myself as light. As I did this, Navaro would always comfort me by saying, "Great work, keep going." If I got distracted, like wondering when I will do the next load of washing or that negative thought about how I was not worthy of this, he would gently say to me, "My beautiful light, there is nothing to fear, you will see how this will help you to expand your understanding of self." So I would sit there, reassuring myself, loving myself as much as I knew at that time, and just allowing myself to feel into my light. Navaro would keep saying to me, with his gentle energy, "Keep going, you're doing great." This would go for two hours or more, just sitting and learning how to remove the negative ego from my heart, by not allowing the mind chatter to distract me. Then the room got brighter. I noticed how the room was filled with a luminous light of love, something that just touched my heart. I became emotional and cried a lot of tears because I knew that this light was clearing my heart of the darkness that was trying to keep me from shining my light. At that moment, I intuitively knew that my time with my medium mentor was actually connecting me to my authentic intuition and through this practice, I was getting stronger and much wiser about my energy. Because during my time with her, she would have me sit with my higher self and journal my communication. So sitting quietly was not new for me, what was new I was doing this alone and I had to really learn to trust my instincts.

From that moment onwards, I now sit in silence every day and tune into my intuition. This helps me to clean my energy and bring other members of my guidance into my space so I can continue to learn about my energy and the universe.

I used this technique every sitting. Suddenly one day, the energies around me shifted and Navaro taught me all about colors and the new shift of new energy that entered my space. Once again the question was asked, "What do you feel?" I would open my eyes and see a particular color, green, and everything that was green in my room became brighter. I would sit in awe because everything about it felt so unworldly, felt fluid, and so kind and loving. And once again, he would keep mentoring me into moving more into that energy so I could understand it from my emotional state because it was a reflection of my own healing energy. So many moments like this occurred and still do.

This led me to know how to differentiate between my own energy and external energies. I discovered what light looks like when I am quiet within my own energetics. One day, as I quieted my mind, once again the energy shifted into a brighter light, and then Navaro said to me, "You have an energetic visitor. I have asked for this energy of a galactic being to enter your space so you can learn more about energy". I said 'yes' with curiosity and excitement and then this beautiful energy of lightness, a flow that is not recognized in the human condition entered my space, so Navaro and I gave her a name and we all sat at my table. She sat directly in front of me, I actually offered her a chair. I used my automatic writing, my knowing and my senses, my sight and feelings, and my hearing to learn to interpret the information I was getting. During my training it took me seven years to activate and ensure my sight and hearing were directly linked to the higher dimensions.

You might ask why it took so long. The answer is it wasn't because I was afraid or I didn't believe I could do these things, it was done this way for me because my humanity and physical body were also important factors in all this. I had to learn to take care of myself at all times during my channeling and connections to the invisible world or it could cause major problems like creating a fragile nervous system, having physical pain and mental issues, and worse, heart attack or stroke. Navaro had to teach me how to get accustomed to this higher vibration.

Authentic Intuition Vs False Intuition/ False Light

Your journey may be different, your inner GPS could be communicating differently to you. You may feel that your process is too slow and it is not working. I can assure you, you are learning about your own process and that is uniquely your own. Keep going, look at what comes up for you when you sit quietly or when you write in your journal. There is no wrong way, once you understand that your way is your intuition bringing you everything you need to create more ease and grace, then you will be able to see your energy versus other energy.

> *"My process to trust my intuition was about sitting in my stillness for hours and hours, at 29 years of age. This taught me how to trust my intuition and connect me to the Universe." Journal entry 2nd December 2021*

This is all a process of trusting yourself and knowing in your heart that you are able to connect. You see, as you grow to understand your own intuition, it will connect you to your higher self and I know once this happens, your life will change and you will be on a journey of self-discovery, which is such a wonderful journey!

During this journey, you will encounter false intuition/light. Everyone has, everyone will, and everyone who works to understand their energy will have to understand what this false light looks like and feels like. This is just another way to learn about your authentic intuition. Your intuition knows exactly the outcome this will bring.

For me, sitting quietly for hours taught me how to listen to the darker energies, what that looks like physically, emotionally, and spiritually. Within all these quiet times, I discovered that our negative ego/false light did not want me to master my own light because it knew that I would not be fooled anymore. I now realised that at 25, I had been moved into the darkness to learn how it operates so I can see the signs and flag poles along my path. This created a strong sense of self and belief in myself. It taught me how to remove the darkness from my space and from others. Because once you master your own darkness, you will become the master of your own light.

I would sit quietly and tune into my heart, place a lot of love within me and around me. As I noticed the energies changing around me once again I was asked, "What can you feel?" and I said I felt a distortion of sorts, like a pain in the heart. Or I would get angry because suddenly I knew this false light wanted me to believe that I was better than someone else, or that my psychic gifts are much stronger than another person. Have you ever had that thought that you are better than someone, from this place of judgment? Yes, that's our ego talking. The dark light brings out your ego and misleads you to broken promises or gives you false hope about an outcome and it doesn't happen. This makes you believe that you are not worthy of all the success in your life. You start to blame others for the mistakes you make and your false light makes you believe that the world owes you something. I learned how to trust my immediate instinct before my conscious mind kicked in and rationalized what was going on. This was a good way to counteract this darkness.

As I sat quietly with Navaro I was made to reflect back on all of this and more to see the difference between my authentic intuition and the false light that I experienced during my years in the dark. The physical sign that helps me now recognise the dark light is a dark spot on the nose. I see this on the spirits who appear to me as golden light. Other signs are the pretend smile of a person, or just simply the inner knowing that something is not right. Or that feeling of sickness in the stomach or the race of my heartbeat. Or suddenly my hearing stands me up and I have to pay much more attention. You will develop your own process and that is a wonderful thing because this will keep you safe and protected.

I work with my authentic light and this light cleans my energy every time I sit in my stillness. I can now notice when a dark thread tries to enter my space and wants to pretend to be the light. All this has helped me to develop my awareness into the grandest light of me.

Not everyone is taught like this, and I don't want you to feel your way is wrong. We all get trained differently. I needed to be trained this way so I could claim my zone of mastery. So that I can be here with you and for you as the bridge between you and your higher self and teach you what I have learned from them.

Working With My Client

As I worked with my client, I gave her my tools of sitting with her energy and learning to understand it while connecting to her higher self. I communicated directly with her higher self to help her understand the unraveling and clearing of her energies so she can communicate directly with ease and grace and without the fear of being tricked by the false light. As we do this, she will discover how wonderful her light is and how that can bring so much joy into her life. We discuss all aspects of the light and dark, so she can gain a deeper understanding unique to her. For six months I walked with her and the results are that she now is able to channel her higher-self through automatic writing and channel directly to me. Her new tool for doing video journals is strengthening her connections. This will assist her to move more into her own understanding of her intuition. I now speak directly to her higher self and she gives me the information I need to assist her. Such an honor to be of service this way for my client.

Trust your intuition and let your heart and soul guide you on this journey. I promise you cannot mess anything up that is meant for you.

I would love to be your guiding light along your journey. Do you resonate with me, shall we connect to see how I can help you? If so, please book a free 30 min conversation at your convenience here: https://bit.ly/3yML5iF.

ABOUT THE AUTHOR

KATERINA LENARCIC

KATERINA LENARCIC is an Evolutionary Life Coach/Mentor, Quantum light Master, and Activator who is working with Universal Life Energy to raise the frequency for humanity and Planet Earth.

She is a Co-Author of the #1 international bestseller Collaboration: *Visionaries Share A New Way Of Living* (2021), in which she shares her journey of connecting with her Higher Self.

Katerina gives her clients a safe place to re-discover their connections with their higher Selves and Spiritual Guidance. Her Intuitive nature takes them on a journey into their own interdimensional energy field where they are assisted in discovering their own intuitive mastery.

Her clients establish a profound relationship with their higher selves which brings them clarity and feeling of greater purpose to achieve the goals they have set out for themselves. They leave her feeling lighter, brighter, and with the courage to stand in their own power of understanding.

Katerina uses her skills as a Reiki Master, Light Language Specialist, and Crystal Light Bed practitioner with Sound and Frequency to connect her clients with their universal life energy. With her Life Coaching skills and her understanding of the human journey, she is able to help you to integrate all of your awareness into your everyday life.

Connect with Katerina here:

Website: https://www.beyourtrueselfkaterina.com

Free 30 min Heart to Heart conversation: https://bit.ly/3yML5iF

For all socials and booking calendar: https://linktr.ee/beyourtrueselfkaterina

FARRAH MILLER

INTUITION IS OUR GUIDING LIGHT

I was smiling but inside I was a complete mess. I tried to pretend that Everything was just fine while my world was crumbling all around me.

I was twenty years old and freshly divorced. I'd been culturally pressured into an arranged marriage that I never wanted, but chose to accept because I was afraid to disappoint everyone around me. The scandal of divorce sent shockwaves through my entire family and my community made me the center of gossip. Divorce was taboo and it still is today.

I couldn't stop worrying about my future. I had fallen down the rabbit hole of shame and depression and couldn't see a way out.

As my life was spinning out of control, I took my frustration out on the one thing I could still control-my body and my emotions. To numb the emotional pain, I began inflicting physical pain on myself as I deprived myself with one starvation diet after another. I avoided confronting the emotions that were brewing inside me and I lived day after day in basic survival mode. I was constantly pretending that nothing was wrong.

So I developed a fake smile to hide my feelings, but I couldn't fool myself.

"These pains that you feel are messengers. Listen to them." -Rumi

Then one day, I decided to take back control of my life. That day, instead of torturing my body, I decided to go jogging. And that's when the magic happened. As I ran through the streets that I had spent my adolescence in.

Suffering heartbreak and pain, I decided to not be defined by my past and to carve a new future for myself. On that day, exercise became my drug of choice, one I have refused to let go after all these years.

Feeling my heart throbbing with anxiety, I had an inner knowing that I must move to a new city where I would expand and grow. I had to move away to know more about myself. This inner knowing inside of me was speaking to me without a voice but with a "knowing" which I followed without looking back.

As I broke the news of my relocation to Washington DC to my family, there were mixed reactions, fear and concern for my safety and well-being. They were so worried and scared for me. They wanted to help, but felt helpless at the same time. My father began to understand the pain I was going through and supported my decision to move. As I packed my bags, I felt an inner voice propelling me and telling me, "you can do this, you are much more than a life inside a box, and you must try new things in order to expand."

After moving to DC I continued running and exercising, nurturing the body that I had previously inflicted pain upon. The cycle was reversed and through physical wellbeing, I began the process of emotional healing. It hasn't been easy but I learned to fall madly in love with my life. Running became a part of my rhythm and helped me create dreams which were possible. The last eleven years have been transformational, helping me experience my higher essence, and connect with the One Infinite. I learned that our intuition is a gift and a power, and we must listen to it and follow its wisdom.

Eventually I came home to my happy place and I discovered the divine spark within me. Now I wake up unconditionally happy every day, eager to take on the world!

I had completely turned my life around. I took ownership of my circumstances, started to make internal changes, and worked on my mindset, emotions, and energy. I did not watch TV for 5 years, but I read, traveled, made connections, and had a successful career in banking. I then became a health and wellness coach, working with 1:1 clients, and collaborating with well-known brands like Clif Bar, Goli Gummies, Isopure, and many more.

Everyday I see myself in the process of becoming more and more of who I am. But the truth is that I didn't do it all by myself. Many have played roles as teachers, providing me with the triggers I needed to get up and make changes.

We can heal our lives, but sometimes we just need a helping hand, a little nudge in the right direction to instill the realization in us.

I can still look around and see that familiar misery in others that I used to live with every day.

I know the struggle because I lived it. But you don't have to suffer. You are worthy of being happy and loved and celebrated and that is why I am so excited to share with you everything I know about connecting with your inner compass and using it for your highest good.

> *I believe we all have the power, wisdom, and love inside us to change our circumstances and choose better life experiences, and the answers are within us, not outside.*

As society becomes more evolved there is a greater emphasis placed on processes, habits, logic, and mental toughness. Modern society can also feel a little empty and meaningless too. We have been ignoring our intuition in order to fit in. We choose comfort over pursuing our purpose. Behavioral patterns over thought. We choose a life that we think will impress others rather than living a life we find fulfilling.

Our intuition is a form of wisdom that is specific to us. Your intuition is different from your neighbor's. Your intuition can guide you to where you should be.

You can call it a gut feeling, a connection to God, or a wisdom that you've developed throughout your lifetime. Regardless of how you want to describe it, everyone knows what intuition feels like.

We all have intuition, but have you been using it? Have you been training for it? These are important questions I ask my clients when we first start to work together because that is such an important core lesson for us to be able to navigate our life's direction towards our highest destiny. We have been raised with no awareness around self-exploration, self-expressions, or wisdom of the souls. No, nada!

> *"Silence is the language of God." Rumi*

Rumi's quote hints at utilizing silence to connect to God, to hear the wisdom answers coming in the form of intuition. What we see with our inner eyes is what will be shown back to us. Our intuition is our guiding scale, aligning with our other guiding tools like emotions, breathing, movement, taste, touch, smell, seeing, and feeling. These are all here for our guidance, helping us shape our lives and evolve as we take the next step. So why are we so disconnected from our true nature?

How do we listen to the wisdom of our own intuition? By quieting the chatter of the mind through meditation we can tap into the whispers of our wisdom-filled intuition. Our intuition is very present in our thoughts before society conditions us to ignore it.

When I was five years old, in Karachi, Pakistan, late on a dark night, on our family's rooftop, staring at the stars, I asked why I was not there in the sky shining with them. Even though I did not get my answer right away, that question connected me with my star family heritage some 20 years later. Our intuition always talks to us. All we have to do is pay attention.

How you choose to view your intuition is entirely up to you. But there's no doubt that most people do experience gut feelings, hunches, an instinct, a sixth sense, or an inkling.

If you are reading this book, I know that you are looking to develop a deeper connection to your intuition and follow its hunches.

As a coach, becoming our highest version and incorporating inner wisdom, is what I love empowering my clients with, because I know the impact and the life-changing experience it can bring. The liberation and the empowerment spiritual development brings, can feel like love, peace, and joy in daily life. Inner work is rewarding and enlightenment is a gift.

One of my clients was suffering with limiting beliefs due to traumatic childhood experiences. Being in a controlling family environment had her feeling not capable of making her own decisions and she had to ask everyone around her for permission. After working with her for 4 months, she started feeling safe in the world, and taking each day as it is, perfect, divinely orchestrated, and now things are working out for her.

Overcoming Obstacles

Your intuition is often quiet and subtle. Distractions and stress are just two of the obstacles you'll face when learning how to tap into your intuition more fully. Eliminating obstacles is an important part of becoming maximally effective at anything.

Obstacle #1: Trauma

Traumas are one of the biggest obstacles that stand between us and our intuition. So many of us grew up with trauma and circled around the lower energies of guilt, shame, fear-based beliefs, and a dogmatic cultural environment creating patterns of depression.

So many live with the pain of the past and fear of the future. However, humans have not been taught to use the gift they have as their guidance, the intuition that is ever-present, a guidance from God.

Obstacle# 2: Self-Limiting Beliefs

Limiting beliefs are subconscious patterns of thoughts and habitual ways of thinking from childhood to past life times. Working on mindset and creating new beliefs but releasing old ways of thinking can help you create new beliefs and enhance your life experience. It helps with intuition strengthening, as you create new beliefs and incorporate your higher mind, you will start to realize the guidance you are receiving, called intuition.

Obstacle# 3: Lack of Boundaries

Diverted focus can dilute the intuition. When you are not present, you are not listening to your soul's wisdom.

Most of my life I was people pleasing, not being able to say no, shy and timid. That's why I ended up in an arranged marriage, even though my intuition was screaming to me not to do it.

As I began my healing and awakening journey I started to get so many insights to my inner values, beliefs, and passions. I knew in my heart that connection, collaboration, and unity was the way to live in peace and harmony where everyone, regardless of race, religion, or color is respected, loved, and accepted.

Strengthening Intuition

It's important to meditate and quiet the mind in order to enhance intuition. As we evolve and create a deeper connection with the universe, simply by raising our vibration and cultivating love for all beings, we strengthen our intuition and its guidance becomes more fluid; instantly available to us.

Breaking the forms which keep you from the thoughts that support the life you want to create is a mindset. Along with the shadow work that I help so many women with, creating the right mindset is life-changing. When we change our beliefs, patterns, and personal energy, we change our life.

> *"If prayer is you talking to God, then intuition is God talking to you."*
> Dr. Wayne Dyer

Managing a large, busy, high-profile branch for a large firm in Georgetown was a great learning experience for my personal and career growth. However I was not fulfilled with the job from the deeper level of my being. One day I asked God what my purpose was and how I could make an impact on others. In the days following that question I was led to a wellness career as a healing practitioner. These were intuitive hunches which I followed as they showed up in my experience. I listened to my higher guidance within.

If your life doesn't please you, the most effective thing you can do is to stop making short-sighted decisions. A few effective long-term decisions and sometime are all that you need to enhance your life significantly.

I share many techniques, tools, and frameworks with my clients to help with gaining clarity on their life's purpose, connecting with inner authority, and realizing personal power.

Use your intuition to make great decisions

Get clear: Begin to relieve yourself of all the opinions, beliefs, values, and ideas of others. These typically have little to do with you. Your decisions have to be right for you. Leave others to worry about their own decisions. If your decision is even 10% based on what others will think, you're playing a losing game.

Let go of your own opinions as well. Release your fears. Ignore your need for comfort. Ignore the beliefs you have about yourself. Reject everything that is not native to you.

Clearly define the decisions that need to be made and look at your options: Perhaps you are trying to decide if you should rent an apartment, buy a house, or sublet a condo. Find a quiet spot and close your eyes. Imagine making each of those choices and notice how it feels.

In one case you are going to rent an apartment. What are the physical sensations you're experiencing? What thoughts are you thinking while you are there? What emotions are you feeling as you move in?

Take a few deep breaths and complete the process with the other options.

Your decision could be very clear to you: The right decision will feel peaceful. You might feel excited. A clear *no* feels the same as eating a food you dislike. It's a clenched, restricted feeling.

If you fail to find a solution that feels right, explore additional options or work further on releasing yourself from the influence of others. It's also possible that you have a limiting view of your future or life in general.

The first two steps of this process are challenging but critical. Imagine at first that all choices are just as right as any of the others. Allow your intuition to guide your decisions.

Find your purpose in life: How do you feel about your current situation? Be clear on what you like and don't like about your current situation. Include the following in your assessment:

- Finances
- Relationships
- Career
- Hobbies
- Health
- Spiritual Health

Ask yourself, "What do I need to feel happy and fulfilled?" Find a quiet place where you are feeling relaxed and open. Ask yourself the above questions and listen to the answers.

Be focused on what you need, rather than what you want. Wants are often ego-driven and get in the way of what you need. You might want a jet or a yacht, but those things aren't needed and get in the way of living your purpose more than they help. You might, for example, decide that you need $50,000/year, three good friends, a cat, a piano, and a career that focuses on helping the environment.

Examine how fear is limiting your life: Fear has controlled your life more than you think. It has limited your education, career, relationships, hobbies, travel, and all of the other aspects of your life. Imagine what your life would look like today if you hadn't allowed fear to impact your choices over the years. If you were fearless in growing your career, you might be in a different place professionally and financially. Projecting what your life could have been without fear demonstrates how far your intuition could have taken you if you had permitted your intuition to direct your life instead of your fear.

What do you love to do? Find a quiet place again and ask yourself what you love to do. Ask yourself when you've felt most fulfilled. Be quiet and really focus on the answers you receive.

Ask your intuition to reveal your purpose to you. The previous steps were just a warmup. This is where things become relevant.

- Do more than just find a quiet place in your home. Get out of the house and find some solitude. It can be a spot in the woods. It could be a hotel room. It can be anywhere you are alone and feel comfortable, but it needs to be someplace outside of your familiar territory.

- Close your eyes, take a deep breath, and tell your intuition to reveal your purpose to you. Listen to what it says.

How did the response you received feel to you? It should feel 'right.' even if it feels illogical or challenging. Your purpose doesn't have to be something that's easy for you. In fact, it might be the most challenging thing you've ever done.

However, it should be exciting, interesting, and important to you. It might not be something that impresses other people. This is your purpose, not someone else's.

Start making a plan. We've all had great ideas that we failed to pursue. Your purpose is too important to leave to chance. Start making a plan that will allow you to immediately begin pursuing your purpose.

A life without purpose can feel like a slow, painful death. You weren't created to go to a job you don't like. You aren't designed to spend your time in the same way as everyone else. Find your purpose and make your life interesting again. That is when intuition is divine guidance.

Everybody has a greatness in them and a genius potential which just needs nurturing and tapping into. We are all filled with divine abilities; we can reach our heart's true desires and create our best health, wealth, and fulfil our life's purpose. No one must suffer. Suffering is a choice in many cases. Some of life's situations are, of course, out of our control, but many times we can make a subtle choice and change the direction of our lives. I want every woman in the world to thrive and get the best education, resources, and respect no matter where she lives. In many countries women are struggling, poor, victims of violence, or routinely talked down to. I want to see a change in these cultures and situations now. It is time that we understand that all humanity is connected, and when we thrive individually, we thrive together. We are the world we create, and following your intuition is an important step in that creative process.

I invite you to be part of my growing community and share your journey with me. I live in Seattle with my husband, two beautiful fur babies, and a lovely view. If I am not working on my blog or doing a live show, you can find me running outdoors by the water, having a creative writing session in a nice cafe downtown, or doing a workshop. As an empath, my superpower is to see the potential in others that they can't see. The childhood trauma and outdated patterns of behaviors always begin to appear, and that's when my work comes in.

ABOUT THE AUTHOR

FARRAH MILLER

FARRAH MILLER is a Quantum Vibrational Healer, Reiki Master, Integrated Nutrition Health Wellness & Life Coach, and Women Empowerment Advocate, who passionately helps women to stop asking for permission from everyone around them, tap into their own infinite potential, and create their best fulfilling empowered lives. Farrah empowers her clients to do their inner healing work, change limiting beliefs, daily habits, and take control of their emotional, mental, physical, and spiritual well-being by being aware of their personal energy.

Farrah launched her wellness practice after going through her own spiritual awakening and learning about healing and well-being and helps many women overcome insecurity and trauma, and move forward with confidence. She has been published and interviewed for her work globally and worked in corporate culture as a leader for many years. She gets featured regularly in platforms like thrive global, elephant journal, thought catalogue, and many more and regularly writes in her weekly blog as well..

Farrah's mission revolves around love, peace, joy, self development, and evolution, and she spreads this message everywhere she goes. She came from hardships just like so many, but she values self development and resilience in the face of adversity. She lives in Seattle with her husband and two cats.

Connect with Farrah here:

Website: www.farrahmiller.org

For Freebie and all other links: https://linktr.ee/farrahmiller

TRACY JENKINS

EMBRACE YOUR INTUITION AND TRUST YOUR PATH

What is intuition?

For me, it's that gut feeling that leads you in a new direction. It isn't like hearing a voice in my ear. It's more like feeling the words from deep within. 2017 was the first time in a long time that I heard myself. It was so quiet and yet powerful at the same time. My inner voice was the eye of the storm amidst the chaos that swirled around me. This was my authentic voice, my intuition, saying, *You need help or you aren't going to make it.*

Some people may call it the voice of God, others may say it comes from an angel or some other guide who looks out for you. Wherever you choose to say it originates doesn't matter nearly as much as your willingness to listen, participate, and move when you hear it.

If you haven't heard that voice in a while, or maybe even ever, I'd like to use my journey back to myself to help you reconnect and create a life where you can live more aligned to the person you were born to become.

1. Heal your mind to open your heart

As humans, we tend to subscribe to the idea that having feelings and expressing them is a sign of weakness. And if you deny your feelings long enough, they kind of shut off and give all the power to your mind.

But the trouble with living only from your thoughts is that's not where your intuition resides. So instead of being able to hear that important soul-led voice, you're functioning on thoughts and patterns that may not even align with your truth.

I started going to talk with a therapist in November of 2017. She agreed with me that I was not depressed and I didn't need medication after two back-to-back years of traumatic events - my mother's death, and a fatal work accident that my husband witnessed. What I did need was a way to "reconstruct all the bad water slides" in my brain.

So imagine that your skull contains the most incredible water park ever. All the slides are running smoothly, with water gushing down them. They are doing exactly what you built them to do. But the problem is that you created them when you were a kid.

And when you were a kid, your perception got a little skewed. Okay, a lot skewed by the events that occurred to you and around you. So you have to tear down all of those well-run, poorly built water slides and check the blueprints for the right way to rebuild. And when it's finished, they'll work well again, but in a much healthier way. It'll be exhilarating and excruciating.

We discussed specific events, but therapy is so much more than a "who did what to you" situation. It's not about blaming other people for their part in the way you built your water park. It's about looking at what you can do to heal yourself now. Thank God for neuroplasticity! My brain is recovering from all of the trauma I dealt with, and I am a different person.

When you can address and heal those subconscious ways of doing things, your heart begins to open. You start feeling more emotions and can express yourself more easily. When you get back to feeling your feelings, your intuition starts to get louder. And the more you listen, the more you'll hear.

2. Accept new possibilities

Maybe you had a dream job placed on your heart as a child. And then somewhere along the way, you watched the actions and heard the thoughts of those around you who made you feel like it was impossible, and you'd better just settle into something that made more sense to them.

But what would happen if, starting today, you decided to go full-on after that dream, accepting that it isn't something unattainable any more than the job you have right now?

Say it out loud, "I'm going to ____ when I grow up!" It doesn't matter how old you are or whether it makes sense to one other human on this planet. If you wholeheartedly accept that it can become a part of your reality and listen for your intuition to be your guide, anything can happen!

My mom was a nurse her entire adult life. She wanted to study sign language and teach students with hearing impairments, but her high school sweetheart (my father) thought it made more sense for her to go into nursing because he would be a firefighter (cute, right?).

Her last job was in a pediatric emergency room. She was the one they went to when they needed an IV started on the tiniest babies. I remember so many nurses sharing stories of what a fantastic nurse she was at her calling hours. If she couldn't be a teacher, she decided to become the best nurse she could be.

I always knew I was a storyteller. But after a year of college as a Professional Writing major, I veered from the path to gain my parents' respect and changed my major to a "real job" in education. I would become the teacher my mom wanted to become. I told myself it was my choice. My mom was so proud of me.

Just like my mom, I decided to be the best teacher I could be. But what I didn't realize then was the toll it took on me over time. If I had to keep doing it until I retired, I might as well be great at it, right? I spent more money in the first four years and took about 20 more courses after my Bachelor's degree. After six years, another teacher mentioned that I'd make a great gifted teacher, so I got a Master's degree. I was late to my first class of a *second* Master's degree in School Counseling because I was at my mom's first chemotherapy appointment. I took the final exam for that course online on the morning of her funeral.

I moved from building to building, thinking that with each move, I'd finally settle in and fall in love with my job. At that point in my life, I was only living in my head. My emotions were actually pretty cut off, to the point where you could ask me how I *felt*, and my brain would jump right into telling you what I *thought* instead. My intuition was barely a whisper in a thunderstorm. So it tried to get my attention physically.

Beginning with the first week of school that first year, I'd get ready to go and suddenly start gagging. I'd never actually vomit, but the heaving of my stomach would bring tears to my eyes. I'd blame it on anything - toothpaste in the sink, a temperature change - and then continue to get ready and go to work.

This would happen at least a few times every week. My two boys got so used to it, my older son could whip out a napkin from the glove box with amazing precision as I gagged above the steering wheel on my way to drop him off at the high school and take my younger son with me to the middle school where I worked. For over 19 years, this was my life.

In therapy, I was finally able to express that I wanted to write for a living. My therapist helped me get to the conclusion that my mom wouldn't want me to live her life - settle for the job that made sense to others, get really good at it to quiet your truth, retire, and die.

And once I said it out loud, everything began to change. Just like that, the gagging stopped. My soul was inching closer to alignment. It was like I stepped out of a box, and when I looked back at it, I realized I never really fit into that old box in the first place. Trying to step back into my "stable job" and forget what I wanted for my life made me more and more frustrated. But getting frustrated can be a sign that you're ready for change.

3. Set your intention and keep listening from within

When you speak your truth out loud, it's as though you proclaim to God, "Hey! I remember who I am and why I'm here." And the response is, "Well, it's about time! Here you go!" And as you move closer to your true self, more opportunities show up.

I started writing again. And I told my husband that by the time our younger son graduated from high school, I would leave education to pursue a writing career. But then I'd wave my hands playfully in the air and say, "But I'm bending time, so it'll happen sooner than you think!"

It's okay to set a goal and put a timeline out there. Remember, time can fly when you set an intention without getting too hung up on how and when. Take the time to focus on what you feel in your heart, and follow along. It's incredible when you start to see all the synchronicities appearing as you begin to listen to and follow along with your intuition.

In the summer of 2020, I was in a Zoom meeting with the principal and other teachers, discussing the next school year. I volunteered to take a student in my class who would repeat the year, and I heard that voice again. *You won't have her in your class.* It's more accurate to say I felt the words in my soul. I nodded my head and responded with, "Okay." It made absolutely no sense at the time, but I wholeheartedly accepted the possibility.

I saw a parent about a month later at a golf outing. He informed me that he planned to request to have his son in my class. And there it was again. *You won't have students.* Another deep breath and a nod to the parent, knowing that somehow it wouldn't happen the way he expected.

On the first day of school, we sat in the gym, masked up and listening to the principal talk about how the school would look different. Without any malice, and with each word spelled out matter of factly, as though my intuition was clapping with each one, I heard *You. Don't. Belong. Here. Any. More.* Moments later, I learned I was selected to have an empty classroom because they assigned the first graders who chose to learn from home to me.

When you start to tune in and trust that little voice, it gets bolder, and you hear it more clearly. In the shower, it was, *You need to write your letter of resignation.* Hours after writing a draft, a request for me to ghostwrite someone's autobiography came in a Facebook message from a new friend.

Update your resume. A month after asking in a writers' Facebook group for help with my resume that listed buildings and grade levels where I'd taught and choosing an agency to help, I ended up getting hired as a writer on their team! This was a turning point because I was getting paid to write. I'd become a professional writer (High fives all around here, kids)!

On my 44th birthday, I sent the final draft of my letter of resignation and closed down a school year for the last time. Since then, by listening deeply and going with the flow, my first ghostwriting project ended with that client receiving a traditional publishing contract. My growth in the agency has moved into project managing and consulting along with writing for clients!

Once you declare your heart's desire out loud, don't let your intuition scare you. My best advice is that if it doesn't make any kind of logical sense in your brain, that's okay. Just hear it, feel it in your heart, and smile to yourself. Maybe even nod in agreement and laugh at how amazing your life is. But don't try to figure it out. Keep going with the flow, and you'll be able to look back and see how the pieces fit together perfectly a bit further down the road.

4. Give your brain some grace

Chances are, when you start moving into the space where you acknowledge who you are and what you really want out of the rest of your life, your brain will have some issues with all the changes. If you're anything like me, you may have let your brain take the wheel for the better part of four decades, so it isn't used to being in the back seat reading a book or calmly looking out the window as you forge ahead.

There will be moments, especially if the change is rapid when your brain starts to get a little on the frantic side. You may notice that you start questioning your intuition. You may feel like you just made a horrible mistake, and the world as you know it is about to end, or you should stop all your nonsense and get back to your safe zone.

All of those kinds of thoughts are completely normal when you're experiencing changes. Give yourself a moment to take a ridiculously deep breath. Consider where the thought originated. Is it something your friend said? Is it your truth? Acknowledge it, then let it go. Thank your brain for looking out for you, but remind it that you've got this, and press on.

5. Let go of what no longer serves you

When you begin to focus inward, you start growing in ways that may not make sense to the people around you. This is to be expected because they're used to seeing the old version of you. When you come into your truth and start living it, you may surprise yourself with the confidence and strength that starts to show up more naturally as you listen to yourself above the noise that surrounds you daily.

Everyone is on a different journey. Some people choose growth, and some choose to put their heads down and try to get by. Some friends won't understand what's going on with you, and they may come across as bitter or downright angry with your changes. I have experienced all of it. I felt hurt at first, but I realized it wasn't my hurt to take on after some reflection.

Consider two parallel lines as you encounter people like this - one on the bottom and one on the top. When you find yourself asking why they can't just be happy for you, understand that it really isn't about you at all. You're on the top parallel line, and they're on the bottom one. You're growing and moving forward, and they feel trapped in the illusion that they can't change their situation. They're too low to reach up and give you a high-five. And you're too high to sink down enough to reach them.

It's okay to move on from people who aren't in the same place as you anymore. You'll start to notice that you gravitate towards others who are growth-minded. As you make new connections, you don't have to feel obligated to continue relationships that you've outgrown.

6. Go forth with gratitude and childlike awe

The best part of your growth journey is looking back and allowing yourself to see how far you've come, just by tuning in to your intuition and trusting what's next. Children get super excited about the smallest things. Why can't adults have the same zest for life?

Here's the secret - we still can! As long as you are here on this planet, you have the right to see the beauty in every moment, just like a child. Smile at the next butterfly that crosses your path. Nod in agreement when you hear your intuition, and it makes no logical sense. Declare your heart's desires out loud and watch them unfold as you choose to move towards them and put in the work while God gets ahold of those desires and moves them into your reality.

When we wake up looking for the beauty in the world, it can inspire others to do the same. And when you go about your days with joy and playfulness, your stress levels lower, and your dreams manifest at a much faster rate.

7. Share your story

Maybe you never wanted to be a writer when you considered what you wanted to do for a living. But guess what? Your story is worth sharing.

Leaping into contributing a chapter to this book was exciting and horrifying, even for me! But if my story can inspire one more person to tune in to who they truly are, follow their intuition, and trust the process to live the life they deserve, it's totally worth it!

When enough of us choose to boldly start conversations by shedding light on our struggles and celebrating our triumphs, it inspires others. And when we learn to live intuitively, there is no need for comparison or judgment. We can trust our choices and live our best lives while encouraging others to do the same. Can you imagine how the world would look with every one of us trusting ourselves?

Thanks to choosing to listen to my intuition, I *do* feel like a superhero version of myself. But it's just me. I've always been here. Safely hidden deep inside. Without all those bad water slides holding me back, life is much more interesting.

If this chapter resonated with you, I'd love to hear your story. And if you need help sharing your voice, now you know where to find me. Here's to your journey!

A poem, from my soul to yours!

The Goddess Within
Beneath the surface where no one else goes
I meet myself there, with the hint of a rose
She possesses more power than you might suppose
Speaking words without sound, I feel, and she knows.

Forever she's been there, but I couldn't see
Whispering watching waiting for me to be free
What kept us divided, a dark mystery
Diluted, dissolving all parts that aren't me

All along, she knew truly this power within
Feeling foolish, I hid it and counted it sin
My eyes slam wide open; it isn't a whim
I finally wake thus my life can begin

Her dress I see flowing and gleaming bright white
Crown surrounded by daisies a glorious sight
The smile we share beams with love's purest light
Two beauties we merge, now our dreams can take flight.

ABOUT THE AUTHOR

TRACY JENIKINS

TRACY JENIKINS lives in the US with her husband, two sons, and three small dogs. After two years of intense therapy, she was able to heal her mind. Then, by taking Mandy Morris' Love and Authenticity Practitioner Course, she fell back in love with herself and made some life-long growth-minded friends while learning that she can inspire others to be who they were born to become.

Tracy was a teacher in public education for 21 years before retiring early. Choosing to heal from within and follow her heart led her to a new career that she absolutely loves. When she isn't ghostwriting and editing nonfiction books or contracting with Legendary Ideas Group as a consultant and copywriter, she enjoys writing poetry, having deep conversations with friends, spending time with her family, and dreaming of a waterfront home on Lake Champlain in Vermont with her husband.

Connect with Tracy here:

Website: https://www.tjenkinswrites.com/

Email: tjenkinswrites@gmail.com

Socials: https://linktr.ee/TracyJenkins

DANIEL WERNER

DON'T FIGURE IT OUT – FEEL

HOW TO READ THE SIGNS AND TRUST YOUR BODY'S WISDOM

From Heady to Embodied

For the first 30 years of my life, I was what you might call a very "heady" person. Not surprisingly: I grew up in a scientifically-minded family, where solving crossword puzzles and watching *Star Trek* were some of our favorite family pastimes. This *did* have benefits: I understood complex matters really quickly, and logic came to me easily. I had stellar grades at school, and people kept complimenting me about my intelligence! It became my greatest pride. Ironically, on the flip side of the coin, I was also the most emotional male in my age group, which the people around me, even adults, didn't really approve of. I learned to shut down my emotions at an early age to avoid being picked on, and the resulting shame I would feel.

With these emotional traits, many things I wanted in my life always felt out of reach: Friends, connection, intimacy, belonging, and most of all, a sense of purpose. For example, I could never figure out how group conversations worked. People appeared to intuitively know when to speak and when to listen. It looked like so much flow and grace, whereas I was constantly trying to "get it right," say the right thing at the right time, and not embarrass myself. What I didn't realize back then was this: Most people were at least somewhat present in their bodies and could *feel* what was next. I, on the other hand, was completely stuck in my head, trying to figure it out.

The first time I came into conscious contact with making big life decisions by *feeling*, not by using my mind, was when I finished school. The big question was clear: What to do next? I was at a loss. The most logical choice would have been to go to university as a Computer Science student. The subject was fun to me, the job prospects fantastic. I had the grades for it, and could have easily gotten into a university close to where I lived. A lot of my peers did just that. Yet, I found myself feeling uncannily unexcited and unalive when I visualized going down that path. To imagine taking some of the advanced classes should have felt joyful and inspiring, but it only ever felt "meh." I simply *didn't feel drawn to it*.

Not knowing what else to do, I drifted along for months, feeling really uncertain about the future, until out of the blue, a large tech company invited my school class to pay them a visit. They offered an apprenticeship to become an IT Specialist — a certification that is generally considered "beneath" a university degree, so I had never really looked at it. Yet, when I listened to their presentation, I suddenly felt so excited! Much of what they offered did not only sound logical to my mind, but I also felt a deep sense of aliveness in my body. After letting it sink in for a couple of days, I just *knew* deep inside my body that this was the path I wanted to take.

The apprenticeship ended up feeling exciting, but also very scary for the first months, taking me far outside my comfort zone. I suddenly couldn't hide anymore, study alone and get good grades. Instead, I was forced to work closely with others. Of course, *all* my social fears and anxieties now showed up: "I'm not good enough," "I don't know how to talk to people," "They won't like me." Having to face these fears, though, without the option of backing out, had the most magical effect on me. I started learning to be with my discomfort, approach people anyway, and slowly, I was getting the hang of being with others. Being thrown into this situation provided all the lessons I needed to finally get the connection, intimacy, and belonging I had desired for so long!

Had I not taken that leap of faith to listen to my intuition and take this apprenticeship, and instead gone to university because it "made sense", those lessons would have taken much longer to arrive. This realization had me *really* start to pay attention to what feels good and right in my body.

Why Is Intuition More Important Than Ever Today?

I am not the only person who has had a seemingly illogical decision turn into a positive outcome that nobody could ever have predicted. You have probably had these experiences, too. Yet, sadly, in today's Western world, intuition is usually seen as "woo-woo", or at best as a way to *sometimes* make *minor* decisions. Even women, who are traditionally seen as the more "feeling gender," are being taught that what they are feeling is not real, or "too emotional".

At the same time, the mind (intellect, knowledge, smartness) is elevated above everything else. There is a deeply-rooted cultural belief that if only we are smart enough, and think about matters long enough, we can solve anything and figure out everything. This is not entirely wrong — after all, it has brought us science, medicine, and lots of other breakthroughs.

The Mind Is Not Good At Making Decisions

On the other hand, when it comes to decision-making, the mind meets its limits. Its ability to project possible futures and weigh several options against each other works well for scheduling things on a calendar, but not so well for the bigger life decisions. Because the mind never has all the data — it can't know about every single possibility that might present itself to us! It can only ever operate based on what it has learned in the past, or the information it is given, which also includes lots of societal ideas about what makes e.g. a "good job", or "a good relationship", or "success" — which boxes to check off in order to get it.

Through my own experience and listening to others, I have come to believe that making mental decisions is one of the main reasons we feel stuck in life, and in situations that don't feel good to us. We feel stuck in frustrating jobs we drag ourselves to every morning. We feel stuck in relationships that feel comfortable, but unalive, or which we might have long outgrown. Our socially acceptable ways to respond to these situations are either, "This is normal, you just have to accept it," or "You'll have to work harder, get a promotion, or maybe find a new job or a new partner that makes you happy."

Getting out of all of this confusion is why trusting our intuition is so important. It allows us to wake up to the realization that there is something deeper inside that can guide us. That we have our own inner knowing, our own "inner GPS". It's an inner authority, not an outer authority. And it's in the body, not in the mind.

This is relevant now more than ever. For the past decades, all around the globe, we as human beings have become more and more self-empowered. Breaking out of the "one size fits all" mainstream, and looking for our own answers when it comes to health care, food, love, sex, purpose, and everything else, instead of trusting corporations and government agencies by default. Today, we have so many options available to us everywhere! This means we need a way to decide *which ones* are right for *us*.

How to Learn Intuition the Hard Way?

All this is easier said than done, of course. After my experience of "intuiting" the apprenticeship, many more followed over the years.

Right at the beginning of my spiritual journey, I discovered that I wanted to not only live to fulfill my own desires. (After all, what good is it to the world when you alone are happy, and everyone around you is miserable?) I also wanted to help others find healing, satisfaction, and meaning in their lives. For the longest time, I didn't know what that could look like. All my attempts at "making it happen" lead to either dead ends or burnout. At some point, while I was taking time off of work to find out what I really wanted to do with my life, something magical happened: Through a series of "coincidences" I was unexpectedly invited to join a professional coaching program. In this program, I would have to fly to London every month for more than six months. Now, *why on Earth* would I want to become a coach? I knew I wanted purpose, but I also "knew" that it shouldn't look like *that!*

Yet, the offer felt really good in my body. I felt a definite, whole-hearted "yes". So I signed up despite my fears (and the rather large investment), and embarked on a journey of transformation, at times far outside of my comfort zone, that had me evolve more and faster than I had ever done before. Halfway through the program, I finally discovered how well coaching *was* suited for me, and how much I love doing it — so much so that it ended up becoming my passion. In the end, this haphazard decision to sign up for something "nonsensical" paved the way for me to find a large part of my soul purpose.

How Can I Use This Myself (The Easier Way)?

My personal process of stepping into my intuition was very gradual, probably slower than most people's. On the flip side, this allowed me to learn many of the lessons thoroughly, which now helps me lead others through their own processes.

The biggest breakthroughs in my life came when I started learning the Human Design System. It describes how intuition works differently for different people, and what a person needs to specifically look out for to perceive their own personal intuition.

Since every person is different, this is the point where I would usually give individualized guidance, and together explore what *your personal way* of connecting to your intuition is. However, interacting through the pages of a book is pretty limited (being a one-way conversation). So I am going to show you the basics that work for around 70% of people, and give you some tips and tricks to experiment further, so that you can find out what works specifically for you.

With all of this, I would really like to encourage you to experiment! Try things out, and learn what works best. Don't just take what I'm saying here for gospel. It has to work for *you*.

What is Coming Toward Me?

The first question of any choice: What do I even choose *from*? If you have a very active mind as I do, it constantly comes up with all sorts of good ideas and projects that you then *think* you *should* put into action. The Universe works in its own timing, though. We can "piggyback" on this timing, and align with it by waiting for signs and cues to respond to: What is coming *toward* you from the outside world?

It can be formal, like a friend inviting you out, or suggesting an event to go to. Less formally, you might come across a newsletter, a Facebook post, or a billboard ad that you suddenly feel drawn to. It can even be a conversation between strangers that you overhear on the street! Once you start paying attention, you'll be amazed at how much there is to respond to!

For example, years ago a friend invited me to the Maldives to visit her. I was a bit hesitant to take such a long flight. Over the next weeks, though, I overheard colleagues at work talking about the Maldives, a couple passed me by on the street mentioning the Maldives, and another friend of mine told me she was considering a holiday in the Maldives. A *bit* suspicious, isn't it?

Do I Follow It, Or Not?

The next question is whether it is actually a sign for you to follow, or just a random coincidence. Now, one reason why making intuitive decisions is not mainstream yet is probably that there is no one-size-fits-all formula to do it.

For example, have you ever heard the following: "Listen to your heart!" "Trust your gut!" "Let your feelings guide you!" Why are there so many different types of advice? Turns out that different people feel their intuition differently.

There are three questions you can ask your body to cover all of the above:

- Does this choice feel good to me?
- Does this choice make me feel alive?
- Do I feel drawn to this choice?

If you can answer "Yes" to any of these, then it's a "Yes". The specific questions that work the best vary from person to person. Usually, it will be a mixture of these.

You may, at times, get conflicting answers. For example, "I feel drawn to it, but it doesn't feel that good." This is where having patience and waiting for clarity is really helpful.

It May Take Time to Reach Clarity

There is an often-repeated adage in the spiritual community that "Your intuition already knows." However, it's totally okay and normal if your intuition doesn't give you a crystal-clear answer right from the start. Some people *do* instantly feel what the right decision is for them, and this feeling stays consistent over time (this pertains to about 45% of humanity). For other people (like myself), feelings ebb and flow like waves over the next hours, days, or weeks, with emotional ups and downs in the process (another 45% of humanity). For yet others, their intuition speaks to them in even more specialized ways (10% of humanity).

My emotionality was the reason why I didn't trust my intuition in the beginning.

For every single decision, big or small, my emotions were constantly in upheaval! One day I felt joy and excitement, and wanted to say, "yes!", the next day I felt apathy, and a strong "no". It took me a long time (and a lot of jumping into things and later regretting it) to learn that both the ups and the downs are just snapshots for my intuition. A clear picture would emerge over time once I allowed myself to feel through *all* of my feelings, and even then, clarity would only ever rise to about 70-80%.

One client texted me several weeks after our coaching session that even this little shift in awareness had created massive changes for her: She had started waiting for her emotional waves to ebb and flow until she reached a state of mostly feeling calm, and *then* making the decision. Now, she didn't feel angry all the time anymore about her choices not working out. Instead, she had cultivated a lot more emotional peace.

Is It Intuition or Fear?

At any point in the process, the mind will likely freak out and want to regain control. "This doesn't make *sense!*" "I *should* be doing X instead!" It's a very faithful and protective servant in this way. After all, its job is to keep us safe and away from danger. Taking new steps into the unknown can seem terrifying.

Be gentle with yourself here. Notice your thoughts without judgment, and come back to your body. How are you *feeling* about the decision? Does it feel good/alive? Do you feel drawn to it?

Even without any conscious doubts, an action you want to take can suddenly feel off, like an absolute "no". It may be your intuition — or it might be a fear so subtle and pervasive that you have gotten used to it.

Are there things in your life that you are regularly afraid of? Do you have fear of failure? Fear of not being good enough? Fear of being judged for your decisions? Once you are aware that these are fears, they are usually *much* easier to move through. Relaxation is generally a good indicator that no fear is subtly impacting your decision-making. Feeling tense, however, is a sign that it's time to press "pause", and become conscious of what is going on.

How to Start: Experiment With It!

Now, how do you use all of this in practice? I usually give my clients the exercise to begin with small decisions at first. For example, next time you decide what to have for dinner, take your time to feel into your options one by one and ask yourself the three questions. "Does choice A feel good/alive for me? Do I feel drawn to it?" Then for choice B, then C, etc. You will likely feel different nuances for every option, and for every time you practice. After the fact, you can always "reality-check": Did eating this dinner end up feeling fulfilling?

Please allow yourself time with this. Learning to trust your intuition is not a quick fix. It does take practice and trial-and-error. After all, this is about unlearning a lifetime of trusting your mind! I really encourage you to trust the process and keep experimenting. The sky does get bluer even after a little while of living by your intuition.

Living Uniquely as You

With this general process you just read, once you get the hang of it, you can already create big shifts in your life. How does that feel to you — do you want to try it? If you want to work with it, and fine-tune your process, or if any other questions come up for you while reading this chapter, reach out, I'm always available to talk.

If you have determined that this way of listening to your intuition is a good fit for you (preferably by feeling into it!), you can take this one step further and together we can take a deeper look at your unique energetic blueprint with the help of the Human Design System that I am trained in. This way, you can uncover:

- Where in your body is your intuition located for you, and how do you best work with it?

- Which energies determine and support your life's purpose? How do you find it, and how do you best live it? (As an aside: Once you are aligned to your purpose, so many other subjects like relationships and emotional well-being work out a lot more smoothly, too!)

- What is your ideal business structure (if you want a business), and the best way to cooperate with people?

- Which kinds of individual strengths, needs, and challenges in relationships does your blueprint bring?

Being aware of this information helps you feel a lot less resistance and more flow in life, uncover tripwires along the way, and live the joy and fulfillment that you were born to live.

In my own life, through Human Design, I found out that I am personally at my best when I motivate myself through staying hopeful and surrendered instead of through "kicking my butt" or "Just do it!", and that allowing myself to feel and express my emotions honestly is my "prosperity law". Once I started to implement these changes, my life began to transform in all areas: Relationship conflicts feel a lot less personal now, we are able to solve them a lot quicker. In my business, I discovered that I love to write, and many of my clients find me this way nowadays. Most of all, though, my life's purpose has crystallized, and the next steps keep appearing almost magically.

Knowing how to consciously work with your unique blueprint, and be in *alignment* with your personal energies, makes an enormous difference. It can save you from blindly trying out a lot of formulas that have worked for other people, but may or may not work for you.

I've seen it happen so many times in this work: Once you learn to know yourself, listen to your body, and trust your intuition, your life will take radical turns for the better, and you will never want to go back to how you lived before.

ABOUT THE AUTHOR

DANIEL WERNER

DANIEL WERNER lived a very mind-centric life for his first 30 years. Growing up in Germany and working as a software engineer gave him plenty of opportunity to learn that the mind is *not* the right tool to figure out how to find fulfillment!

Fast-forward to today, his passion now is to use the Human Design System to help people who want to change the world root deeply into their bodies, and find their own unique way of listening to their intuition. He loves supporting revolutionaries to discover their purpose in life, as in his experience, this is where the real juice and satisfaction live. Daniel is also an international speaker and certified Orgasmic Meditation© trainer.

Do you feel impacted by what you just read?

Reach out to Daniel at The Alignment Coach:

Website: https://aligned.by

Free Offer: https://aligned.by/freebie

Socials: https://linktr.ee/alignment.coach

PART II

THE FEMININE AND INTUITION

BRENDA K. JOHNSON

STRENGTH PLUS SISTERHOOD EQUALS SUCCESS

PRINCIPLES FOR LIVING INTUITIVELY

I wasn't even supposed to be here.

Experiencing the death of an abusive father at a young age and growing up mainly in a single-mother home helped strengthen me.

On Easter Sunday, we were all ready to attend church and my father was mopping the kitchen floor. Suddenly he threw the bucket of water all over my mom, who was in her Easter Sunday Dress.

We moved in with my mom's identical twin sister that day. The following Monday my mom was at work and he called her. Apologizing and trying to talk her into coming back home. She said no. I'm sure the noise of the shotgun rang in mom's ear as he shot himself in the head over the phone. It caused a ripple effect throughout the family. My aunt went into premature labor; their brothers came from all over the country to help out. Later we found out my father had cut up all our photos and most of my mother's clothing. He wanted to kill her, and possibly us too.

I wasn't even supposed to be here.

My mother took the life insurance money from his job at the Department of the Navy and had a new home built for us in Haven, Michigan, outside of

Detroit. Within a few years she started a restaurant in New Haven, across the street from the foundry where most of the men in town worked. My sister and I worked at the restaurant helping serve food and cleaning. I was five years old at the time; I started discovering my untapped strength early in life. My inner intuition guided me to fight for life.

I was supposed to be here because I had a mission.

I loved high school after hating junior high school. Being a junior varsity cheerleader was an early goal. It was achieved. The excitement thrilled my heart. At the end of basketball season, our junior varsity team made it to the finals. We celebrated with a party at a friend's house.

Never liking parties, I left early. We lived around the corner so I started walking home. A car pulled over with two star basketball players from the opposing team and another quiet guy who was a senior from my high school. "Want a ride," one of the star basketball players asked. "No, I only live around the corner," I replied. "We don't mind dropping you off," he said again in his nice voice. Quickly thinking with my sixteen-year-old mind and feeling safe seeing a familiar face from my high school, I accepted the ride. Bad mistake.

They quickly speed past my home and the two star basketball players raped me at gunpoint while the familiar quiet guy from high school continued to ask them to stop as they waved the gun in his face. Lacking maturity meant lacking intuition, the intuitiveness to sense danger.

After being brutally raped at gunpoint, I went into myself. That time in my life was horrible. While walking one day thinking in a daze, I met a girl sitting on the curb of the street crying. Maybe she was an angel. I sat next to her and cried too. We both did not speak for a long time. We just met with our shared tears, sharing our awful stories of being raped while hugging and crying. It was a life-changing moment. Now I had someone to talk to and share with. This was the beginning of sisterhood for me. A stranger turned sister.

After that, I began to dance at my high school, trying to regain my balance. Jazz dance helped me regain who I was. Locking myself in our high school dance room at lunchtime and after school, and every free moment watching intuitively the good and great dancers. Determination and drive became my best friends: I learned from those who already processed the gift of jazz, model, and ballet dancing. Spending hours alone in the dance room after school, teaching myself and watching as they prepared for the seasonal dance events at our school. A knowing inside was driving me to live, to survive. With no one else besides a stranger to discuss this terrible event, dancing helped me to survive.

Collaboration and determination became survival tools. Collaborating with those who had the skills that I was determined to learn. Within a year I was ready.

Have you experienced something tragic in your own life that forced you to take a different path or perhaps you would not have made it through? My life mission was coming into focus then, my mission to transform lives.

A transformational journey in our lives can be the bridge needed to change course when tragic events or trauma happen. When events happen at whatever point or time period in life, we must survive. We survive or we die. When given a choice after a deep emotional scar has occurred, we make a choice as to which direction we choose to go.

Dancing became a focal point of sisterhood in my life. Moving forward, women's empowerment was embedded inside of me. I wanted to work with women and help women. Everything that was done from that point forward was to help others. Help women. Changed forever, deep inside I chose life. To overcome and never quit. We can entertain Angels unaware at our lowest points in life. Some relationships last for a moment in time. Others last for a lifetime.

My commitment to empowering women is my lifetime commitment. Strangers have become lifelong friends. Women share an emotional bond. A kinship ingrained in our feminine nature. Our safety zone. From the lowest point in my life, I knew Sisterhood was a key element to a woman's life. Sisterhood at that moment provided me with the strength to survive. Stop and think of your sisterhood moment.

In times of our greatest weakness, strength plus sisterhood equals success. Working together in unity is the key to our empowerment as a woman. Success thru Sisterhood. How, you ask? By being each other's cheerleaders. By working together as women and encouraging each other, by knowing our Divine Right as Women, our Divine Birthright is to have wealth, we can obtain success through sisterhood.

That is what I teach as a part of owning and operating a business. Do you feel it is important to know how much money you want to make? Why is that important? Because without a target there is nothing to hit! By encouraging each other we become stronger as a group than by standing alone.

Sisterhood through Success

By being sisters in a sisterhood that is excited about the success of our fellow sisters opens us up for our success. How? Because, what we give we receive. What we want for others comes back to us. That is the way the universe operates. Whatever title we want to put on it, it works. It will work for you. It will work for me. That is the number one reason why sisterhood can be your Superpower!

Coaching is my Gift

Coaching basketball for girls in Kindergarten through twelfth grade was exciting. When living in Doha, Qatar I experienced one of the most impactful and enriching coaching experiences being the establishment of a women's basketball team for the College of the North Atlantic in Doha. Working with those young ladies was a gratifying and unique life experience. Working out alongside them challenged them and was challenging for me. We won every game of the entire season, but lost the final game. They did it. They didn't think they could do it. But working as a team of women, we did it. Teamwork was the key. They found their untapped strength: it was teamwork and having a coach. It was a sisterhood of women. Working together as a team. Inside of me, I felt a deep intuitive knowing that working with women as a team was an effective way of overcoming insurmountable odds.

Have you noticed all great athletes have a Coach? Great business people get guidance too. Think about back in grade school, that wonderful teacher that helped you learn math, Spanish, or whatever it was that you struggled with? That goofy professor that you thought was funny in college, but who in the end was one of your best instructors and this became one of the most fulfilling learning experiences. Your mom who taught you. Your dad who instructed you. Normally we had someone, or a situation in our lives that pulled something from deep within us that was hidden inside. That untapped strength within us that only needed to rise to the surface like cream in coffee.

Was it always so great and easy? Of course not, I moved to Afghanistan and opened an office in Dubai to start my coaching contracting business. All I needed was one big contract. That million-dollar contract. Ok, settling for a five hundred-thousand-dollar contract would have sufficed. But the short version was that the business only won small contracts. Then my ex-husband became sick right as things were turning around, and I had to leave Afghanistan and I couldn't return. I was devastated. Failure seemed to be staring me in the face at the loss. Heartbrokenness did not even describe the feeling.

Those are the times we either stay down or get up fighting! You either allow yourself to stay in the hole or, "get back up, dust yourself off, and start all over again". That's when I start singing my battle song: "I am woman, hear me roar...If I have to, I can do anything! I am strong! I am invincible! I am woman!" By Helen Reddy. Whenever I feel defeated, I sing it loud and strong. Reminding myself that if I have to, I can do anything. Driven by the intuitive deep-down desire inside of me. Inside of us. Something that we sense based on something deep within us. And yes, I pray!

As the founder of Powerful Women Business Academy, I mentor women to fill their toolbox with business-power tools to take their businesses to 6-figures. If that is your goal, I can help you. Together we will explore your untapped desires. Your untapped dreams and visions of your business. Using the strength of sisterhood and working together as women, we are powerful and strong. That is a coaching tool that I teach the women that I work with.

As I already mentioned, my mission is to transform lives, helping women with a mission. Helping women who want to take their businesses to the next financial level. Does your instinct drive you to take the next step to go to the next level? If you are not excited about what you're doing for a living let's work together to change the direction. I could show you how to do something you've always wanted to do or be. There are tools to open your long-lost desires for a business. Do not let your brain tell you it is too late. You're not too old or too young. You're the right person at the right time! Now is the time to move forward in your own life. Crazy negative thoughts will always cloud our minds. Yes, you can. You can do it. Use that inner strength that lives inside of our feminine nature. Those are the talents that are often dormant inside of us. The gifts that we do not want to die without even having lived. You have the gifts. I believe in you. Now you must believe in yourself. Use those talents inside of you for your future now. The untapped strength is there. Using that inner strength for your future success that is inherent inside of you as a woman. Do it now. Make the course correction today. Not tomorrow.

Each of us is gifted with an intuitive instinct, a feeling, a knowing, a belief deep inside our heart of hearts. For some, it is God in their hearts. For others, it is being guided by an intuitive feeling, a knowing without any proof of its existence. It can make you a visionary. A woman destined as a future leader with an entrepreneurial drive towards success. A success-driven modern-day warrior. Are you motivated to become a leader, driven by your strong desires for leadership without knowing where or how to start? Or, perhaps, you have started your business journey and need collaboration? The Powerful Women Business Academy was developed for women just like you. Helping you is my goal. Supporting you to upscale your business to the six-figure level is what I do for the women that I coach and mentor. Think about what a successful business could do for you? Together we design a program specifically designed for you. There are thousands of stories of women who have achieved unimaginable goals in their lives and businesses. Your name is on one of those actions. It is only waiting for you to move into action.

Have you ever wondered why many businesswomen do not have a coach for business? I have read that ninety percent of people who invest in coaching get results. We want you to have results. I believe that if we follow an individual program and have accountability partners, we're more likely to succeed. Does that sound like something that you would be interested in? If it does, jump on a call with me, and let's get going.

Did you realize many women that start businesses don't know how or what to do? Therefore, they do not even start. That is why a coaching solution exists for women. Selecting the right coach for your business is similar to selecting the correct coach for an athlete. The well-being and financial success of your business are in direct line with having the right coach for your business.

After serving over twenty-two years in the military training troops, and the other portion of my life working with women, I love the Sisterhood of Success! Laying the groundwork for a lifetime of giving back to others. That is one of the birthright gifts that women have in their nature. Did you realize that women outgive men and men make more money? Our organic feminine nature always kicks into gear and wants to help others. That is who we are. That drive and nature are the perfect characters needed for a successful business. With one of my Business Dream Breakthrough calls we dive right into what is needed for your successful business.

Another one of my business goals is helping women increase their income using their businesses. Because as women we wear a million hats! So, we need at least a million dollars!

Mother, wife, sister, CEO. We never quit. We never give up. That is who you are. That is the toughness built into us. The bold. The strong. The powerful.

Military women. Corporate leaders. All women are leaders. And that power stays within us. It never leaves. That is part of our Sisterhood.

The Three Golden Keys of S: Strength, Sisterhood, and Success

Strength

The strength to push through. The strength not to quit, stop or become so discouraged that you do not finish the course. Those are the characteristics you need in business. The strength and determination to go the distance. The drive to see it through. The desire to go it alone if necessary but of not feeling alone because you have a team.

Sisterhood

This is where the superpower of sisterhood comes into play again. To encourage each other. Using our own determination and drive. Working as a team can be a motivating factor at times, we need a push. At times your strength is low. When life gets in the way of strength we focus on sisterhood, a built-in nature that will help us through. Being in business by yourself but not alone because you are part of a sisterhood. Part of a Team. Teamwork and sisterhood are already in our DNA.

Having a sisterhood to undergird you and help motivate you through. Having those around you that are on the same journey, just on a different path. Having sisters who will hold your hand, so to speak, by encouraging each other, telling each other that you can do it. You can make it. I am on the journey with you as a sister. That is sisterhood. We are a group of powerful women all with different goals as to what we call an achievement. One may be running a publishing company, another may be a spiritual healer, another with a message business. The wonderful thing is the business principles are pretty much the same for all businesses. Therefore, we can run ideas past each other without feeling someone is going to steal your information. We are women from all over the world and from all walks of life united in purpose, goal, and achievement.

The final golden key: Success!

Your success is my success. Our success. Cheering you onward. Encouraging you each step of the way as you complete each block by block, brick by brick on the ladder on your journey to success. We each have a different definition of what success means to us. You will clearly define your end goal. Together we will direct you down the road from a dirt road to a paved road over the bridge to your high accomplishment. Building your business bigger and better than before. That is, you! That is us! You can do it! You are doing it! That is the sisterhood. Let that intuitiveness inside of you grow so that intuitive living becomes a part of who you are. Allowing that instinctive nature for fulfillment and winning thrust you beyond where you ever thought possible for your life.

Now it's time for you to have and grow your own business without a glass ceiling overhead. With the name that you chose on the marque whether it's brick and mortar or online, belongs to you. With your blood, sweat, and tears that will be put into it. S + S = Success elevates women leaders, providing them with the tools to achieve their ambitions! You can do it through the three S's of S + S = Success. Strength, Sisterhood, and Success is our superpower to business victory.

ABOUT THE AUTHOR

BRENDA K. JOHNSON

BRENDA K. JOHNSON is a multi-focused retired U.S. Army Officer and businesswoman who has lived and worked internationally in both beautiful and dangerous locations. Brenda grew up in a single-parent home with a business-owning mother. She has volunteered with many veterans and prison reform organizations and currently is a board member for Keystone College in Pennsylvania. Coaching basketball for girls, led to establishing a women's basketball team for a College in Doha, Qatar. Brenda is a writer and motivational speaker.

Brenda K. Johnson is using her years of experiences as a military training officer and business-owner to write and share her professional heartfelt experiences as a co-author in *Intuitive Living*. Her chapter entitled "S + S = Success" elevates women leaders, providing them with the tools to achieve their ambitions. As the founder of the Powerful Women Business Academy, Brenda coaches and mentor's women empowering women to live their business dreams and contribute to the world by assisting others.

Jump on your free 20-minute Business Dream Breakthrough Session where we take a deeper dive into what you want to accomplish in your business, click below.

Connect with Brenda here:

Website: www.powerfulwomenbusinessacademy.com

Free 30 min Session: https://bit.ly/3qkXrLj

Socials: https://linktr.ee/bkjohnson

RANDA SULTAN

BANGING MY HEAD AGAINST THE WALL

AN EMPATH'S JOURNEY FROM DELUSIONAL OPTIMISM TO AN EMBODIED LIFE

*L*iving guided by love is the mantra of any empath. As an empath, I feel your pain and I have the deep desire to help, to fix, and to hold you until the pain dissolves so you can be released from the heavy burdens you are carrying.

What I did not know in my early years is that there *is* a way to do this, without becoming exhausted, without losing self, and without carrying the weight of other people's pain.

Empaths also have the gift of being able to see the purity, light, and soul essence of each person. To see where the soul *wants* to go. This can lead to what I call *delusional optimism*. Having the utmost faith and trust in people and believing that each person is ready to step into their beautiful soul potential. I was steadfast in this belief.

For me, this gift has also caused a lot of pain, grief, and disappointment, as I was unable to accept the reality of how others were choosing to live.

I was on a mission to prove that the purity and innocence of my love could fix anyone. I just had to try a little harder, love a little deeper, take on a little bit more of their pain. I fought repeatedly for this to be true. Until concussion after concussion, I was forced to listen and learn. To eventually *see* the reality of what is, instead of sitting in the delusional optimism of what I wish would be true.

It has been a lifelong evolution of learning, acknowledging, and accepting that each person is on their own journey, and that it is not my job to fix or carry their pain for them.

This is a story of not only my journey, but the journey of any empath. The empath that tends to get pulled away from intuitive living when matters of the heart are involved.

The lessons learned here are intended to guide you back to being in tune with your own inner voice, living in alignment with who you are, and being able to *see* clearly. To evolve from the lower aspects of fear and loss of self to the higher aspects of love, wisdom, and empowerment.

Intuitive Living

Living guided by intuition is such an incredible experience. Imagine a meandering river and you are floating on it effortlessly. The river bends and turns, divides, and rejoins. As you float along this river you are relaxed, in body, mind, and soul. This is as life is when you are living in alignment. A life full of ease. Isn't this the ultimate dream? To live with inner peace, joy, love, and balance?

My life has felt like this, in phases. I am a free spirit, who has lived life guided by my intuition, not necessarily knowing why or how, yet allowing, listening, moving toward what felt in alignment, what lit me up, and following my passions. Yet when my heart was involved, in relationship, I fell into the role of the *unevolved empath.*

The unevolved empath lives in ego, believing that they are capable of and responsible to fix others, yet the evolved empath learns to be guided by their intuition. To hold the space for others to live their journeys of growth and evolution, by *representing* love.

Life is a journey of exploration, expansion, and evolution. Yet when we find ourselves repeating similar patterns with, no doubt, similar outcomes, we are stuck in the exploration phase. It is the ego that keeps us in the known pattern of comfort, whether it is "good" for us or not.

When we are stuck in the phases of repeated patterning, the Universe *will* send us messages. When we learn to listen more deeply, see with clarity, and are willing to shift out of the patterns, our expansion and evolution is possible.

My journey of evolution began with inheriting the empathic self from my mother, pushing against it, and moving away out of fear - to then moving toward it with love, embracing, and aligning it with my highest values and stepping into my soul purpose. Moving from the unevolved to the evolved empath; from *unevolved egoic living* to *evolved intuitive living*.

The Empathic Mother, My Role Model

My mother is an empath. She is an incredible healer, strongly intuitive, and a solid presence in my life to this day. She has always been there for me, my 2 siblings, and my father. People are drawn to her. They automatically feel safe enough in her presence to tell her everything.

All of these things I saw as an incredible role model of how a mother *should* be: nurturing, loving, caring, always present, and generous with her time and her love. I can still feel the safety, solidity, and security of her hand on my head as she would hold me while I was up in the middle of the night with yet another flu. With her, I always knew everything was going to be ok. She would take our pain away by listening and allowing our hurt to be shared with her.

When I was 10, everything changed. My father had a massive car accident which led to weeks of hospitalization, and months of rehabilitation. Broken ribs, clavicle, collapsed lung, and a brain injury. My father was a stoic doctor who had emigrated from Egypt. He was the *man of the household*; a man who also struggled with diabetes, OCD (obsessive compulsive disorder) and depression. It got worse after the accident.

At the core, he was an incredibly talented and caring physician, and a loving father, in the ways he knew how. Yet his internal struggles caused such emotional angst it was challenging to keep it all inside, and anger and rage would erupt. This angst my mother would deeply empathize with. She, in turn, was the receiver and carrier of his externalized pain, and emotional trauma.

It wasn't until many years later that I noticed she was *still* feeling and carrying all of our pain. She was exhausted. She had lost a large part of herself, felt little worthiness, and was physically carrying the weight of others by the extra weight she carried on her body. She had become not only the *rescuer*, but the *victim* as well.

Denying My Gifts

I knew at a young age that I could sense things. I was aware that something bad was going to happen before it actually did, and I could feel the energy of the room before I entered. I could feel the tension, the pain, the hurt in others and wanted to help to alleviate it. Exactly like my mother, an empath and an intuit. At the same time, the turmoil, conflict, and angst at home was too much for me to be able to handle, so I unconsciously shut that down.

When we are uncomfortable in a space, we go into fight, flight, or freeze. As a child, who was averse to conflict, fight was not an option, nor was flight, so instead, I froze. I put walls around my heart, a cloak over my third eye, and marched forward with less attachment to people, to the possibility of hurt, expectation, and disappointment. I became ultra-independent, a typical trauma response.

What I was doing was setting boundaries, put in place by fear. This was the only way I knew how to protect myself, for I didn't want to lose myself and become the *victim*, as I saw with my mother. When those boundaries weren't enough, I set a large physical boundary by moving 4,000 km away from where I grew up. This is something I was not consciously aware of at the time.

Finding Comfort in Mother Nature

I have been drawn to Mother Nature from the very beginning, connecting with her so deeply to taste her soil with my lips, hear the trees whisper, watch the snowflakes fall with such grace, feel the mud between my toes, drink her tears of joy and happiness. Constantly drawn to swim in her waters, I let her wash over me and through me to let me know everything was going to be ok. Immersing in the water, I could feel her flow, and allow myself to flow with her. Water, an empath's perfect companion.

Growing up in the City of Toronto (Canada) made it more challenging, yet I would consistently find my way to a forest, a creek, or a patch of greenery, even amongst the sprawling paved infrastructure.

What is it about Nature that draws me to Her? She *embodies* love, unconditional love, and acceptance. There is no judgement, no comparison, no expectation, no pressure. She exudes a rhythm, and if you pause and pay attention, you can hear and feel it. She is beautiful and raw and always present. She holds space in a way that feels supportive and safe. She is the ultimate *evolved empath*, who draws away and transmutes your pain without it burdening her so. She is inspiring. She is grounding. By tuning into her, there is no external noise, there is only intuitive listening and guidance.

This intuitive path to Nature guided me to become an avid environmentalist, and study Her in depth, to protect Mother Nature. Traveling from Toronto to the Rocky Mountains, exploring glaciers, mountains, alpine lakes, hiking trails, fossils, rocks and planting the seed that one day, I would find myself living here. By allowing the flow of life and my intuition to guide me, I now live in a beautiful small town in the middle of the Rocky Mountains.

In the winter, it is the blank canvas of a snow-covered mountain that draws me in. Can you imagine it? Seemingly barren, yet the snow itself adds an element of magic to the scenery. Mystical creatures form out of trees and rocks covered in this blanket of snow. Sunlight dancing off the sparkling snowflakes. Icicles dripping from branches. Backcountry skiing, for me, is the full immersion of body, mind, and soul to the incredible landscapes of winter.

It is a meditative experience. Sliding one ski in front of the other as you carve out your path through the mountainous terrain. Following your inner guidance and being fully aware of your surroundings. Always looking, listening, and feeling; into the wind direction, the sun's warmth, the strength of the snowpack, the angles of the slope, the complexities of the terrain.

There is no space for ego in the backcountry. We must be quiet in the mind, in tune with the messages we receive from Mother Nature, as she directs us to trust our inner guidance, and find our flow through Her landscapes, as in life.

Trapped in Old Patterns

Whilst I have always been guided by my intuition, when in relationship I would fall back into the unevolved empath role. Conventional advice teaches us to "listen to our heart", yet for the empath, this can be a severe downfall, and lead to being blinded by delusional optimism. Without healthy emotional boundaries, I allowed my heart to guide me with more certainty, or more power, than my intuition. Every empath goes through this, most certainly whilst in relationship, until they learn to empower themselves.

I recreated that for myself, repeatedly, in relationships with men who were sitting in the lower vibrational state of being. They were in mental distress and emotional pain, which I could see and feel so deeply. The pain which I attempted to hold and carry for them. I could see their soul essence and potential, wanting to reach a higher vibrational state, and yet was not *seeing* the reality of the situation.

If only I could love more deeply, could take away more of their pain, could show them what it would be like to step into their light. This delusional optimism led to years of emotional abuse. Manipulative relationships with men who would threaten suicide, resulting in my inability to leave for fear of them doing physical harm to themselves.

I did not have the emotional support at the time to help me through it. I did not have a role model with healthy emotional boundaries in place to learn from. I remained in empathy and made excuses, "it's not his fault", "he is hurting", "I can help". When a counsellor mentioned to me the words "manipulated", "emotional abuse", I cringed, I denied. Yet it was true. Again and again, this was happening to me in relationships.

How was this possible? I abhorred watching my mother recede from her empowerment, I moved far away, set up boundaries of all kinds to protect myself. I denied being an empath as I saw it as a weakness. I was a highly independent woman. Yet in relationships, those boundaries weren't working. I was vulnerable and raw, the unevolved empath at her core. Unaware that my boundaries were set up out of fear. Not having yet learned it was possible to embody the empath, setting up healthy emotional boundaries out of love instead.

Banging My Head Against the Metaphorical Wall

When we are given messages from the Universe, but we do not listen, the messages will keep coming until we do. Louder and louder, until we pay attention. For me, the messages came with repeated impact to the head.

WHACK... passed out on the slippery bathroom floor, a pool of blood around my head.

SMASH... tumbling down an icy slope, slamming into avalanche debris, landing with a thud, ears ringing, seeing stars.

CRASH... landing 20 feet away from my bike, dizzy, broken bike helmet, brain swelling, at risk of a brain bleed, which could kill me.

TRUTHBOMB. One that I was not ready to listen to. My concussions externalized and demonstrated that in my life, I was "banging my head against the wall" trying to fix the men in my relationships, and they wouldn't hear me. It took me a long time until I realized, it wasn't that they didn't want to, it was that they couldn't. That wasn't their path and I wasn't meant to rescue them.

Concussion Number 7

Biking downhill, accelerating through a berm, I see three options of jumps in front of me, I steer to the left, and quickly realize as it shoots me up in the air, higher than I have ever come off the ground before, that I am way out of my zone of ability. The thoughts are racing "I don't know how to land this", "This is going to be BAD". The ground comes fast, *too fast*, my head, my shoulder, my hip taking the brunt of the hit. I SCREAM... I know... this is bad...

That was 7 years ago. Concussion number 7. The one that stopped me in my tracks.

And this time I had to listen, for I could do nothing else.

At the time, I was in relationship with an alcoholic. A man who was in denial, as was I. As always, my gifts allowed me to see the incredibly beautiful essence that was at his core. My heart could feel the emotional pain and trauma that lay beneath the external persona, and that drew me closer. All the while, my ego chose to ignore the reality of the situation.

I knew I shouldn't have been out there biking on that day. I was tired and emotional from a long night of attempting to be heard in the relationship, to no avail. Yet I ignored my intuition, dragged myself out of bed, perhaps if I just pushed a little more, I would be heard.

Moving Inward – Exploration and Expansion

For months after the accident, my days were spent in dark rooms and quiet spaces. Alone for the most part. Muddled with emotions of blame, grief, anger, and disappointment, I sat in the darkness feeling more and more alone. It was in that aloneness that I found the silence, and now I was ready to listen more deeply.

Endless hours of reflection, meditation, qigong, grounding, and self-healing practices. I came to recognize that with each of these concussions, there was a lesson to be learned. Eventually, I was able to reconnect with myself, my heart, my intuition, my deep desires, my essence. I found my way back to the *magic* inside of me. Slowly, breathing into that light, letting it expand to fill me, and then outward enough to begin to feel the glow and share with others.

I reached out to my soul group of energy healers with whom I had trained years earlier. Through their unconditional love, healing, and guidance, I found myself ready to receive. The boundaries I had previously set up out of fear were shifting. I found myself able to connect with my intuition on a deeper level, and my abilities to see and feel the energies around me became heightened.

It was time to use these life lessons and embody my soul purpose as an evolved empath, as an intuit, as a healer. I called in incredibly soul aligned coaches and leaned into their support and guidance to further strengthen this newfound vision.

No longer in denial of my intuitive nature, I vowed to live guided by it. I vowed to do things differently.

Embodiment as the Evolved Empath

Moving away from the conscious state of *doing*, of ego, and into the subconscious state of *being*, and allowing the intuition to guide, is the soul evolution of the empath. I had learned to represent love by holding space for others, whilst maintaining healthy emotional boundaries, embodying the evolved empath. With this empowerment, the egoic empath that had surfaced in relationships was healed.

I stayed in relationship with this man, again with someone who was struggling with trauma and emotional pain. Yet, this time, I was able to hold space, with love, and allow for him to travel the journey of growth and evolution without the prior need to step into ego and attempt to fix or carry the pain. Even when his trauma led him to the darkness of depression and attempted suicide, I was deeply aware that the most loving thing I could do was to be present in my light.

It was within this space of love that he found his way back to himself. He chose to step into his full soul essence; explore, expand, and evolve into the possibility that I had seen inside of him. It has been an honour to witness him travel the soul path to his light, to fully *become*.

It shows that these men were literally fulfilling their part of the soul contract until I would eventually empower myself to create healthy boundaries and embody the purity of love.

Finding the Light from Within

We are all walking on our own path, and journey of life. Your experiences and circumstances may be completely different from mine, or they may have similarities to what I have experienced. Exploration, expansion, and evolution is available for any one of us.

> "I will not rescue you.
>
> For you are not powerless.
>
> I will not fix you.
>
> For you are not broken.
>
> I will not heal you.
>
> For I see you, in your wholeness.
>
> I will walk with you through the darkness.
>
> As you remember your light" - Sheree Bliss Tilsley

Today, I fully embody my role as a healer and acknowledge the empathic and intuitive nature I have as my gifts. I know that it is not my job to fix something I didn't break, but to hold space for healing to occur.

I see the light in you, and I will guide you toward it, yet it is your job to ignite the torch inside, own your worth and empower yourself to travel the journey when you are ready. I will hold the space for you to do so, out of love. I honour myself and I honour you in this way.

As a transformational life and mindset coach, I help women come home to their internal magic. Learn how to shut off the external noise by calming their minds and becoming in tune with their own inner voice, finding clarity, and gaining the confidence to allow themselves to be guided by intuition. I support women in creating healthy emotional boundaries and living in alignment with their truth, beliefs, and values, so that they too can lead their lives with more ease, joy, balance, and fulfillment.

We all have the light within us. Perhaps it is time to set it free, so you can shine brightly and feel the glow.

What would it be like if you could live in flow? If you could hear, trust, and let your inner voice guide you? If you could step out of your own way?

ABOUT THE AUTHOR

RANDA SULTAN

RANDA SULTAN is a transformational life and mindset coach, leading women to their intuitive guidance and empowering them to embody the magic within. She is passionate about living life in alignment and supports women to find their place of inner calm, clarity, and confidence so they can live with more ease, joy, balance, and fulfillment.

Her mastery lies in creating sacred, supportive, and nurturing spaces for women to find their way back to their inner light. In these spaces, she weaves together her extensive training and experience in energy healing, breathwork, meditation, qigong, life and mindset coaching to create a unique experience for each woman to heal and transform. She works one-on-one, in groups, in person and remotely.

Guided there by her intuition and love of rocks, water, mountains, Mother Earth and all things magical, Randa lives in a small town in the Rocky Mountains in Canada. She is often found exploring the mountains in her backyard, scaling cliffs, floating on planks in the snow, riding on dirt trails, paddleboarding rivers and lakes, and meandering on foot. Most frequently sharing these passions with her young son.

I see your light, even when you cannot. Let me guide you to your magic, so you too can live an embodied life.

Connect with Randa here:

Website: https://sacredprana.com

Free Embodied Light Meditation: https://sacredprana.com/embodied-light-meditation

All Socials: https://linktr.ee/sacredpranahealing

CHRISTIANE AMEYA

WOMB AWAKENING

RECLAIMING OUR FEMININE POWER AND WORTH

The Life of a "Perfect" Modern-Day Woman

From the outside, my life looked perfect. I was a 28 year-young woman, physically healthy and very beautiful. I had a leadership position at the Federal Employment Agency in Germany, I was in a long-term relationship and surrounded by family, friends and colleagues that adored me. I lived in a gorgeous 2 bedroom apartment in the city center, just bought a brand new fancy car and always had enough money. But the truth was that deep down inside I felt empty, numb, and incredibly sad. There was no spark of aliveness, pleasure or joy in me.

For the previous 15 years, I had tried very hard to fit into all the different boxes society puts a woman in. I was pleasing everyone, while in the meantime filling my lack of self-worth and confidence either with diets or emotional eating. My hobbies were shopping, getting my fake nails done, and partying. I was wearing tight pants, high heels and never left the house without makeup. I spent my weekends in bars and clubs escaping my day to day reality in alcohol and drugs. I found myself over and over again in unhealthy intimate relationships with emotionally unavailable men. And I was constantly stressed, exhausted and overworking in a job that I was unhappy in.

For a couple of years my body gave me clear signs that my lifestyle wasn't right for me, but I didn't listen. I had recurring abdominal pain and dizziness without any physical cause. Due to the constant stress and being in fight-or-flight mode, I had severe tension in my head, neck and shoulders and my energy was chronically low. I couldn't sleep at night and felt tired most of the day, which made me gradually withdraw socially. I lived from weekend to weekend, from holiday to holiday, from one little moment of exhale to the next. I saw various doctors, started talk therapy, took time off to slow down, and went on antidepressants. But nothing seemed to work. I felt like there must be something fundamentally wrong with me. Why would I not be able to function in the world like everyone around me?

The day I finally collapsed, I was sitting in my gray office as I had every day for the last ten years and handled countless documents and papers, deciding about peoples' financial situations and lives, who had often, like myself, lost passion and purpose in life. I found myself in a poisoned mud of superficial safety, thinking that this is what life is all about, and what I will do for the rest of my years on this planet. This thought brought a huge dark cloud that came from above and melted over my head and slowly inhabited my whole being. It filled me with an incredible emptiness I had never experienced before. Like in a trance I closed my countless emails, shut down my computer while witnessing the two screens becoming black, almost as a reflection of my own inner state. I left the huge amounts of paperwork and complaints behind, without worrying about who would take care of them and what would happen to my already stretched co-workers, and asked my workmate to drive me home.

What followed were the darkest, most scary weeks of my life. I went from anxiety to a deep depression. I thought I was dying and in some moments considered taking my life. Nothing seemed to make sense anymore. I had hit the rock bottom of my own so-called perfect life.

The Fall and Rise of the Feminine

Imagine, there was a time in history where the feminine in all her aspects was worshiped. If we look closely, we find so-called mother goddess figures in every ancient culture. Back then women had a high status in society and their magic ability to create life was honored in sacred rituals and celebrated in temples.

The world we live in now is deeply imprinted by masculine principles and completely disconnected from its original feminine essence. When I talk about the feminine and the masculine I am not talking about genders, but about universal principles and energies that we all have, women and men. We are growing up learning that the logical mind, being strong, productive, in control and goal-driven is all that matters. Feminine qualities like intuition, creativity, receptivity, surrender and nurturing are not valued and often seen as weak.

For thousands of years we looked up to a male role model somewhere out there in the sky for answers and the only option for women seemed to either be a virgin or a whore. The patriarchal suppression, conditioning, shame and guilt around being in a woman's body left psychic scars in our collective consciousness. We as women all carry the witch wound as a shared memory. In the middle age women who were in their feminine power were feared, hanged or burned. A woman connected to the wisdom of her body, her intuition, and sexuality is incredibly powerful. She is not second guessing herself or letting herself be manipulated because she is anchored in her own essence and truth. Over time, we as women began to deny our bodies and with this our intuitive feeling nature, and moved into our minds.

We don't have to go back that far to see that our mothers and grandmothers faced a very different world than we do. They had less rights and protection and they had to be very strong. Many of them not only had to escape from their homes and experience the brutality of war, but they also lost their husbands and had to build up a whole country, brick by brick. They had to hold back their sensitivity and their feelings in order to survive, and often became internally hard or bitter.

Expressing our emotions is a very feminine quality, yet from a very young age many women haven't felt safe to express their emotions. We were usually made wrong for it, experienced withdrawal of love, or even worse, got punished for our sadness, anger or fear. Most people feel so much discomfort with their own emotions that they usually try to either fix them or push them down. For little girls being sad might have been slightly ok but anger, no! Good girls aren't angry.

As we become young women our society offers an amazing variety of possibilities to suppress our natural capacity for feeling even more. The birth control pill, for example, but also alcohol, cigarettes, and drugs are substances which make us feel even more numb. We become tough and disconnected from ourselves. If you desire to feel more as a woman and connect with your intuitive nature and the wisdom of your body, you need to learn to get comfortable with the whole range of your emotions - not only the so-called 'positive' ones. You can't feel truly joyful if you do not allow yourself to feel your deepest grief. You won't be able to surrender into deep orgasms if you suppress your sacred rage. Anger also helps us to set healthy boundaries in life. If we don't learn how to express anger it will turn inwards and make us collapse.

Women lack education about what it means to be a woman and how it feels to live in a woman's body. In a culture of Barbie dolls, processed photos in high-gloss magazines, and beauty surgeries, women are suggested to from a very young age what a "perfect" woman (and especially her body) looks like. But no one in the mainstream teaches us how we can access our feminine energy from deep within. So we often begin to compare ourselves with other women or pin our desirability and our sexuality onto a man, and with this, lose our connection to our body and our intuition, and can no longer feel our own essence and aliveness from within.

Through Feminism we managed to liberate ourselves from the outside by expressing our sexuality freely, but most women don't feel truly liberated from within. Many women nowadays find themselves stuck, burned out and depressed.

The rise of the feminine is a movement that brings balance to the patriarchal and masculine structures that have long dominated our society. Now is the time that we, as women, collectively reclaim our feminine essence, because it is here that our true power as a woman lies. A woman connects to her power by turning inwards and releasing old pain, suppressed emotions, and past trauma in her womb space. It is when she loves herself deeply, follows her intuition, owns her worth, implements boundaries and embodies her magnetism, that she taps into her true feminine power.

Listen to the Voice of your Womb

She asked me with a loving and caring voice of a mother, "What is it that you really desire, Christiane?" The question was simple yet powerful. No one had ever asked me about my needs and desires before, nor did I even dare to ask myself. I looked at my therapist with a tiny spark of light in my eyes and said, "I want to travel." The answer came all the way from my deepest core. So I took the decision to quit my job, ended my relationship, sold everything I had and booked a one-way ticket to Asia to follow my intuition. Following our intuition can be scary. No one taught us how to do that. But a part of me knew that there must be more to life than I was experiencing so far. Do you know that feeling?

Inspired by the book "Eat, Pray, Love", I felt Bali would be a great place to start with for a woman who has lost everything and wants to find herself. Arriving on the island of the gods and goddesses on the other side of the world gave me an instant dose of relaxation and magic. I spent most of my days practicing yoga, sitting in health food cafes and indulging in the pleasures of delicious food. I began to meditate, and offered flowers and incense to the temple. Each morning I woke up and gazed from my terrace into the luscious green rice fields and I asked myself, "What is it that I really desire? What brings me pleasure?", and I began to listen to the silent voice within, and kept following its guidance.

One day my intuition told me to go to India. I had no idea where to go or what to do there but I kept trusting the message. On my flight from Bali to India I met a woman, her name was Katja. She told me that she was going to an ashram and that there was an Indian woman and they were doing beautiful meditations on the beach. I knew immediately that I had to go there. The same evening I met Amma, an enlightened master and teacher. I will never forget the moment she stepped onto the stage with her white sari, bowed in front of the thousands of people who were waiting patiently for her arrival before she started the evening bhajans, which is devotional singing. I couldn't stop crying. This meeting changed everything for me, because I was able to experience a taste of truth. She reminded me of the unconditional love of the Divine Mother and the deepest love within myself.

I began to immerse myself deeper into spiritual practices and tantric yoga. Tantra is an ancient tradition and spiritual path that can awaken you to the truth of who you are through embodiment practices like yoga, meditation, breathing exercises, mantras, visualization, energy work and rituals. While other modalities create a split between spirit and matter, Tantra embraces the full spectrum of life and teaches us that all is one and that all is divine. This includes our bodies, our emotions and our sexuality. We don't have to give up our own tradition or humanness in order to be "tantric". Having regular yoga practice helped me tap deeper into my intuition and strengthen my self trust. However, after a while I could sense that there was an important piece of the puzzle missing. One day during my morning practice I felt a deep inner longing for more feminine energy in my life. I wanted to learn about goddesses, sacred sexuality and womb power, and so I embarked on my first tantric women's retreat.

The facilitator asked us to find a place in our body where we feel like home. I was scanning through my whole body, trying to figure it out from my mind as suddenly a bigger force, more subtle but crystal-clear, guided me all the way into my womb. I placed my hands over this vast earthy space inside of me and began to breathe into her. For the first time in my life I experienced a feeling of belonging. Never before had I felt so connected to myself, grounded and safe within my own body. It was like coming home.

I invite you now, to place one hand on your womb and begin to breathe into her. Send her some love and ask if she has any messages for you. You might be surprised what your womb has to tell you.

The Magic of the Yoni Egg

The deepest pain and the brightest light of a woman are held in her womb. That's why my work is dedicated to teaching women how to connect to the intuitive wisdom inside of their womb space, and through this reclaim our true feminine power. If you are now wondering about how to awaken your womb in the fastest and most profound ways, then let me share more about the Yoni Egg with you.

The Yoni Egg symbolizes our womb and ability as women to create both within and outside our bodies. The word Yoni in Sanskrit means "sacred space" and refers to a woman's genitals: Vulva, vagina, and womb. A Yoni Egg is an egg-shaped crystal originally made out of Jade. The use of Jade Eggs is an ancient practice that originated in China to improve a woman's wellbeing and strengthen their sexual organs to activate more life force energy. The Yoni Egg is used by inserting it into the vagina in a very loving and gentle way. While practicing with the Yoni Egg, we awaken our sexual energy through awareness, breath, muscle squeezing, body movements and other special practices. The Yoni Egg opens our sexuality, unlocks our full orgasmic potential and helps us develop a deep inner love for ourselves. It also gives us a direct experience of embodied femininity and feeling whole as a woman. This beautiful practice allows us to release blockages, traumas and awakens and empowers our intuition and trust through pleasure. How amazing is that?

Martina messaged me because she wanted to join my Awakened Woman program. She told me that her Yoni was tense, her heart was in pain and she couldn't feel herself anymore. Martina carried a lot of fear, shame and trauma in her womb space. She didn't experience any real joy in her life, she never self-pleasured and she never had an orgasm. She thought she was broken and a burden for others. Even though her intuition told her clearly that she had to be there, her mind had a lot of good reasons not to join: "I don't have the time", "I'm not ready", "'I don't have the money". But she kept listening to the voice of her womb and said yes!

The Awakened Woman group program is an 8-week online journey where I'm guiding women through powerful self-love practices, womb meditations, breathwork and other feminine embodiment practices. We do powerful rituals together to create the essential foundations for deeper sexual exploration. I teach the women how to do breast massage and how to prepare their bodies for the Yoni Egg practice. We do audio-guided Yoni Egg and self-pleasure practice together and have live sessions and peer-support groups where we share about our experiences.

During the Awakened Woman program I saw Martina blossoming. She was able to let go of so much emotional pain. She said that she had never experienced so much love, openness, warmth, and had never felt that safe. Martina fully dedicated herself to doing the Yoni Egg practice. Two weeks later she messaged me and said that she had gotten her menstruation and instead of ten days of heavy and painful bleeding she had her menstruation for four days and with a super-easy flow. We continued to work together one-on-one and she released even more layers of shame around her body and sexuality. She opened herself deeper than ever before to let all the love, goodness and support in. She began to be playful, to dance and to make love to herself. Martina initiated her partner into Slow Sex and with this experienced her blissful orgasmic potential.

Six months later she left therapy. Her psychologist told her that he could have never helped her as much as this work, the practices and the connection to other like-minded women did. At the same time Martina started her own business and is now supporting other women to connect to their wombs through vaginal steaming and menstrual awareness. Whenever I see Martina now I see a completely different woman. The Yoni Egg opened her up to more love, deeper pleasure and helped her follow and trust her true purpose in life.

Martina's story is one of many, many women's who reclaimed their feminine power and worth through this deep inner work. The womb represents the next important step back to ourselves as women - the return to fully inhabiting the wisdom of our bodies, and reprogramming our sexuality, intimate relationships and work environments. When we as women open the gateways to our womb we begin to step into our desires, creative gifts, and take inspired actions. We follow our intuition and deeply trust the cycles of life. The path of the womb also shows us that the divine is not somewhere out there but instead to be found in the sacred chamber of our womb space. Then feminine spirituality is no longer a concept but an embodied experience that allows balance and healing to arise. Women in their true feminine power lift up their families, their communities and with this, our whole society. Let's birth ourselves into a world we truly want to live in. The whole world is hungry for more feminine energy. Start listening to the voice of your womb and trust your desires.

I invite you to be really honest with yourself. Ask, "What is it that I really desire?", and keep following your inner guidance.

ABOUT THE AUTHOR

CHRISTIANE AMEYA

CHRISTIANE AMEYA IS an embodied leader of the new paradigm of conscious love. Women call her "The Queen of Femininity" and "The Voice of Feminine Worth". She is also a love, sex & relationship coach with a holistic and tantric approach, female intimacy expert and modern mystic.

Christiane helps female entrepreneurs to reconnect to their feminine essence, have meaningful sex and create loving relationships. Since 2015 she has worked with more than 1,000 women privately. Her work has touched women's hearts in more than 50 countries through her 1:1 sessions, online programs, retreats and trainings. German-born, she currently lives in Ibiza. To receive her free guided meditation "Awaken your feminine essence" click the link below.

Connect with Christiane here:

Website: www.christianeameya.com

Freebie: https://christianeameya.com/freemeditation/

Linktree: https://linktr.ee/christianeameya

JUSTINA CASUARINA

YOUR BLOOD IS SACRED

RECLAIMING THE POWER, BEAUTY & WISDOM OF YOUR MENSTRUAL CYCLE

Dedicated to my mother Kath Kelly (30/06/1944 - 15/05/2021)

In this chapter I will attempt to break down the negative imprints placed upon women's menstrual cycles, to help clear the oppression and suppression of our intuitive & cyclical natures, and reclaim the sacredness of our bodies and our blood. My mission is to inspire the clearing of shame, taboo and disgust that so many carry in relation to women's period's, whilst assisting the transformation of bringing it back to a place of sacredness, honour, reverence and respect.

"This is what happens to us women each month when we are not pregnant and carrying a baby in our bellies", my mother would tell me in a very grounded, easeful manner as I followed her around our home enquiring as to what she was up to in the bathroom, and why she had tampons and pads in her possession. These are some of the earliest recollections I have of her. My mother raised me to be excited and proud of becoming a young woman. She would always answer my questions relating to my natural curiosity around my body and female anatomy with age-appropriate responses, providing me with books on becoming a woman, periods, and how our bodies work. When she was pregnant with my sister, and I was only 8 years of age, she would fuel my inquisitive nature about reproduction, sex, and child birth in a similar way. I devoured this information. I was thrilled that I was to become a woman and that one day I too may be pregnant, gestate, birth, and raise my babies in this world.

It's no surprise that the most positive and profound imprint my mother had on me was that of excitement and anticipation around becoming a woman. My first period would be the beginning of that journey. I was literally the 11 year old who would run to the bathroom to check whether anything had "shown up" that day on my underwear. I could not wait to become a woman, to have my first period, and enter the magical & mysterious realms of womanhood, discovering the secrets of my feminine form and nature.

I was a competitive & avid swimmer, in the water at any opportunity, so the only concern I had about entering the world of women's business was that it might complicate things in the water for me, possibly limiting my swimming time. It didn't. I never cramped, had migraines, felt sick, or struggled with tampons like so many of my peers. It just wasn't an issue for me at all. I wasn't disgusted nor embarrassed. I was extremely proud of myself and wanted the world to know I was now a woman. I attribute the excitement and celebration I had about becoming a woman, to the message my mother carried within her and impregnated me with, that having a period is completely normal. For that I am truly grateful.

My experience is however definitely and very sadly not the norm for women globally. In fact it's quite the contrary. Reflecting on this and what I've discovered throughout my extensive work with women, I believe that the shame and guilt women carry around their menstrual cycles may very well contribute to pain, hormonal imbalances and disharmony throughout a woman's monthly cycle.

For more than 2 decades I have had the honour of being a women's educator, working and guiding women in the areas of feminine embodiment, dance, childbirth education, menstrual awareness, and the healing arts. The past 13 years, I've had the incredible opportunity to be specialising in the field of women's pelvic and sexual health & wellness, with a body of work that supports women to come home deeply to their bodies, anchoring greater self-love. It involves the ancient & sacred jade egg practice, which revolves around an embodied psycho-sexual method. Throughout this time, something that has profoundly impacted me, over and over again, is that in all the tens of thousands of women I have connected with, my experience and imprint around menstruation was and still is, in an extreme minority. That is, most women entered into menarche, their first period, with exceptionally low amounts of education or preparation on this most important and profound process of the feminine anatomy, or they had absolutely none at all.

I have heard endless stories of the horrific experiences women had at this time in their lives. Stories such as, thinking they were going to die, that they were extremely abnormal, being frowned upon or brushed aside by their parents, bleeding through their clothes in extremely embarrassing circumstances in front of their peers, using socks to "block up their flow", the list goes on. First experiences like these left imprints on women of great shock, shame and trauma. The awareness of this gave me a burning desire to inspire and empower women by helping them learn more about the magic they hold within, to support them to become fully educated on the magnificence of their bodies and to clear the psycho-sexual imbalances that play out, so they can enjoy more of the fullness and totality of being a woman.

Statistics On Menstruation

To assist in some perspective of how important it is we embrace, learn to love and work with our cycles, here are some simple yet potent statistics I have gathered from numerous sources over the years: approximately half the population on the planet, roughly 3.5 billion or so humans are women, and will menstruate for roughly 40 years, every 21 - 35 days, between 3 - 7 days on average each period, during a healthy menstrual cycle. If we look at the average menstruating woman, we can say, as an estimate, that she will have 450 - 480 periods throughout her lifetime. She will bleed for approximately 3500 days, which equates to bleeding roughly for 10 years in total. Women will literally be menstruating for around 10 years throughout their lives. Astounding right?! Let those figures sink in. My wish is that by realising the enormity of the amount of time a woman bleeds for, that we may reassess the importance as well as relevance of education, care and respect for this time.

History & Menstruation At A Glance

Over the past 25 years, I have studied the way our ancestors related to their menstrual cycles with fascination and awe, and will share a very brief summary of my understanding to help bring things into perspective.

Since the beginning of life on Earth, women have menstruated, and in order to continue the procreation of the human race, women will be menstruating forever more.

If we look to the past as a reference point, there was a time in this world where women's bodies, their natural rhythms and cyclical ways were honoured as a magical, organic and powerfully potent part of life. 11th and 12th century art works such as Sheela Na Gig's, which were found above the doorways at the entrance to churches, cathedrals and temples, offer prime examples of this. Throughout time this picture changed. Many women lost their connection with their body. They stopped trusting their body and the guidance it was offering them.

Numerous communities, tribes and cultures understood that menstruating women, (as well as pregnant women and the crones who had already transitioned through change of life, beyond menopause), were in an altered state of being, and were looked to, in fact often revered as oracles to varying degrees.

The reason for this is because the menstruating woman enters into a slightly altered state of being during her menses, through a combination of hormonal, brain and bodily changes which occur each month. Have you ever noticed that when you're pre- menstrual or menstruating, not only are you lower in energy, your brain may also feel not as sharp or switched on? If during these times you are able to take space for yourself, to rest, rejuvenate and replenish, you will find that you have heightened intuition and knowing. You are more likely to gain clarity on correct forward movement on subjects and situations in your life that you have not been clear on. You will also regain energy as after all you are losing blood from your body.

When a woman bleeds, it's akin to a portal being opened for access to her higher insight, wisdom, her intuition. As she approaches this phase within her monthly cycle, it would be of great service to her as well as her family and community, to set things in place so she can benefit and drink at this time between realms more fully.

In the ancient and not so ancient times women and priestesses knew this. They would create places and spaces, in fact many even had temples built where they could take time out from daily life and tasks to rest, rejuvenate, replenish and reflect. They would do this with other women weaving in rituals, supporting one another and enjoying this time for the pause and reset it would give to them.

They recognised their bleed as an indicator of fertility and that this is something to be celebrated. They also considered their lifeblood to be sacred.

By sacred I mean something to be treasured, that is precious as it is not here forever, only for a certain amount of time, even to be in awe of. We could learn a lot from the common practises and the wisdom of our ancestors. Like them, if we are open and willing to work with our body's natural cycles, our wellbeing and lifestyle will be enhanced.

How did something so profound and sacred become such a taboo subject that has most of the human race completely disconnected from it? With so many negative thoughts surrounding it? Could the disconnect women experience, as well as the shame and guilt related to their menstrual blood, be a major contributor in the pain and discomfort, as well as imbalances women experience with their cycles?

The Disconnection

Throughout time, it was decided that menstruation was dirty, shameful and something definitely to be hidden. Many men feared our gender as we could bleed without dying. The significance and importance of our cycles was misunderstood. Women who were deeply connected to their bodies, also held a great connection to the Earth. This combination brings a woman more fully into her power, and this too was something many men feared. Women who were menstruating were seen as gross, unclean and disgusting. Many were ostracised and shamed from some sectors of the community. Today, unfortunately, the same continues in some parts of the world where menstruating women are put in outhouses under dangerous and debilitating circumstances which can lead to death (New York Times: "Where Taboo Is Leading To The Death Of Young Girls").

Women, over time, began giving their power away to the patriarchal medical system, which has also been a major contributor to the disconnection women experience from their bodies and cycles. Sadly, so many women now distrust their own body, looking outside of themselves, rather than within, or to wiser, older women, for guidance on what to do when, in order to support their feminine health and vitality.

Let us reflect for a moment on the collective story that has been told about menstruation. A fabulous way to start is to look at what stories you hold around women's bodies & their menstrual cycles. Reflect on your first experiences. If you're a woman reading this, were you educated on periods before your first bleed? Was your first period celebrated or at least positively embraced in some way? If you didn't have a positive experience, what would you have loved in place of this that would have set you up for a life of happy periods? If you're a man reading this, when did you first become aware of periods? What beliefs and stories were you told? What are your thoughts and beliefs on menstruation today, and do they possibly need updating?

The Impact The Disconnection Has Had On Women Physically & Emotionally

Women are like the seasons, cyclical and ever changing. Like mother nature herself: sometimes unpredictable. We don't expect nature to produce all year around, we accept that it has its quiet, internal, down times. What if we were to allow, or encourage our women to really tune into themselves, their body, and take time out to nourish and replenish when they need it. We never rush the bud of a flower to blossom into full bloom, yet we have been conditioned to push aside & override our own needs, expecting the same from one another. I believe it is of great importance that we become acutely aware that women are literally designed to be in an outward giving, external mode for half the month and an inward receiving, internal mode for the other half. Our bodies, brains and hormones have been hard wired for that.

In the body of work I teach women, for their pelvic & sexual health & vitality, we understand that the psycho-sexual nature of a woman, i.e.: the way she is feeling, has great influence over her sexual health and wellbeing. It is clear to me the amount of feminine imbalances such as: endometriosis, PMS, bloating, sore / tender breasts and nipples, mood swings, brain fog, ovarian cysts, fibroids, polyps, PCOS, clotting, severe cramping, and pain, are huge indications that our psycho-sexual selves are not in balance, and wreaking havoc on our delicate endocrine systems.

Cultivating Deeper Connection To Your Menstrual Cycle

If you wish to return to harmony and respect within your body and desire to trust yourself deeply, tune into and trust the wisdom of your menstrual cycle and your beautiful body.

My invitation to you is to come back home to your body, honouring it as the sacred temple that it is. Tune in and ask yourself what feels good? What doesn't feel good? Learn to trust her to guide you on what is a 'yes', and what is a 'no' for you, remembering that a maybe is a 'no' until it is a 'yes'. This is a powerful practice you can use in all areas of your life for clarity.

I am a passionate believer that women are equipped with their own internal guidance systems, their intuition. If we are carrying shame, guilt, repulsion and or mistrust in our body, this will absolutely disconnect us from it.

The more a woman listens to and tunes in to her body, the greater her knowing and intuition will be, therefore she will learn to trust herself deeply. On the flip side, if women override their needs and disconnect, it can throw our body into all sorts of imbalances, represented by disease. When we are at home, anchored in, and at peace with our body, we are able to hear and feel the subtle cues and nuances she gives us as to what our needs are, what is the right action for us, e.g.: When our bodies need to rest, being able to hear, rather than override that, and take time out. The opposite of this is waiting for our body's major loud cues to scream at us, developing conditions such as adrenal or chronic fatigue.

A couple of easy-to-implement ways to support you to tune into your body, understand more about your cycle, and access greater levels of trust within your body and your intuitive nature are to:

> 1) Track your cycle on a chart. (An example of this can be found as a free download via my website: www.femininevitality.com). This is the number one step to begin with to allow you to know how long your cycle is, when it is next due, and you can start to plan life around this, based on internal/low energy times and more external/higher energy times, or, the phases of our cycles. It is great if your partner can see this as well, as it's priceless information for them to be aware of too. You can, of course, access apps for this, however, I am old school and am a big believer in pen to paper for this practice. The main reason being that apps miscalculate sometimes and can lead you astray. This is particularly important to be aware of if you are wishing to avoid pregnancy. A good chart will also allow you room to track your moods, libido, appetite etc., so you will begin to see patterns emerging and understand what time of the month various rhythms and patterns occur.
>
> 2) Use period products that are gentle on your body as well as the environment. There are so many products available which are full of bleaches, dyes, chemicals, perfumes, pesticides, etc. that all wreak havoc on women's delicate endocrine systems, tipping it out of balance, and causing many problems, so go natural, preferably organic.

3) Cultivate and stay deeply connected to the Earth. Spend time in nature regularly, preferably daily. This is especially supportive during the premenstrual or luteal phase just before our periods. Ground, calm, clear, replenish and rejuvenate. This is vitally important for any woman wishing to have a profound connection to her body, intuition and wishing to trust her instincts.

4) Block out time each month when you will be bleeding to do as little as possible, resting, replenishing, rejuvenating and dreaming, and

5) Have nourishing food prepared in advance for your bleeding time, so you don't have to cook.

Can you lean into accepting that you are a menstruating woman? The more you embrace, celebrate and accept this as the beautiful, sacred gift it is, the more ease and flow, (literally), there will be in your body, and your life.

Considering all of the above, I encourage you to sit with everything I've shared, allow any thoughts that may have been stirred to arise, move through you, and observe how this feels within your body and your heart. Perhaps some of this spoke deeply to you, possibly even all of it. My wish is that something, even one little piece may land for you, and help in the positive, empowering and uplifting transformation of the global perception of women and our menstrual cycles.

Your blood is sacred. We all require a menstruating woman to enter this world, as a menstruating woman will ovulate, and through ovulation a new life may be conceived. Now is the time to reclaim with reverence and respect, the connection this process gives us to all women everywhere, to all life, and to the earth. To our bodies and our deep intuition. It's time to reclaim the sacredness that being a cycling woman brings to us, as it allows human life to continue on the planet and indicates the state of health of each woman.

If this chapter has spoken to you and you would love to deepen your exploration and understanding of your menstrual cycle, cultivating more harmony with your body, I invite you to connect with me via my website or social media for the programs, courses and sessions that I offer.

Imagine for a moment now, how different your life and this world would be, if this completely healthy, natural and organic process that most women will go through for decades, every month throughout their lifetime, was more fully embraced and understood. Let's put it in its rightful place of being an indicator of our health, a guide to what activities are best for us to do when, our portal to access our intuitive nature, a time to rest and replenish, and if we choose, the fertile ground to which brand new life can be brought onto the planet. Miraculous, marvellous, magical, extraordinary, beautiful, and yes, sacred.

ABOUT THE AUTHOR

JUSTINA CASUARINA

JUSTINA CASUARINA a is an educator, focusing on feminine embodiment, sexual sovereignty, menstrual awareness, peri-menopause and beyond. With over 25 years of experience, she specialises in Jade Eggs and their teachings, for women's pelvic and sexual health and vitality.

Justina is a leading expert in women's psycho-sexual health & healing. Featured on numerous podcasts and facilitating at conferences throughout Australia. She is known for speaking the unspoken and bringing fresh new perspectives to light. Justina created Cultivating Lifelong Pleasure, Embodiment & Feminine Vitality, to support women of all ages to have empowering practices they can carry throughout their entire lifetime.

Justina holds a vision of a world where women carrying shame and guilt in their bodies is a thing of the past, and the new norm is women coming home to themselves, holding great love and reverence within, seeing their bodies as the sacred temples that they are. She knows that as women do this, men and children will too, creating profound transformation on the planet.

Mother of two, 20 & 16 years, Justina lives in Byron Bay Australia and is often found swimming or dancing somewhere fabulous.

Connect with Justina here:

Website: www.femininevitality.com

Freebie: www.femininevitality.com/offer

All socials: https://linktr.ee/Femininevitality

EVA ARISSANI

SHE PHOENIX: THE RISE

*A*sha started to feel cold, then dizzy, sleepy... soon she lost consciousness. Her fourteen-year-old body laid still on the floor. Her breathing slowed down. The growing life inside of her probably did not understand what was going on. How did things come to this? How did little Asha end up in such a mess? How? What could have happened to push her to the edge?

> *Have you ever been in a situation where you feel as if you were in a horror movie where you are the main character and you feel almost struck by fear to such an extent that you see no way out?*

A few months earlier...

Asha was looking fondly at him and thinking how blessed she was to have found someone who made her feel so alive and loved. Since her parents split up, home had never been the same. Every day was a reminder of everything they had lost. Every day came with daunting questions: "Will we have something to eat?" "Will we survive the day?" It was a lot for the young soul who only longed for a life filled with joy and blitheness. So, every morning, she left all her worries and hardships at home and looked for an escape at school. Asha found that escape in Sefu. The seventeen-year-old was a good looking hunk. When Asha and Sefu met, they immediately clicked. Every time she was with him, Asha forgot about all the difficulties she and her family were going through financially. One day, they decided to take their relationship to the next level. They met at his home. Asha did not think that through. She blindly and naively wanted to be like other girls and be a *real* girlfriend to Sefu. He took Asha's flower. As this was done without any protection, he planted a seed that would change the young girl's life forever.

A few weeks later...

Asha's mother came straight to her and touched her tummy. "Asha, are you pregnant?" She shouted in a voice filled with horror. As she uttered those words, everything around Asha became blurry - probably because of the tears that began to fill her eyes. Her chest was all knotted up. "How could you, Asha?" said her mother, crying. "We are done, Asha! You destroyed our family! How will we feed that child when we barely manage to survive!". Asha's heart was beating so fast, it was as if it wanted to break out of her chest and flee from her body.

A few days later...

Asha's mother and Sefu's mother met. Asha tried to speak to Sefu, but when she tried to open her mouth, he stopped her and said, "How do I know for sure that this is my child? This is not my child!" As he uttered those words, he turned around and went to his mother, leaving Asha in horror. She could hear how Sefu's mother was defending her son and telling her mom what a bad girl she was. She was saying that the child Asha was carrying was certainly not her son's. Sefu was standing there, quiet.

Asha felt alone, judged, condemned and betrayed. Sefu had betrayed her trust, love and their relationship. She suddenly was drowned in regrets. She should have listened to that voice deep inside of her that was telling her not to have sex with Sefu. All the signs were there but she chose not to listen. She suddenly remembered how her chest tightened when she crossed Sefu's door. She could almost hear that voice telling her: "Do not do that Asha! Be careful! Do not cross that line." She had ignored that inner voice.

> *Have you ever been in a situation where circumstances suddenly changed and everything in you immediately screamed DANGER...DANGER and yet you managed to turn the voice down and ignore all the red flags? It is incredible how the mind can easily, and in a fraction of seconds take control over our instincts.*

Well, reality was starting to sink in for Asha. She knew that things would never be the same again. "How am I going to feed that baby when Mom is struggling to make ends meet? Will I still go to school? How will I survive the shame and humiliation? There is no hope for me and the baby," thought Asha.

A wave of destructive thoughts was rushing through her mind, causing her heart to be extremely sore.

Asha felt nauseated. Her legs were shaking. Her breathing was staggering. Her throat was dry and her voice seemed lost. She tried to whisper something, but the only sound she could hear was the one inside of her telling her, "This is it. There is no way out." Her mouth did not respond to her orders anymore. Tears were rolling down her cheeks. She could taste them as they fell on her lips, salty and with a taste of loss.

Have you ever felt lost to the point where you feel that sense of loss at cellular level?

Every fibre of her being was sending a red signal. Everything in her was reaching the breaking point. She walked through the kitchen door. In a robotic way, she reached one of the upper cupboards that her mother used as a medication shelf. Grabbing her mother's sleeping pills, she walked to the bedroom, with a haggard look, pale, crying, breathing heavily, shaking, she sat down on the floor, took a pen and a piece of paper and started pouring words onto that paper:

Mom,

When you read this letter, I will be no more. I think it is better this way. I realize that I screwed up big time. Your life is already so complicated; I do not want to make it harder than it is already. I am sorry for my mistakes. I cannot change what happened. If I could, I would turn back the wheels of time but I cannot. I hope one day you will find it in your heart to forgive me. I have reached the end of the road. Considering the state of our finances and all the hardships we are going through, I do not see any bright future for me or for my unborn child. I wish Sefu had taken responsibility for the pregnancy, but he didn't. I am sorry. You deserve better.

I love you,

Asha

A tear fell next to the last phrase, "I love you." It looked like a seal, a stamp that was making this official. Asha folded the letter and put it on her pillow.

Asha choked down the sleeping pills, about 50 of them, becoming more resolute with each suffocating swallow. She wanted to see her mother for a last time, so she went to the living room. What she saw destroyed her even more. Her mother was being humiliated by Sefu's mom. Asha could feel her mother's anger and disappointment from afar. At that moment, her eyes caught her mother's. The way her mother looked at her made her feel wracked with even more guilt. Asha wished she could go back in time and say, *No*. She stepped back, went back to the bedroom. She was feeling cold, dizzy, light, sleepy... soon Asha lost consciousness.

Darkness. So much Darkness. That was it, or was it? Asha was gone. With her, her unborn child, her desires, her future, her youth, her hopes. Darkness. Her fourteen-year-old body was between worlds.

Have you ever felt so guilty, every part of your body and soul ached? Have you ever felt so much remorse, it haunts you? Did the feeling blanket you, the way the guilt, remorse and loss of hope engulfed Asha?

A few hours later...

Background voices. "It's an emergency!" yelled Asha's mother. "She's lost consciousness. Is she still alive?" she continued crying. "I can feel her heartbeat," said Doctor Liz. "It is weak, but we can save her!" she added. A sharp scent of antiseptics was floating in the air. A slither of light. A light.

Asha's eyes flickered open and she saw a bright light. It was so bright, it made her eyes blink. As she opened her eyes, she was not sure if she was alive or dead. She realized that she was still alive. "Oh my God, I am still alive. I am still alive!" thought Asha while breathing heavily. Everything rushed back to her. Asha began to cry. Her tears were tears of fear, shame, sadness, uncertainty, guilt.

She was scared of the present and even more of the future. "How will the baby and I survive?" As she asked all those questions in her heart, she heard a voice. It was a voice deep inside of her. That voice was different from the one she had heard before when she took the pills. It was warmer, comforting, soothing. That voice told her: "Don't worry, Asha, you will make it." That voice resonated in her and made her feel hopeful. Regaining consciousness, Asha felt stronger. She could not explain that feeling but she felt ready to take on life. Asha felt as if she had been touched by an angel. Every cell in her body was fine. It was as if all the stress, disappointment, distress and pain had deserted her. She was inexplicably ready to step up. She was ready to take full responsibility for her life and her baby's. She somehow knew deep inside of her that she was going to make it. The doctor who saved her life was very kind.

"Are you ok, Asha?" she asked.

"I will be, Doctor," Asha answered calmly. She had no idea how she was going to make it. The financial difficulties her family was going through, her pregnancy and everything else were issues she would need to deal with, but something deep inside of her was telling her that out of no way, a way would be made. Asha chose to believe it.

Twenty-six years later...

From being a fourteen-year-old mother with no financial means to feed her baby and no assurance that she would make it in life, relying on the divine connection she had discovered on that hospital bed, Asha is now a fulfilled woman. She is a mother of 3 daughters, married to the most handsome, empowering, loving life-partner. She is a published author and inspirational speaker, running a successful business and a non-profit organization that caters to teenage mothers, filled with gratitude. She started a non-profit organization with the aim to help young girls get from where they are to where they can be or want to be. The organization she built with love and passion is there to give teenage mothers hope and to restore lives, one girl at a time. Asha never thought that it was possible to live such an extraordinary life. If someone had told her twenty-six years ago that she was going to find peace, love and harmony, she would certainly never have believed it possible. If she had managed to kill herself, she would have missed a life full of excitement and blessings. Asha was touched by the very same Holy Spirit that raised Christ from the dead. 1 Corinthians 6:14: "And God raised the Lord and will also raise us up by his power."

***

Our intuition is like the post box through which God sends messages to us. Sometimes, depending on our state of mind, our baggage, our fears, our pain and our hurt, we fail to receive it. We fail to tap into that incredible power that has always been within us. Like Robin Sharma so eloquently put it, "Instinct is wiser than intellect."

Not everyone's circumstances and experiences are the same. Asha's story is my story. She was a teenage mother who learned the hard way how to journey through life. In the process, she almost lost her life, but made it through. Adversity shaped her. Like a Phoenix, she died and rose out of her ashes to become who she was meant to be. You might have gone or might be going through something different. It might be a disease, a loss, a divorce or anything else. Whatever you may be going through, listen to that voice, look for that little light. We all have that seed of power inside of us. It was planted in each and every one. It is up to us to nurture that seed and transform it into something beautiful. Can you believe that Asha would have missed a beautiful, fulfilling, blessed life if she had died following her suicide attempt? Life is a bumpy journey, made of ups and downs. As long as you breathe, you can turn your life around if you are ready to work for it. Sometimes, the traumatising experiences that we have gone through are the manure that we must use to grow our seed of greatness.

A principle that helped Asha to make it is that she took 100% responsibility for her life. Asha had been so disappointed by Sefu and felt so guilty for everything that was happening, she decided consciously to stop looking for scapegoats or easy ways out and she took 100% responsibility for her situation. She first tried to run away. How was she supposed to know that out of impossible circumstances, ways would be paved? It is only when she made the decision to take full responsibility for her actions, when she synced with her divine connection and allowed her intuition to guide her that she started to be in control.

Taking 100% responsibility for your life is one of the hardest things to do, and yet it is one of the most powerful tools to use. One thing that worked for me was to have a conversation with my inner self:

"Am I happy with my current circumstances? Do I blame anyone for where I am now? Will blaming others make any difference? Do I consciously or unconsciously let things happen by not being present, by not being fully aware of what is going on or by ignoring my intuition? Do I listen to that little voice inside of me? Do I want to feel better about my inner self? What would it mean for me to take 100% responsibility for my life?"

If you put aside some quiet time and allow yourself to have that conversation with yourself, you will start your transformational journey.

Revisiting some dreadful past events of my life, I have found similar patterns in the way I reclaimed my power and deepened my divine connection with God and these can be summed up into 8 steps as follows:

1. **Accept and grieve** - Let the hurt that is suffocating you get out of your system. Some cry, some scream, some talk it out. Just let it out. Running away from reality will not help. As bitter and painful as it is, bite the bullet and let your pain out.

2. **Dig deep within / trust in God's plan** - Trust in God's design even when you don't understand it; everything that you encounter in life is meant to help you grow as a person. Keep this in mind, repeat it to yourself. Forgive whomever you feel may be responsible for what you are going through. It

could be yourself or anyone else. It happens in layers. Forgiveness will happen if you see the circumstances or the people who hurt you as a means to a greater end.

3. Use your misfortune as motivation to find a new purpose - In Asha's case, her baby's survival became her source of motivation. As she grew, her motivation evolved. She ended up finding a life purpose where she started helping teenage mothers. You too can find your source of motivation and ultimately, your life purpose.

4. Make the decision to rebuild - Take some time off. Meditate and/or pray about what you need. Rely on the divinity in you. Listen to your instinct, the little voice inside of you. Write down every single idea that comes naturally. Take a look at your list and choose what seems right.

5. Visualize / pray with an end goal in mind - See and feel what you want. Speak it to life (through journaling, a vision board, speaking to a friend).

6. Plan your next course of action - Perhaps have a brainstorming session with your partner, your best friend or someone you trust. Write down anything that comes to mind and draw a mind map.

7. Keep yourself inspired & motivated: Read inspirational stories of people who went through the same thing you are or went through. Listen to motivational speakers such as Les Brown. I love his "It's Not Over Until I Win" motivational speech. Read the Bible; it contains verses that would definitely soothe your wounds and inspire you. Surround yourself with people who can bring you joy, constructive criticism and who will support you. Whatever you do, you want to develop an overcomer's mindset.

8. Receive: Allow yourself to be happy. Allow yourself to dream again. Expect better things to happen in your life. A practical way to achieve that would be to do a vision board and look at it on a daily basis (step 5.) Perhaps write down positive statements. For instance, I usually say, "I have the power to reclaim my life."

Changing your life is not a piece of cake, but it is exciting because like Asha, you can turn your life around. There are many Ashas, and many people going through seemingly insurmountable situations, but if you only get one lesson out of this story, remember that every difficult circumstance has within it the potential to make you grow if you are willing to trust your intuitive powers. A fourteen-year old managed to do it, so can you. Teenage pregnancy is not a dead end. Neither is anything else. We all have a past, but how it influences our present and our future is up to us.

ABOUT THE AUTHOR

EVA ARISSANI

Originally from Libreville, Gabon, residing permanently in South Africa, EVA ARISSANI went from being a teen mom at 14 to becoming a fulfilled woman who lives life with gusto. Through the disappointments, hardships and mistakes of the past, she felt a divine connection that led her to a purposeful life where she inspires women, young women, and girls from all walks of life to get through adversities, while deepening their relationship with God through her charity She Phoenix Femme Phoenix.

She is the Founder and Director of Transcentral Pty Ltd; the Co-Founder and Executive Director of the charity She Phoenix Femme Phoenix (SPFP); the author of the book entitled *New Moi New Life: Five Ways to Build a New You and Live an Extraordinary Life*, and is currently writing her second book.

She holds a Baccalaureus Artium Honores from University of Pretoria and has over 15 years of experience in the language industry, where she has held several leadership positions.

She is a multidimensional global woman juggling business, family, spirituality, philanthropy and much more. Her motto is: "We all have a past. But how it influences our present and our future is up to us".

If you feel inspired to support Eva in her mission to end teen pregnancy and help teen mums on their path forward, make sure you reach out.

Connect with her here:

Translation Website: https://www.transcentral.co.za/

She Phoenix Website: https://shephoenixfemmephoenix.com/wp/

Socials: https://linktr.ee/EvaArissani

PART III

INTUITION IN PERSONAL DEVELOPMENT

ISABELLE TIERNEY

YOUR INTUITION'S GREATEST OBSTACLE

As I sit on my cozy couch to write this chapter, looking out my bay window on a snowy winter day, I feel deeply connected to Peace, Love, and Joy. I just finished leading over a hundred people through a guided meditation in listening to God, right after enjoying a leisurely french toast breakfast with Brian, my husband. I know without a doubt that the way I feel right now is not "accidental". Rather, it is due to a sacred journey that I have undertaken, the journey from separation to Unity, fear to love, ego to God. While this journey, sometimes called "the hero's journey", is often considered arduous and even confusing, I'm about to share with you a simple, life-changing method to help you shift out of suffering and access *everything* you long for, peace, love, joy, intuition, in short, your "True Treasure".

The Beginning of the Journey

As with many powerful transformational journeys, the hero (me, in this case) begins in a place of pain. Living in Peace, Love, and Joy was *not* the way I used to live! In fact, I lived the opposite way, stuck in the Stress Response, anxious, overwhelmed, and disconnected. I looked good from the outside, a highly successful psychotherapy practice, 3 kids, a husband, a beautiful home, and lots of friends. But on the inside, I felt constantly overwhelmed, irritable, and empty. I overworked, seeing 8 clients a day, 5 days a week and struggled with a raging eating disorder. I had no connection to my intuition, to my soul, to God.

Do you recognize pieces of yourself in my story? I know I'm not alone. I speak to countless women who become my clients for that exact reason. They feel rushed, depleted, disconnected from their Truth, separated from Source. I remind them that this is normal, that we live in a society that values external success (the "false treasures" of money, thinness, status...) no matter the stressful consequences on our body, mind, or spirit. Many of us wait until we experience a crisis before we are finally willing to stop and question the way we are living our life.

The Wake-up Call

I experienced two wake-up calls that led me to say yes to the journey of transformation. The first one occurred when I was diagnosed with adrenal exhaustion. I had literally so overused the cortisol in my body that there was almost none of it left to function. Cortisol is one of the hormones that gets secreted to engage in the Stress Response, a physiological response designed to help you fight, flight, or freeze in the presence of danger. This evolutionary response is vital if we experience danger, but it is unnecessary and actually highly damaging when it is constantly engaged, to rush to the next appointment, complete our endless to-do list, or raise a family, to name a few examples. While we need some cortisol to function in our daily life, my chronic stress had completely depleted it. My tank was empty, and I barely had the energy to get up in the morning, let alone run my life.

My second wake-up call occurred when Brian and I divorced. There are of course many complex reasons that lead a couple to divorce. But I can tell you without a doubt that one of the primary reasons was because of my near-constant living in the Stress Response. While we all have a preferred stress response, mine happens to be 'fight'. I spent years fighting and bickering with him. Because our perception of the world gets distorted in the Stress Response (more on that later), Brian became my adversary, the person I needed to compete with rather than collaborate with. He became the person that all of my frustrations, irritations, and discontent got thrown at, and that, combined with mental health and addiction issues, led to the demise of our marriage.

After these two crises occurred, I was forced to stop and take a good, long look at myself. I had to own how miserable I was in my pursuit for external treasures, how disconnected I had become from my True Treasure, my Higher Self. I had to find out *why* the way I was living was so powerfully blocking my soul and *how* to live differently.

Identifying the Obstacles to our True Treasure

I dove deeply into research about what really happens to us in the Stress Response. I was blown away by what I found. Did you know that the Stress Response doesn't just affect us physically and psychologically, but spiritually as well? This is because there are 3 foundational problems with the Stress Response that lead us to be so deeply disconnected from our True Treasure.

Three Problems with the Stress Response:

Problem #1: The Stress Response is the great fault-finder. In the Stress Response, our brain is wired to only see the negative. We can literally only see what's wrong with ourselves, others, and the world. Our brain has an evolutionary bias towards negativity that helped our ancestors survive in a hostile environment. This biased brain, by dwelling on unpleasant possibilities, was "better prepared for the unexpected". Today, this is helpful in times of danger, when it is vital to pay attention to what could go wrong. For example, if you are walking the streets of New York City at 2am, it is vital that you notice moving shadows more than the clear night sky.

When you are not in danger, though, this "negativity bias" is quite destructive, as it only allows us to see ourselves and others from a place of "what's wrong" rather than "what's right". Can you recall a time when you could only see what was wrong with a loved one, even if you had felt affection for them a few hours before? When I'm kidnapped by the negativity bias, even Brian's chewing drives me crazy!

Additionally, this bias not only causes us to see ourselves and others from a negative lens *in the moment*, but it also causes us to remember negative experiences *from the past*. When I'm in the Stress Response, I have at my immediate disposal every unkind word and action Brian has ever said or done to me! The negativity bias is corrosive and toxic, distorting our view of ourselves and the world and creating unnecessary suffering.

Problem #2: You can only experience aggression, anxiety, and fear. In the Stress Response, your brain is emitting high beta waves which are designed to help you most effectively fight, flight, or freeze. These high beta waves lead you to experience aggression, anger, anxiety, or impulsivity. Can you see how that might be helpful when you are in actual danger, but not so much in daily life? Additionally, because the Stress Response forces us to focus on incoming danger, it forces us to focus on the body, the environment, and time. As Dr. Joe Dispenza says: "We become absorbed by the outer world because that is what those chemicals force us to pay attention to. And because we are overfocused on the outer world in order to survive, *we forget who we truly are. In the Stress Response, we become less spiritual, less conscious, less aware, and less mindful.*"

Problem #3: We can only make reactive, fear-based choices. In the Stress Response, our prefrontal cortex, the rational, decision-making part of our brain shuts down so that we can make split-second decisions in times of danger. If you're on a hike, for example, you don't want to take too long to figure out if it's a golden retriever or mountain lion that's coming towards you. You want to act *now*, think later. This is fabulous if you're in actual danger. Not so fabulous when you're trying to live a conscious life. Can you remember a day when you promised yourself that you wouldn't overeat/overdrink/snap at your loved one, only to find yourself doing just that, especially at the end of the day? That's a clear consequence of the Stress Response and of who you become when you're in it. You literally can't be the conscious, intuitive, responsible human being you want to be.

Let's look at the many ways the Stress Response separates us from our True Treasure:

In the Stress Response,

- you can't access your true power, your creativity, your infinite capacity for peace, love, and joy.

- you are literally wired to be reactive, aggressive, impulsive, anxious, disconnected.

- you can't make the life choices that you actually want. You can only make reactive choices that hurt yourself and others.

- You can't be present. You can only ruminate about the past and worry about the future.

- You are burned out from overusing cortisol and adrenaline, rather than inspired by infinite Source.

- You can only engage in competition, unable to connect to collaboration.

- You are disconnected from your body, from your sensuality, from your sexuality.

- You are disconnected rather than plugged into the infinite currents of God, the Peace that passes all understanding.
- You are disconnected from your deepest intuition.

How does this information land with you? Isn't it just amazing that a simple physiological response can turn off our capacity to be the kind, loving, compassionate, intuitive, conscious human beings that we long to be? This simple physiological response keeps us away from God, from Love, from Unity. It keeps us away from the treasure that every hero's looking for on her journey.

Identifying our True Treasure

Now that the hero has identified the obstacle, she must now identify the treasure, the point of the whole journey. Many spiritual teachings tell us that our greatest treasure lies *inside* ourselves, what I call the "True Treasure". What I discovered in my journey was that my True Treasure was accessible in the physiological state of the Relaxation Response, the antidote to the Stress Response. In the Relaxation Response, our bodies and minds believe that we are safe from potential danger. This allows us to experience trust, which in turn allows us to effortlessly access the qualities of peace, love, joy, creativity, intuition, sensuality, pleasure, presence, compassion, kindness, and more.

Every quality you long to embody becomes accessible to you when you connect to the Relaxation Response!

In the Relaxation Response, **you can see "what's right".** Your brain orients towards seeing yourself and the world with a positivity bias, seeing from the lens of love rather than fear. Remember the last time you fell in love. Do you remember how you could only see your beloved's highest qualities? Not only that, but the whole world looked and felt like a multi-colored, magical, joyful, loving, and heavenly place? Unfortunately, few of us can maintain these high frequency states of being for very long, because we falsely believe that they are due to something outside of ourselves, in this case, a new lover. But if you can understand that it is possible to live in this world, *exactly as it is*, from this lens of love and gratitude and awe and inspiration, wouldn't you want to do everything in your power to learn how to do it?

In the Relaxation Response, **you can connect to non-dualistic, blissful states of being.** You become capable of accessing slower brain waves that can shift your consciousness. In these deeper states, the two sides of the brain become so balanced that the "transcendental" experience of oneness and harmony with the entire universe is revealed. You see life more objectively, without fear and judgment, without a need to manipulate others, without need for approval. You become more productive; peaceful; connected; happier; capable of more intimacy, creativity, wholeness!

In the Relaxation Response, you recover your capacity to **make conscious choices**. You can access your prefrontal cortex, allowing you to make conscious, love-based, wise choices. You can "think straight", focus your attention, predict the consequences of your actions, control your impulses, manage your emotional reactions, and plan for the future, to name a few.

This is why I love the fact that Dr. Andrew Weil calls the Relaxation Response "The God Response". Every quality we are looking for lives in that state, including a deep sense of trust and intuitive knowing that can never be taken away from you.

Accessing our True Treasure

So at this point, you might be wondering, how do I access my True Treasure? Every hero needs to know this in order to fulfill her destiny. After researching how powerfully the two responses influenced every aspect of my being, I became determined to find a way to sustainably live in the Relaxation Response where my True Treasure could be easily accessed.

I began putting together a step-by-step healing process informed by neuroscience, mindfulness, psychology, and spirituality. Because I had just gotten divorced and still suffered from adrenal exhaustion, the changes were subtle at first. I still woke up every morning in a state of depletion and disconnection. But as I kept up my new practices, I slowly but surely started feeling more energy, more inspiration, more joy, more peace, more love. Brian and I fell in love with each other all over again and have been together ever since. I stopped using food for comfort and instead found that my connection with God nourished my body and soul more deeply than anything. I started trusting my intuition, my soul, my deepest Self.

And then I started teaching the same process to clients, naming it The Feel Good Life Methodology for its capacity to help us feel good and feel God. They too started healing in powerful and miraculous ways. I then began teaching it online, and the results were astounding. Many of the students loved it so much that they became certified to teach my Methodology around the world. Today, this powerful process is even being taught in businesses, where the effects of the Stress Response can severely impact engagement, productivity, and most importantly, well-being.

Learning How to Access our True Treasure

Are you ready to embark upon your transformational journey and discover the True Treasure that's always lived inside of you and that's just waiting for you? I am so excited to introduce you to the Feel Good LIfe Methodology because it is a simple, powerful, 3-step process that can help you shift out of the Stress Response and into the Relaxation Response in minutes. This Methodology can help you become the person you've always wanted to be, someone connected to peace, love, and joy no matter the external circumstances. It is scientifically and spiritually designed to help you feel good and feel God.

The key to the Methodology lies in your practice of this simple equation: Awareness + Action = Transformation.

Bring Awareness. If you really want to find your True Treasure, you have to become skilled at identifying whether you're residing in the Stress Response or Relaxation Response.

The Methodology teaches an extensive list of signals divided in 4 life categories, body, mind, emotions, and relationships. Here are just a few:

Stress Response signals:

- body: rapid heart rate and shallow breath;
- mind: worry, rumination, and obsession with past and future;
- emotions: anxiety and irritation,
- relationships: criticism and blame.

Relaxation Response signals:

- body: slow heart rate and deep, abdominal breaths;
- mind: slow thoughts, present-moment orientation;
- emotions: joy and gratitude;
- relationships: love and kindness.

If you notice that you're experiencing any Stress Response signals, immediately practice the next step, *Take Action.*

Take Action. Now implement the 3 steps below. These are scientifically proven to shift your physiological, psychological, and spiritual state. I use a traffic light metaphor to help you remember them when you need it most.

Step 1: Stop (Red light)

Step 2: Slow down and breathe (Yellow light)

Step 3: Go! Act on a positive habit to anchor you in the Relaxation Response (Green light)

Step 1: Stop. This step reminds you to NOT trust your thoughts, feelings, impulses, and actions when you're in the Stress Response. These will *always* be distorted by your inability to access your rational brain and by the engagement of the negativity bias. Any action you take from the Stress Response will create more destruction, more stress, more disconnection.

Step 2: Slow Down and Breathe. This step has been scientifically proven to be the fastest way to help your body shift out of stress and into relaxation. Deep, abdominal breathing lets your body know that you are safe, that the world is trustworthy. This immediately moves you closer to your True Treasure.

Step 3: Go! The third and final step invites you to implement a habit that anchors the Relaxation Response or God Response. I call these Feel Good habits, because they sustainably help us feel more good, more God. For example, you might want to call a friend, take a walk, meditate. Or if you feel more frantic energy, you might want to dance wildly to a favorite song, sprint around the block, or do a few jumping jacks in the office bathroom.

Make sure to practice fully embodying the pleasure that your habit creates for at least 30 seconds. Anchoring the pleasure of a habit for at least 30 seconds has been scientifically proven to rewire your brain to store positive memories rather than negative ones.

The Completion of the Journey

A great transformational journey ends with the hero not only powerfully transformed but also equipped with the tools she needs to undertake the journey again and again. I hope, dear reader, that you feel this for yourself, as it is truly my greatest mission to share these tools for you to use for the rest of your life. I could share countless stories of how people's lives have transformed because of the Methodology. But you can go to my website to find out more. My hope, in this moment, as I close my computer and get on with my day, is that you feel inspired and committed to become more deeply connected to your True Treasure for the rest of your life. There is no greater gift you can give yourself or the world.

Your Free Gift

I am so excited to share the next step in your practice of the Methodology with you. This is one of my favorite tools to help you access your True Treasure: The Hell-Yes Hell-No Practice. This two-step practice invites you to consciously choose habits that connect you to the Relaxation Response and to let go of those that keep you stuck in the Stress Response. If you practice it daily, you will find your life transforming in the most miraculous ways.

For your free download, visit: https://thefeelgoodlife.com/ebook/

ABOUT THE AUTHOR

ISABELLE TIERNEY

ISABELLE TIERNEY, M.A., is the creator of The Feel Good Life Methodology™, a simple yet powerful process to take you on a journey from a fear-based life to a love-based one. She's also a licensed marriage and family therapist, stress management expert, and eating disorder specialist with a 20+ year international private practice. She uses a variety of modalities to inform her work, including science, mindfulness, psychology, and spirituality.

The Feel Good Life Methodology is taught as an online course to a global audience and, because of its rapid growth and success, as a facilitator certification program. In addition, it has been adapted for use in the workplace, because of its effectiveness in enhancing engagement, collaboration, and well-being.

Isabelle is a highly-respected speaker, having presented at a multitude of venues, including mental health conferences, YPO retreats, radio stations, universities, school districts, addiction centers, and retreats, including her own. She's been a keynote speaker around the world, including South Africa, Madagascar, Nicaragua, Morocco, and throughout the United States.

She speaks three languages, including English, Spanish, and French and is the mother of three children, and a proud new grandmother.

Connect with Isabelle here:

Website: https://thefeelgoodlife.com/

Free eBook Download: https://thefeelgoodlife.com/ebook/

All Socials:: https://linktr.ee/thefeelgoodlife

JULES SCHROEDER

INTUITIVE ACTION

THE BLUEPRINT FOR LIVING A 'HELL-YES' LIFE

*A*fter suffering a near-death experience in 2015, everything changed for me.

I remember that morning like it was yesterday. It was a beautiful summer morning at Stanley Lake Reservoir in Colorado. I was out wakeboarding with the boys. We were all playing a game to see who could launch off the wake to get the most air. As the oldest of five and a former competitive gymnast and snowboarder I became fixated on winning. Finally, after an hour of mis-attempts, I succeeded. I hit the wake, launched higher than I ever had and immediately came down, caught an edge and face planted.

Lying in the water, I did a quick check to scan my body, all my limbs still seemed attached, and very slowly I made my way back onto the boat.

About an hour later I began to lose feeling in my arms and legs, and immediately knew something wasn't right. A few friends rushed me to the hospital and my next memory was coming out of the MRI and being approached by a white figure and six black shadow council members. I remembered having a conversation in this out-of-body experience where they said, "Jules you have more work to do in the world, do you want to do it?"

At the time the doctors thought my neck might have been broken or I might have been paralyzed, and I remember saying, "Yes, as long as I don't come back as a vegetable". In that next moment I was zapped back into my body. I felt this energy forge my neck back together and shoot down my spine, and the moment I woke up everything shifted.

It was the start of my life being created through me rather than being created by me.

Weeks later I got a call from a friend who was partnering with the 17 Sustainable Development Goals at the United Nations who asked me if I wanted to be a global ambassador for the People & Planet Foundation for education. I remember being on the phone, laughing silently to myself, still in a neck brace, being like, "this isn't really the best time, having just had this accident," and yet I heard this voice tell me to tell her about "Create U", an initiative to reimagine higher education.

She asked if I could be at the UN in NYC, and with no website, no business plan, no idea what 'CreateU' even was, I told her I would be there.

Weeks later, on the way to the UN I got invited to Forbes 30U30 (30 Under 30) in Boston, and then months later they asked me if I wanted to start writing for them. I heard this 'voice' yet again guide me to share that I wanted to launch a podcast and call it 'Unconventional Life', to tell the stories of people following non-traditional paths. They offered to partner with me to have it be on Forbes 30U30 and embed the episodes in my *Forbes* articles.

I still remember the day in early 2016 when I was sitting outside of the Iceland hot springs on a portable wifi device with my then-boyfriend, and (thank God) copywriter who was with me when I hit send on my first ever blog post and podcast just three weeks later.

Flash forward to 2022, *Unconventional Life* has reached millions of people in over 75 different countries with 150+ *Forbes* articles and 300+ podcast episodes and has been ranked the #1 event for entrepreneurs to attend by *Inc Magazine*. I have created sold-out retreats on six different continents from castle towns in Italy to private islands in Madagascar, to a super yacht in Croatia, to tree houses in Nicaragua.

I've built a global community of high-performing entrepreneurs, creatives, and thought leaders. People just like yourself who are saying yes to living a life outside of what is conventional or predictable. People who realize, "so I can make money in the world, but now what?" How do you also have great relationships, lifestyle, health, travel, impact, and so much more? People who crave the 'and' reality - a holistic perspective of success.

People, like myself, who have felt like they have been lone-wolves in the world. Like they have never really fit in. Where from the outside everything "looks" pretty good. Yet on the inside there is this nagging feeling telling you that there is more. It may even be nagging at you right now. You may feel it when you wake up in the morning or in the shower or on the way to work.

For most of us we have been conditioned to ignore that feeling or knowing. To pretend it's not there or to stuff it down. That you "should" be happy for your job, or stable income, or kids, or family, or what you have and to not rock the boat. That is what I did for many years before I had my near-death experience.

I fixated on setting more goals, creating more companies, more clients, more money to avoid the inconvenience of feeling there may be another truth of why I am here.

It took me almost dying and coming back for me to realize there is another way.

Deep Listening

Deep listening is the ability to hear in the moment what wants to happen versus what I want to happen, so that you make micro-changes or course corrections in real-time that are being asked of you or the situation so you can live in greater harmony, ease, and flow.

Deep listening is the foundation to cultivating a relationship with your intuition, and the more you engage with this practice the more consistent and reliable your intuition becomes over time.

Deep listening is part of what I will teach you to master in this chapter. It is the code by which I live my life and how I make decisions. It is how I have been able to generate the success I have for myself, my clients, and for the world. By the end of this chapter you will be able to master this blueprint in your own life so you get to experience full freedom, aliveness, and congruency in your self-expression.

The first step in deep listening is acknowledging that that voice or knowing you feel inside of you is real.

If it wasn't real that feeling you have wouldn't have been planted inside of you to feel. It is okay that your internal knowing doesn't match your external reality yet. Our instinct is to want to "know" what that feeling is before we take any action about it. Yet the only way, in my experience, to get clarity about that feeling is in the action itself. It is in being the environment of what you want to call forward that presents what next is to come. It is counter-intuitive. How can we act if we don't know which action to take? What if it messes things up? Or we lose our relationship, or our friends don't like us, or our kids hate us, or we aren't able to make enough money?

That is the ceiling, the threshold, that you must overcome to be comfortable with feeling and being in action anyway in order to play in this new domain.

I call this new domain, the blueprint I will teach you, intuitive action. It is the sweet spot where deep listening meets action and if you choose to master it, it will completely transform what becomes possible and available for you in how you live your life. It is how you consistently access the quantum field, the place where infinite opportunity flows from. Where you get to order off the "secret menu" of life, where God, the Universe, the greater intelligence, delivers you things that are beyond what you can even think to want or ask for or comprehend.

I have seen this happen for me over and over again when I release control of "if or how" something can happen and I allow this energy to lead. If you would've told me in 2014 I would reach millions of people through a podcast, or create one of the top events for entrepreneurs to attend, or that I would go on to be named by *Inc Magazine.* as, "1 of 27 female entrepreneurs changing the world", or one of the "Top 40 millennials to follow", or receive a prestigious international grant by the Canadian government to record a major music album, I would've told you that you were crazy as those were things that I didn't even think to desire in the realm of possibility.

Yet all of those things were in the field, as opportunities, at a split second, through cultivating the practice of deep listening that was ready for me.

I like to think about it like an air traffic control center where there are hundreds of "planes" or opportunities trying to land in your life at any given time. From your current vantage point all you see is a gap from where you are now and where you want to be. In order to close the gap, you take more action, or read more books or listen to more podcasts, in hope that you will get the golden nugget that will give you the clarity you are looking for to send you on your way.

The thing is that you keep accumulating more information, i.e. more planes, which create a traffic jam overhead. What you need is more space and to clear the runaway. That way everything you want that is already available to you at this very moment can land.

One way that I clear that space is through a practice I call "cultivating the aliveness muscle" or the 'hell-yes' or 'no' test. It is a consistent and reliable way to practice deep listening and exercise your intuitive muscle while playing in the domain of intuitive action.

Step 1: Get into a relationship with your 'yes'.

Oftentimes we say yes to things that we feel like we "should" say yes to, even though they are not a hell yes, like going out with a girlfriend, or attending a networking event, or helping our significant other with something on the weekend, or having an extra drink to be social, whatever it might be. We know that it doesn't feel like a full yes, yet we give our yes anyways.

What I have found is that those "so-so yes's" often have "so-so" outcomes. When we give our "yes" to a full yes, like, "want to come on an all-expense-paid trip to Mexico", or "want to be a speaker at this amazing online event", we have a 'hell yes' outcome. For those full-bodied yesses or f*ck yea's, we don't even have to think about it, the yes just compels us into being.

A few years ago I started to get curious about what would happen if I stopped saying yes to all of those "should yes's" and to only the "hell yes" ones.

I played a game for 60 days, you could start by even doing this for 7 days. I started charting what I was saying yes to and what the outcome was. I told people in my life that I was playing this game and for this period of time, I was going to be a 'no' to a lot more things than normal.

I was data collecting.

At the end of each day I would tally up what the invitation was, give it a number on the hell yes or no scale from 1-10, with 10 being the maximum yes and give it a number of how it felt. You could make a note in your phone, or on a spreadsheet, as I recommend to my clients.

For the first half of this week-long game you will want to collect data without trying to interpret it, as step one is getting in relationship with your 'yes' and bringing awareness to all the things you say 'yes' to without thinking about it. Then for the second half of the week, practice saying "no" if the 'yes' is lower than a certain number you decide on. For me, it was an 8 or higher on the scale.

What I found is that the more I said 'no' to things that were not a 'hell yes', which at first was a lot, the more I started training my environment to stop bringing me 'maybe yes' opportunities and to start bringing me hell-yes ones instead. Or said another way, when I ranked all the things I was saying 'yes' to on a 1-10 scale, you can also do this as a separate experiment on a piece of paper, I found that most of what I gave my energy to was a 5 or 6. So most of the opportunities I got were 5's and 6's. When I started only saying yes to the 8's, 9's, 10's, I then started getting more of those 8's, 9's, and 10 invitations in return. I had to make space for what I really, really desired to land.

In the process I also started to trust myself and my intuition more as the more I was in intuitive action, with my 'yes' the more the secret menu became available to me. I also got to release guilt, judgment, and fear around decision making as I knew that if I couldn't get a clear read on an invitation it was a 'no' or 'not right now'. I started to become in relationship with my own process for deep listening which is unique for each one of us.

In this 'hell-yes' or 'no' test, I found out that I feel my 'yes' in my gut. It is a clear sacral 'yes' or 'no' right away. It is a clear knowing. You may feel your 'yes' in a different way. Maybe your heart starts to beat faster or you feel heat or chills down your spine or a sense of peace or calmness or you see it in external signs. My partner gets it in random street signs or billboards or in text that jump out at him. Every single one of us is different.

Discovering how you feel and hear your 'yes' is the foundation to intuitive living. You may hear and feel it in more than one way. The point is that you establish a baseline with yourself that you get to keep testing, so that you can keep building on it from small decisions to larger ones.

Step 2: Intuitive Action and Rapid Visioning

The second and most important part is once you anchor in the listening is to be in action, in real-time with that listening.

Intuition is only as good as its anchored in the physical. We are human beings in bodies and what I have found is that you can have all the insight and knowing in the world, but without grounding it, that knowing doesn't translate. This is why intuitive action is so important as the more you take consistent action the more intuition or knowing becomes available to you. As I said earlier, it is only in the environment, or in the process of doing, that you get the clarity you are looking for.

I call this process 'rapid visioning' where you start by asking yourself what do I know to be true in this moment. We often think that in order to act we must know how it will all turn out and we wait until we have a plan through step 10 to even begin step 1. In rapid visioning you start with a feeling, a knowing, half-formed idea and throw a dart, let your environment give you feedback, then use that data to take the next step, throw another dart, then let that inform the next step and so on.

You may even choose to experiment with that knowing you feel inside of you right now.

Ask yourself, "what is one small step I can take with what I know to be true so far that I can take in this moment to be in the domain of action?"

One-time I practiced rapid visioning and accidentally generated an $80,000 revenue stream from one Facebook post in the span of 3 days.

I was sitting, heartbroken at my mountain house in Colorado after a relationship ended and was feeling disconnected from my female friends and craving some adventure. I got the ping (step one of rapid visioning) to post on Facebook, which I never did, with a post saying, "Are there any women out there who want to take a bucket list trip together somewhere exotic in the world".

I thought to myself if no one comments I'll delete the post in 10 minutes. I got up, went to the kitchen to get a glass of water and started hearing notifications going off. People began commenting like crazy. The next morning when I woke up I had over 125 comments, my most viral post at that point in my life, with men messaging me asking if I wanted to partner with an all women mastermind, etc. I then thought to myself I should put all of these women in a Facebook group as commenting was getting crazy and invited them (step two, take the next logical action and get feedback).

80 women joined and then I thought to myself what makes sense is to gauge interest for a trip. Instead of spending a ton of time planning and working out details, I decided to (repeat step two, take the next logical action step again from the new data) send out a form for a $2,000 experience and 40 women said yes. Generating a $80,000 revenue stream in the span of 3 days.

It doesn't have to be complicated. When you learn to listen and act in real-time it is actually quite easy. It becomes less about "getting it right" and more about being a translator for what is coming through. The more you stay present with what you know and let go of what you don't, the more you will become an intuitive action master.

If you want to learn more about how you can create these kinds of results in your own life, check out "The Unconventional Blueprint: Discover Your Pathway To Profitability In Your Highest Zone Of Genius". It is a resource that I have made available for readers of this book (normally $147) at www.unconventionalifeshow.com/blueprint for free. If you have an idea or a business you want to start or take to the next level, I highly recommend you check out this free resource. It will take you through exactly how to align your zone of genius with your income. It is a system I teach my clients and those who attend the 5-day Unconventional Life & Business Accelerators in exotic locations all over the world.

Remember that you can have anything you want for your life because you say so. To dissolve any uncertainty, say this aloud:

I release the need to know.

I already know.

The need I know,

I know what I know.

I know. I know.

Say it a few times out loud making any slight modifications as necessary until you feel complete, then take a deep breath and say:

It is in my divine right to live a life for me, through me, and for the world.

I love who I am.

I receive who I am.

I am. I am. And so it is.

ABOUT THE AUTHOR

JULES SCHROEDER

Ranked by Inc. Magazine as #1 of the "Top 27 Female Entrepreneurs Changing the World" and one of the "Top 40 Millennials To Follow", JULES SCHROEDER is a musician and visionary on a mission to inspire people to create a life by their own design. With this vision, Jules created Unconventional Life, a Forbes column, a destination retreat company and top-ranked podcast for entrepreneurs that features the stories of millennials living from this new paradigm. Unconventional Life has reached millions of people from over seventy-five different countries and has become a global community of like-minded entrepreneurs, influencers, creatives, and thought leaders.

Jules Schroeder has founded multiple six and seven-figure companies since the age of eighteen and written over 150 articles on Forbes.com with the Forbes U30 channel along with over 300 podcast episodes on her top-ranked show Unconventional Life. She has also released three intuitively channeled music albums with her most recent release, Vancouver, having been awarded a prestigious recording grant by the Amplify BC fund in Canada with top musicians from Nickelback, Mother Mother, Dallas Smith, and Elephant Revival.

Jules herself has always been multi-passionate as an avid cross fitter, yoga teacher, social impact activist, writer, avid traveler and overall life enthusiast.

Connect with Jules here:

Website: www.julesschroeder.com

Free Gift: www.unconventionallifeshow.com/blueprint

Socials & music: https://linktr.ee/julesschroederlife

NIKI WOODS

THE LIES I TOLD MYSELF

Do you know that you are beautiful? Do you know that you are kind? Do you know that you are emotionally safe? These things can be hard to believe because we lie to ourselves and give our power away. Anytime we use the comments, rules, beliefs, and actions of others to meet our own needs, we have given our power away. And anytime we have given our power away, we are in a persona. Our personas help fulfill our needs. Needs like safety, certainty, love and connection. Personas often fulfill our needs in unsatisfactory ways.

In this chapter we will learn to get curious about ourselves and the events in our lives that have led to distorted beliefs. I will use my story of healing from the lies I told myself to help you discover the areas in your life where you may have given your power away. We will discuss false identities and personas and the trigger management tools to overcome them. We will pull subconscious thoughts into the conscious mind so that we may begin to remember that we have always been whole and we are all connected to the Divine. When we recognize this, we can manifest the life we truly desire and deserve.

You know the saying, "You can take the girl out of the country, but you can't take the country out of the girl." It's referring to an identity. It's a belief that runs so deep that it is part of WHO WE ARE. I am a country girl. So, even when I moved to the suburbs where I share a fence with my neighbors and I hear cars instead of crickets at night, I have not lost that country girl essence.

We tell ourselves stories based on our identities. They can be positive, negative or both. They can serve our wellbeing or contribute to our discontent. Being a country girl might imply that I am self-reliant but also naïve.

Growing up, my mom helped me develop the ability to feel all my feelings without shame. She did not need to be needed and this allowed me to express myself freely. The Knowing within her that my teenage anger wasn't about her showed me that I am loved regardless of my actions. A positive identity was being formed due to this delivery of unconditional love. When she passed away in a car accident my subconscious mind began to tell me lies. "I have no one left who truly sees all my *goodness*."

My dad was a quiet soul. He let Mom do all the child rearing as far as I could tell. I never really knew if he was at my sporting events because he never said, "Good Job!" And I never remember him saying, "I love you," until my mom passed away when I was twenty eight. As children, we create lies to deal with emotions we can't resolve. "Maybe he doesn't show up because I am not important." The lie I told myself then created an identity that would sabotage me until my forties.

I believe the lack of attention from Dad affected my brother quite deeply. They did not throw the ball or go off on adventures together. My brother learned to fend for himself and would be sure I knew how to as well.

One day in high school my brother came and found me to tell me there was a girl that wanted to fight me over a boy. He said he wasn't going to do anything to stop it. I remember the hurt feelings as another male in my life was proving the idea that maybe I wasn't worth showing up for.

The idea that nobody had my back sunk in so deeply that I would not even ask a friend to accompany me the night the girl came to my school dance ready to follow through on her threat to fight me.

I'll never forget the excited look on an upper classman's face as he pushed his way through the bodies on the dance floor to get to me. He told me the spot where she was waiting for me right outside. After days of letting my mind race and allowing the the fear to increase over whether I would be in a fist fight, the time had come.

I mustered up the courage to go out into the cool night air to the meeting spot. I waited, and waited. I looked around and listened to the crickets chirping as the adrenaline slowly faded. She wasn't coming? Was she sitting down in the dark parking lot watching to see if I would show? Did I just call her bluff?

All I know is she never bothered me again after that. My persona of 'Nobody has my back, so I'll do it myself' was born that night.

Identities and Personas

Our personas are tied to our identities. The 'I'll do it myself' persona supports my 'I am not worth showing up for' identity. Anything we believe where we conjure the words 'I am...' is an identity. When we believe something at an identity level our brains will do everything to defend it. Many of our identities and personas are created from dealing with someone else's persona!

Any negative identities my dad carried around may have led to a persona when he decided to be emotionally distant from me and my brother. He may have felt that was better for us. My own identity and personas as a child were created based off his fear based behavior! Therefore, they are not truth! Personas are created by our ego to help us fulfill our needs and are typically responding to a trigger. What personas do you have that were created to help you carry out the belief of an identity on a day-to-day basis?

My experiences up until college seemed balanced between intuitively knowing I was loved and whole, and also doubting it at times due to listening to my ego. When we have thoughts that are doubtful and full of negative self-talk, those are thoughts from ego. Our ego is there to make sure we survive to live another day. Our intuition is calm, peaceful, and usually quite precise. It is trying to help us live life full of love and connection. The balance, or imbalance between these two is what creates our current experience of life.

I'll never forget the night, as a teenager, I was at a party and I chose to not listen to my calm inner knowing. I didn't want to believe what it was telling me, so I ignored it. That night I was raped by someone I trusted. I didn't tell a soul for many years. The disappointment in myself grew to a size I could hardly contain. So, the lies came in to resolve the situation. "It's my fault. I am weak."

Quite soon after I began to tell myself I was weak, I developed symptoms that would later be diagnosed as Crohn's Disease. It's like an entire set of genes flipped on like a light switch. My body is designed to survive and since my mind was saying, "I am weak," my immune system fired up. However, since there was no actual foreign invader to fight, it attacked my own healthy tissue. I went on to have many stays in the hospital and eventually had twenty two inches of my small intestine removed.

Our thoughts are powerful. Our thoughts create our reality. If only my white blood cells knew it was my thoughts I needed protection from. Perhaps you too have thoughts that your body has taken on the task of dealing with. When we learn to identify the thoughts, emotions, and actions of our personas, we can create a new reality.

After the rape, the distrust of myself and others would attract a certain type of man into my life. Men who would somehow show me they were not worth trusting. I was completely unaware it would take ME changing my own subconscious thoughts about myself for me to attract a different type of man. I built up a huge protector persona to help me survive my identity of "I am weak."

My protector persona would keep me from having both feet in a relationship. My boundaries were strict and non-negotiable to make sure I was safe. I was determined to never experience certain things like lies, manipulation and cheating ever again. Others would perceive me as stubborn, and I would pick up that identity even though it didn't feel true to me. All of this remained in my subconscious.

The Medium Place

I went on to live a life in the medium place. A place where things never get fantastic, but they also never get really bad. A life that was just ok and when people asked, "How are you?", I was "fine." After all, I didn't really have anything to complain about.

The medium place is trying to fulfill a need for certainty and safety. If life gets too bad we do something to bring ourselves back up to safety. If life gets too good, we sabotage and bring ourselves back to where our identity tells us that we fit, meeting our need for certainty.

I gained a new identity: 'I am resilient'. I was always ready for a problem to arise because I had the skills to overcome it. And so, they did.

My mom died in a car accident on her way to a family reunion. My connection to feeling fully seen, heard, and loved was gone in an instant. I was incredulous at first. That did not fit into the realm of possibilities for what my life was going to look like. I was going to get married and have kids and enjoy bringing my family home to experience the bliss and safety of that country life I loved. She was supposed to help me pass on the feeling of wholeness to my kids!

I ended up falling in love with a boy who I was on a date with when I got the call about my mom. For the most part he treated me well but would occasionally remind me that my identities were in fact true and, therefore, my personas were absolutely needed. Unlike my relationships of the past, this time the pain I felt regarding his actions didn't lead to me leaving. I was already hurting with a deep sense of grief and that level of pain now felt like my destiny. And so, I couldn't stay in the medium place any longer.

When your thoughts come from a place of low vibration, they create a downward spiral of emotions. Sadness, doubt, anger, worry all begin to attract more of this. Our negative identities seem to have more say than the positive ones.

Knowing that the glue to my family was gone I tried to use my new boyfriend's family to fill my gaping hole. I felt if I could keep one area somewhat stable in my life then I could deal with the uncertainty of grief.

Unfortunately, with control comes chaos. This family dynamic was much different than the one I grew up in. No longer feeling the right to free expression, I slowly stopped speaking up to avoid the emotional rollercoaster it sent me on. And with hurt feelings and frustration I began to concede to whatever his parents wanted so as not to disrupt my relationship with my boyfriend. He seemed to want to keep the peace with his parents first and foremost. 'I was not worth sticking up for,' blared in my head.

My boyfriend and I got married and had two children. The family behaviors that caused me great discomfort began to be used on my children and I could no longer just brush things aside. Time and time again I would say what I wanted and needed in this new family environment just to be dismissed or seemingly validated (so they could avoid the conflict in front of them) and then have them continue pushing through a boundary later. This made it feel like my entire experience was falling on deaf ears.

My husband's anger became so unpredictable I truly feared him. One moment I felt it was ok to be light hearted and having fun and the next moment another version of him would appear to inflict pain on those around him. I walked on eggshells and put up a fortress around my heart to avoid the hurt of his demeaning words and physical retraction from me. I felt alone and I feared what his anger meant for our children.

The Game of Codependency

I finally found a therapist and some validation. She would describe my 'loss of self' as learning to play the game of codependency. Codependency is when you rely on others to take care of your feelings. Love feels quite conditional in this atmosphere because everyone involved is needing things to be done in a certain way so they can *feel* good.

It would take my first full-on anxiety attack to shake me out of my codependent coma. Today I describe anxiety as a way for our soul to communicate to us. A literal shaking of our body to help us wake up and pay attention to our intuition. "This is not ok! Something is very off here!"

The anxiety attack was my rock bottom. I was not ok with that being a part of my life. It was time to get myself back to the medium place. And once I created that momentum, I realized there was a place beyond that even. A place where life is peaceful and effortless. A life lived with the guidance of intuition and a connection to Divine knowledge rather than my limited ego.

Through therapy my husband realized he resented me for the life we had. He had been people-pleasing me since the beginning of our relationship to try and uphold a façade. And as far as I could tell I seemed to be the one to blame. This was the moment my ego had proof that I wasn't safe with this person. I had been deceived again. I had been lied to and manipulated. Deep distrust in myself and others resurfaced.

My desire to understand codependency began rocking the boat of this family I married into. It was like I had thrown a huge stone up against the façade of their 'whole' family and it had cracked. Pieces began to fall away, and *truth* was being revealed.

By listening to the whisper of my intuition to 'keep rocking the boat', I had set course for a new reality to emerge. The old one was disassembling and crashing like the waves on the beach. Still, I was more scared of staying stuck in codependency than I was of moving even though I could not see my destination. I decided I needed a divorce.

I wanted to be the parent that would tether my children to what wholeness feels like while they experienced the world. And to do that, I had to stop giving my power away to others to fulfill my needs. I found myself having to have the courage to show up to a fight again. This fight would be against all my identities and personas that had been created by my ego as a safeguard. I had to discover them so I could remember how to model wholeness for my children.

Having the courage to look in the mirror and stop telling yourself lies is a humbling experience. I found a program that helped me do it with such love and grace towards myself. This program would introduce me to the idea of personas, identities, and trigger management.

Triggers and Pattern Interrupts

A trigger is not just about feeling uncomfortable in a situation. It's when our body is experiencing some type of trauma from the past. It's moving us out of the present moment.

Pattern interrupts can be used to stop negative thought patterns that lead to a triggered state. Staying in the present moment allows us to uncover the story we are telling ourselves and reframe the thoughts to be more aligned to truth.

We can retrain thoughts of fear to be thoughts of love. "I am in the process of knowing my worth. If I don't let others's deceitfulness mess with my own emotions about myself, then I. Am. Safe. Their behavior isn't about me! I will not stop until I have achieved my goal, not because I am stubborn but because I am tenacious!"

The Voice of Intuition

Strengthen the voice of intuition and you strengthen your trust of self. Trust of self puts us in a position to offer love to ourselves and others instead of the many forms of fear that can otherwise arise. As you move into this place of trust you create new positive identities. I am strong. I am beautiful. I am kind.

I AM LOVE.

And if I am Love and I know love is important, then I am important. I am now worthy of being seen and heard. My subconscious mind is no longer sabotaging my desire for true happiness. No lie we ever tell ourselves can change the fact that we are whole. It's not necessary to give our power away anymore when we realize this.

The more I practiced, I began to stop my triggers from sending me out of the present moment and into a persona when I was with my ex-husband. This allowed me to see and hear him in an entirely new way. I began to listen better and understand his needs better. I could ascertain whether he was in his own persona trying to get his needs met. He learned to do the same for me.

Through understanding personas and identities, we can stop telling ourselves lies. I can see my dad was in his own persona most likely from the trauma of Vietnam. He showed me love not by saying it but by showing me. Like how he was at the dinner table every night. And my favorite was when he would tuck one of my stuffed animals into bed on nights I was out late with friends. My brother's persona was doing his best to prepare me for life since my dad didn't seem to be doing it. My husband's family had forgotten they were whole due to their own traumas. And it was ok if we showed them it wasn't our job to take care of their feelings and vice versa. We learned my husband's anger came from his own attempt to hold up the weight of personas.

My husband and I worked through each trigger that had caused our distorted views of each other. We began to get to know the authentic versions of ourselves and create a more beautiful reality for ourselves. A reality where we realize there is an energetic part of us that can not be broken. That part of us is pure *goodness*, pure light, pure love. That is what we can return to at any given moment when we listen to intuition over ego.

And with a trust in the Divine knowledge that always has our back, my life partner and I decided to make our family whole again. We are adamant about remaining on a path of growth and cultivating interdependent relationships rather than codependent. Thus, keeping our power and modeling unconditional love and wholeness to our children.

I encourage you to use the examples of my story to reflect on your own. For more information on understanding trigger management so that you too may retrain your thoughts of fear to thoughts of love, please visit my website www.blankcanvassoul.com.

ABOUT THE AUTHOR

NIKI WOODS

NIKI WOODS is a certified Love and Authenticity Practitioner. She is also a certified Whole Healer which is a modality that works on the entirety of a person through mind, body and soul.

She is a speaker and trainer at a retreat center in Colorado and has been featured on a radio show dedicated to improving relationships with self and others. She is also a part of the First Responder Trauma Counselors for Northern Colorado.

As Niki worked through her own transformative healing she found her calling in life and is now dedicated to helping her clients rediscover their authentic self. Niki believes that everyone has the ability to heal deeply, if they so choose. The only requirement is courage.

Niki is the founder of Blank Canvas Ltd., a project dedicated to freeing people from beliefs, patterns and rules that were born of fear. Blank Canvas Ltd.'s mission is to guide people in choosing to discover subconscious thoughts so that they may live from a place of true awareness.

Connect with Niki here:

Website: www.BlankCanvasSoul.com

Freebie: www.BlankCanvasSoul.com/freebie

All Socials: https://linktr.ee/BlankCanvasSoul

SOPHIA HARVEY

EMBODIED REMEMBRANCE

*I*t's Christmas Day. My 21-year-old belly is still warm and full. Cheeks are permeating with kisses of family embrace. I'm looking out the front of the car, taking in the beauty of ancient gum trees, gracefully stretching beside and above us, as we glide through their archway, along sun-drenched bitumen. I hear a loud crack. It's a sound foreign to me, screaming danger.

My sister and I look up. The cracking belongs to a huge, old gum, stretching so high and wide, its perimeter is beyond our vision. The cracking diagonally snakes its way up the trunk, slowly tearing this elder in two. My sister and I exchange glances. Linear time disappears. Hand on hand, we resign to our fate. Love and fear in our eyes. My life races by me. I don't want to let go. I grasp at the ungraspable: life, just beyond the reach of my fingertips.

Then something shifts. I accept. I surrender. I drift upwards, out of my body, through my crown, through the car roof. Slowly, gently and gracefully, I feel a magnetic pull upwards. I look up and see a pastel orange sky beckoning me through falling branches. I look down and see hand upon hand in pure love. I keep drifting upwards. The sounds of the splitting tree become more distant. I'm at peace. A peace I have only dreamed about. A peace that's so pure and so encompassing.

BANG! I'm jolted back. Back into my body. Back into the car. Back into this dimension of reality. My sister is swerving skillfully, avoiding tumbling branches, as the roof indents with falling limbs. We halt. Behind us lies the huge trunk, imprinted across the road. Taller than our car. Missing us by a millisecond. We look at each other, knowingly, lovingly, in disbelief, trying to integrate our experience.

No longer could I deny the existence of something greater than me: something so powerful, so peaceful, so enigmatic and deeply familiar. A consciousness beyond and inclusive of me. A consciousness that exists to be tapped into, every day. A consciousness that's wise beyond the rational mind. A consciousness that encapsulates intuition.

I, like many, come from a lineage of intuitive women, who are deeply connected to this consciousness. That day, my mum "had a feeling" about us driving home. She insisted that we take her car, rather than my sister's, with better brakes and responsiveness. I don't know if we would have survived in my sister's car. That day, I had a feeling not to drive down that road. I didn't trust it enough to insist that we take a different route home.

Have you ever had a knowing, or a feeling that something is not ok, but dismissed it? Or do you tune into this expansive consciousness where intuition resides, but sometimes doubt that connection? Our intuition always supports us, yet in my teens and early adulthood, I repeatedly doubted or dismissed it.

Growing up, I was highly intuitive. I was often labelled "too sensitive", "too emotional" and "too deep". Perhaps you can relate. My imagination was expansive. I saw fairies and garden spirits. I talked to animals and could feel their distress. My special place was a naturally formed bamboo teepee, hidden within the garden wilderness. There I sat and pondered life, tuning into a cellular knowing of the sacredness of this space and my nature-connectivity. I followed a flow that brought me joy and magic. I knew things without reason. I sensed when someone I loved was in danger. I added up mathematics equations without thinking, just knowing the answers. These were not cognitive experiences. They were embodied. They were things that just came through me. I was open and connected to this consciousness inclusive of us all.

Then it began to stop. I started to question. Fear crept in.

"Be careful. If you open yourself up, bad energies will enter. It's not safe."

"You could do anything with that brain and academic skill."

"Prove it. What you are saying is not rational."

"That's not real. It's just your imagination."

The rhetoric of others, rhetoric that may be familiar to you too, was swirling around and around in my head. This rhetoric is fed to us through the patriarchy, eroding trust in the self and connection with intuition: trust and connection that we are slowly and powerfully reclaiming.

Reclaiming our Intuitive Wisdom Can Be a Bumpy Road

In a world that considers rational *truth* as paramount, we can become entangled in the disbelieving, doubting, or desire to prove intuition's existence to others, even to ourselves. I delved into science, including quantum physics, cellular biology and physiology, to explain what I could sense intuitively. Now I use this scientific understanding to support others in their *proof*. I've danced between listening, not listening, trusting, not trusting, despite multiple reminders that, yes, my intuition is looking out for me. Does this sound familiar? I guess sometimes we need a kick in the guts, or a flattening into the ground, to truly listen.

It's 2005. I'm a 26-year-old burned-out criminal lawyer on the trip of my life. I'm about to embark on a rural horse-riding adventure in Cuba with my then-boyfriend. I wake up in the morning of the scheduled outing feeling sick in my stomach. It's like knives wrestling in my intestines. I want to vomit. I hear a voice whisper to me, "Don't go riding today". I tell my boyfriend. He says I am probably just nervous and it should be fine. I value his thoughts over my own feelings. I think, "He's probably right". I still feel uneasy, but I don't trust myself. I don't listen to myself.

That unease doesn't leave me as we ride through serene farmlands. It has no logic. I try to focus on the beauty, but can't shake the desire to leave. As our waterfall destination approaches, I see a huge oncoming tractor, laden with sugar cane. I beckon the others to move away, so the horses are not spooked. We do. My horse is the most tranquil it has been the whole trip. I sigh with relief, prematurely. With no warning, my horse bolts straight into the front wheel of the tractor. I feel it being sucked under the wheel. I throw myself off, as far from the tractor as possible. It is not far enough, I realise, as the tyre squashes into my body, squashes me into the earth. A second tyre heaves over my fragile form. I cannot move. I see the load of sugar cane rolling towards my head. It stops, centimetres away. I'm in a living nightmare, on the precipice of life and death, fighting for my breath, with a punctured lung, internal bleeding, and shattered bones.

Time slows. My breath, my struggling, gasping breath, becomes my focus. Each one, I think, will be my last. Each one, extracting a sliver of oxygen from the atmosphere. Eyes open, blinking in disbelief. Head pressing into dirt, feeling the connection of me with Earth, Earth with me. Slowly, my consciousness starts to shift. I am the dirt. The rich, red-brown dirt. I am the tractor, glistening in the sun. I am the tyre tracks, the bushes, and all that I can see on this earthly plain. My glazed eyes tilt upwards. I am the sky. The bright blue, spacious sky. My consciousness expands further. I am the world and all that exists within it. I am the cosmos. I am everything. Everything is me. I feel a surge of gentle warmth and tranquillity enveloping me, becoming me. I am universal love. Universal love is me. At this moment, I understand that this love is the essence of everything and everyone. This is something we seem to have forgotten, as humans.

It is from this space of love and connectivity - or even through glimpses of it - that we can freely access our intuition. In this state, we are open-hearted, deeply present and receptive. Our consciousness is expansive, allowing us to listen to the signals which guide us into our flow. This becoming love by becoming everything, is a state not commonly accessed or prioritised in our modern world. It is possible, however, without finding yourself under a tractor or having near-death experiences.

Meditation is one way to access this state more gently. Stillness, presence and embodied connectivity (with self, others and nature), are preliminary steps to becoming this. It takes practice. It takes commitment. I have a simple exercise I do daily, to support engagement in this deeply connected state. It works your intuition muscles, expanding your sensing through stillness.

Sensing in Nature Practice

- Go for a walk with your journal and pen.

- Find a place you are drawn to in nature that is nourishing. Allow your body to choose the place. Connect with your breath and feel your feet connecting with the ground as you move. Yield into your connection with the ground. Bring your awareness towards your core. Wander around until somewhere invites you in: Somewhere that *feels* right, that you *know* is nourishing, that entices you through *sounds* or *smells*. Just let yourself be guided there.

- Sit in silence in your nourishing place for 5 minutes, remaining connected with your breath, core, and the ground. Then ask yourself the following questions:
    - What do I see?
    - What do I hear?
    - What do I feel?
    - What do I know?
- Pause, observe and listen after each question. Allow your senses to expand. Is there anything new you are noticing? Is there anything out of the ordinary you are sensing? Really listen in stillness. Be open. Refrain from judgement and include everything you sense in your response. Listen in stillness before responding.
- Write or draw your insights and observations in your journal.

Why Don't we Prioritise Accessing this Natural, Intuitive Wisdom?

In ancient cultures intuition was a way of life. Following the flow and listening to Spirit was second nature. Tuning into the landscape to know where and what to hunt and gather was a given. Being, listening and symbiotically existing was the human way.

In our modern Western world, we place our authority in external reasoning, at the expense of wisdom lying within and between us. We value the material over the spiritual. We favour rationality at the expense of intuition. We devalue feminine qualities. An early example of this disregard of the feminine is our movement to a 12 month yearly calendar. Prior to that, a 13 moon calendar, in sync with the 13 menstrual cycles of women, was followed. Evidence of this can be found with the Essenes, Ancient Egyptians, Polynesians, Mayans and Incans.

Our prioritisation of the rational mind has taken our Western civilisations far away from being open to life's mysteries and the wisdom dwelling beyond reason. In addition to our *head brain*, we have a useful *heart brain*, or emotional intelligence centre, and an active *gut brain*, which emerging research indicates is the physical centre of intuitive intelligence. This physical centre reaches out through the physical body and into our energetic field and the collective field beyond. Quantum physics research is supporting this idea that as energetic beings, we tune into this global energy network. This ability is amplified when we are deeply embodied and grounded. When these three *brains* work together, we access a superpowered intelligence system.

What Holds us Back from Accessing this Integrated Intelligence System?

Collective, ancestral, and individual trauma have a huge impact on embodiment and trust, two things needed to effectively access intuition. As energetic beings we are impacted by the collective. Epigenetics research shows us that trauma can be inherited. When trauma occurs, the person's gene expression can change and this modification can be passed down to subsequent generations. Many of us also experience trauma in this lifetime.

Unprocessed trauma is stored in the body and creates a belief that it's not or "I'm not" safe. Trauma keeps the autonomic nervous system switched on, in fight, flight or freeze mode. What do you want to do when in this state? Control everything. Trust is terrifying. Deepening into heart and gut connection feels scary.

The social and cultural rhetoric can feed into this fear and control paradigm. We are often told that if we do particular things we will receive health, wealth and fulfilment. Righteousness reigns and there is little space for the unknown. If we sense something without logical *proof* we can be dismissed or ridiculed. This typically amplifies the fear of the traumatised soul, that wants to feel safe. Going along with a narrative can often feel like the best thing to do, especially when this narrative is promising safety, security and stability.

Trusting the Signals Through Challenge

Trusting in our intuition can be difficult when our intuition is guiding us through a challenging path. When these challenges seem monumentous, it is often easier to ignore or dismiss the intuitive signals appearing in our field. Believing that our intuition *has our back* in these instances can seem unfathomable.

Numerous signals were yelling at me to leave my Latin American adventure and relationship in 2004. I was on a drip in my room with horrendous dysentery that no Western or natural approach would resolve. I was robbed three times and kidnapped by police. I had dreams of leaving and travelling alone, but that petrified me. I was unhappy in my relationship. I persevered in it all, despite multiple setbacks as it seemed easier than heartbreak, solitude and the unknown. I was labelled the "unluckiest traveller" even *before* being run over by the tractor. I could look at the tractor experience as an unlucky incident or one that brought me back into soul alignment. Yes, I didn't listen to my intuition that morning, but it was deeper than that. I wasn't listening to my intuition to courageously leave it all and step onto a different path. Being run over forced me back into myself. Back on track. Literally.

As grateful as I am for this experience, it was one of my toughest times. When I returned to Australia in a wheelchair, with tractor tyre marks imprinted across my torso, I entered a victim-focused slump, momentarily forgetting about my intuition and universal love epiphany. I kept ruminating on: "Why me? Why couldn't this have happened to someone needing a push in a more spiritual direction? I am already on this path. I don't need this setback".

I trudged through my early rehabilitation, feeling sorry for myself. My trip of a lifetime was cut drastically short. I felt the unfairness of life weighing heavily upon my broken body. I felt like a failure: I was living at my parents' house, with no money, no job, no status. I compared myself to my lawyer friends, climbing ladders of legal success while I relied on my parents. I cried tears of pain, despair, and loneliness. A key thing that got me through those days was remembering a moment under the tractor when I chose life. Something deep inside me knew I had to be here: I had to share my wisdom and I had to heal.

Slowly, I reconnected with myself. Meditation, nature and the love of my family were my greatest allies. My determination was my blessing, a trait that came in handy when having to commit to five hours a day of intensive rehabilitation.

Day by day, my lungs grew stronger and my bones re-knitted. Day by day, I grew more strength to move, walk and appreciate. My slowly increasing physical strength supported me to become mentally stronger. I became committed to shedding limiting patterns that were no longer serving me: being the victim, self-blame and judging my worth according to external markers of success. I started to see success as synonymous with how I was being, rather than what I was achieving. I started to understand the learnings of this challenging experience more deeply. I could see all those signals that I didn't listen to, beckoning me to change course. I could understand that this *accident* was a blessing, extracting me from a path destined for an even greater disaster, a disaster through the misalignment of my soul. I touched upon strength within me that had been buried deep within the crevices of my being. I felt more empowered and embodied than ever before. I felt confident and clear. I learned how to *be* once again, in my forced slow down and reconnection. This beingness opened the doorways of my intuition way beyond moments of danger or crisis ever had. I started to really understand the *how* of cultivating intuitive wisdom: a *how* that is deeply integrated into this *being* state, where stillness resides. I wonder whether I would have learned this, had I not been forced to slow down and focus on embodied living for those 18 months of rehabilitation.

Living an Intuitive Life is Extraordinary

Our intuition often takes us on profound pathways our rational minds could not have anticipated. My intuition has taken me on a journey across cultures and countries, traversing the rich tapestry of human nature. I have been guided into professional landscapes I would not have imagined in my early adult years: criminal law and community development in remote Indigenous communities, humanitarian work in Island nations and bustling global cities, therapeutic and advocacy support with refugees, to name a few. The various places I've explored and incredible people I've connected with have deeply changed my life, in ways I could not have dreamed of. What about you? Where has your intuition unexpectedly guided you?

These diverse experiences have taught me that people do the best they can according to their inner and outer resource availability. Most awful behaviours that people engage in come from a place of disconnect: disconnect from self-love, self-worth and universal love. When we reconnect with ourselves and the world more lovingly, we act more lovingly. As I have highlighted, this loving connectivity also supports intuitive receptivity. It's a win-win.

Supporting human reconnection with this loving state is my passion. I love supporting people to remember who they really are, in relationship with themselves and the world, beneath the noise. When people can experience this level of loving connectivity, they *come home* to themselves. Getting there often involves a courageous journey through trauma processing, or letting go of limiting patterns and diving into unknown territory. For me, this has been a necessary pathway home, as it has also been for so many others. How about for you?

I affectionately call the people I work with the "zebras of the world". They are curious, courageous and don't fit in a box. Like zebras, each of us has a unique expression, or set of stripes, that paints a glorious picture. We encompass the dark and the light, the black and the white, and everything in-between. Like zebras, we thrive in community, with our feet (or hooves) on the earth, shining our dazzling light when deepening into our inimitable selves.

My *Zebra Crossing Program*™, which encompasses my empowerment courses, guides "zebras" along the rewarding journey home to their unique connectivity and expression. It is a safe journey from the ordinary into the extraordinary, where authentic and intuitive living is cultivated, to harness a life of deep peace, purpose and personal power. My *Zebra Crossing Framework*™ underpins these programs. It is the intersection between science, psychology, and spirituality.

Intuitive living requires courage: courage to listen to and follow our soul's calling, even when that pathway seems hard or misunderstood by others. When we do so, we live in flow, in synch with our natural rhythms. We are innately fluid beings, who harmoniously evolve in symbiosis with the natural world around us. This is our way forward. This is our way home to ourselves. This is our way home to the peace that dwells in connection with that expansive consciousness, beyond and inclusive of each and every one of us.

ABOUT THE AUTHOR

SOPHIA HARVEY

SOPHIA HARVEY is an empowerment specialist who is passionate about living an authentic life. With a background in criminal law, human rights, community development, research and holistic psychology, Sophia has a wealth of cross-cultural, international and multidisciplinary experience, which supports her to understand the depth and breadth of human experience. She holds a Master in Psychology, Honours in Law, Holistic Psychology Diploma, Coaching & NLP Certifications and various certificates in embodied movement and energetic healing modalities.

Sophia has published research papers in psychology and has been a guest speaker in various conferences and training institutes regarding her psychology work and expertise in working with trauma. Sophia has developed the Zebra Crossing Program™, which is a number of courses, 1:1 coaching pathways, and a membership group, designed to support the zebras of the world to safely cross from the ordinary to the extraordinary. It is a deep journey cultivating authentic and intuitive living, to harness a life of peace, purpose and personal power. In her spare time, she loves going on adventures with her beloved cheeky pooch, dancing anywhere she can and immersing herself in nature.

Connect with Sophia here:

Website: www.sophiaharvey.com

Freebie Quiz: *What's Your Intuitive Archetype?*

Socials: https://linktr.ee/sophiaharvey

STACEY HOLLOWOOD

FEEL IT AND HEAL IT

Let's face it, we all need help unpacking our problems! I have unpacked a lot of my own to get to where I am today and one thing I have learnt from my healing journey is you cannot hide from your own BS! Your energy will introduce itself before you do and it's your job to be brave enough to walk straight into it. So often we bypass our own healing and develop coping mechanisms to keep our traumas packed tightly in boxes, storing them deep down within the unconscious mind so we feel safe. But the truth is, these traumas are controlling us.

If you have been like me, you may have felt a lot of resistance. I came from a 'normal' family, with a 'normal' upbringing and never thought that I had any problems, or rather, that my problems were just a part of life and I shouldn't make a fuss about feeling misunderstood, alone and insecure. I remember my parents saying to me as a child, "there are starving children in the world." This programmed me to believe that I didn't need to go back and work through trauma because compared to others I didn't have any. Even though I knew I had experienced levels of trauma throughout my life, I didn't think I was worthy of the word TRAUMA! I began to focus my energy on healing the world and what was happening outside of me. Even as a child I would raise money for children by doing the 40-hour famine. Instead of giving gifts I would sponsor animals in need of help such as elephants or orangutans. I understood the world needed healing and being gifted as a psychic empath I naturally fell into the role of becoming a healer. Because I compared my problems to others on a daily basis and thought mine weren't bad at all, I resisted my own healing for years. I ignored all the intuitive signs, niggles and nudges. It wasn't until the universe brought me to my knees that I was forced to stop and look within my internal world.

For me, the pandemic was the catalyst for my deep inner healing and trusting my intuition. I was forced to stop working and helping others, be at home with my own toxic thoughts and I was being triggered into fear left, right and centre. But I had nowhere to run this time, nowhere to hide, nowhere to focus my energy on helping others instead of healing myself. Even though I had done spiritual work on myself in the past, this felt very different. My body was responding in a way I had never felt before. I was suffering from severe anxiety, overwhelm, stress, and panic attacks. Medication was not an option for me. My intuition was screaming at me that this was something I needed to look at within myself and I knew I could do it.

I remember hearing my most intense intuitive hit for the first time, I was listening to Gabrielle Bernstein's 'The Universe Has Your Back' and the universal lesson she said was, "To be free you must acknowledge your resistance to love." The words shook my very being. I had goosebumps. OMG I have been resisting love. The physical reaction I was experiencing in my body was my triggered state to all of the mirrors happening around me showing me the parts of my internal world I didn't want to see. I was resisting even acknowledging they were there and I chose fear every time.

I felt like I was seeing my shadow for the first time. I felt the veil being lifted and I was seeing the truth. I knew within myself that I had to learn to love all of the parts of me and I had to acknowledge the parts I didn't accept in myself. Even though I couldn't change what was happening in the world around me, I could change how I was perceiving it.

I wrote down the universal lesson from Gabby on my mirror and I decided that I was willing to learn through love in every moment. I was willing to take my hands off the steering wheel of my life and trust the inner guidance of my intuition. I was committed to this. I finally knew WHY I had to unpack the wounds no matter how big or small I considered them to be. If I wanted to feel understood I first had to understand myself. If I wanted to feel connected to a power greater than myself, I first had to connect to my body. If I truly wanted to heal the world, I first had to heal myself. I listened to my inner guidance on a daily basis, if the guidance was to rest, I rested. If the guidance was to take inspired action, I would be inspired to take action. I gave myself the space to heal, I spent months off social media so I could truly sit with myself without judgement and projection. So, I could see the world through the eyes of love without fear, influence and comparison.

Before you can sit with your intuition, you must be willing to sit with your ego.

When learning how to decipher what ego is and what intuition is, it's important to remember that ego is fear and intuition is love. To be free of fear you must learn to observe your ego and the best place to do this is in meditation. There is no escaping your ego when you're sitting with it. You must learn to witness your ego without judgement.

Ego is neither good nor bad, every person has an ego it is simply a function of the mind. However, being unconscious to it can cause resistance as it likes to create stories and meanings around who we are, who others are and how the world is based on our past experiences. The ego is linked to our identity and likes to keep us separate. It is the voice inside our head that reminds us of fear-based thoughts, that keeps us in our old, familiar and predictable patterns. It does this to protect us from painful experiences that we have had in the past, most likely in our childhood. The ego loves to create stories and projects them on to our future. So just say you are thinking of starting a new venture your ego will create a story that usually stops you from pursuing it and leads you to self-sabotage: "I am not good enough", "I am not worthy", "I am a failure"; this is all ego talk. The ego likes to compare so it's either inferior or superior in some way. The ego also is not flexible, it's either right or wrong. You must learn to witness your ego, without judgment, by paying attention to how you think, how you speak, how you react and respond in every situation. Absolutely nobody can skip over this step. To feel connected to love you must trust, surrender and have faith. The energy of frustration, control, impatience, annoyance, distrust and fear are all energy blockers and will disconnect you from your intuition.

This took a lot of determination for me, when I was trying to meditate, I caught myself thinking and attaching to the thoughts that were entering my mind I found myself getting frustrated and annoyed with myself when I wasn't able to quiet my mind, and the experience of this made me want to give it up. I wasn't meditating at all! I was consciously thinking instead of letting the thoughts move past me. I decided if I wanted to get in touch with my intuitive side, I had to face the negative thoughts head-on. I would acknowledge my negative thoughts with love that came up in meditation as they were a part of me and named them as fear, without judgement. I would then imagine detaching from these words and state, "These beliefs no longer serve me; I surrender this fear back to the universe and realign with the energy of love". The longer I sat with myself in stillness and shifted my ego talk the more I began to hear the subtle whispers of my intuition.

This process can be a tough journey no matter the level of trauma you have experienced. You are opening yourself up to old wounds which can be very real and painful at the time. Everyone's trauma is significant to them. What is significant to you and what is significant to another can be very different. It is very common for people to judge their trauma by saying their trauma isn't worthy of them feeling a certain way. You know within yourself when you have healing work to do. If you are not waking up feeling totally aligned with positive emotions and you're being dragged down into self-doubt and worthlessness, and your behaviours and patterns are toxic, then you are out of alignment with who you want to be and you have stuff to unpack and heal. Accept where you are and trust that you are supported.

I want to share with you a personal experience of mine to help you better understand intuition and what that can actually look like.

There was a moment when I moved back home with my family during the pandemic, a decision I made to give myself space to heal.

I was sitting on my bed in the middle of my anxiety, stress and overwhelm. My mum was sitting in front of me trying to figure out what was wrong with me as this was very out of character for me to be behaving this way. I remember saying to her, "You don't understand me." I felt misunderstood and alone. As I broke down and my Mum tried to give me a hug, I said, "Please, leave me alone," and she walked out. I was in fear and I couldn't receive the guidance I needed to see the situation clearly. I could feel myself being triggered into an internal state. I sat into meditation straight away, tears rolling down my face. As I sat in stillness, I heard the subtle, soft, comforting words of my intuition, "You are looking into a mirror". My mum was holding up a mirror to me and that feeling of being misunderstood was coming from my projection. I had believed so deeply for so long that I was misunderstood that I was only seeing in my reality the experiences and conversations to support that projection. I said to myself, "This belief system no longer serves me." When I came out of the mediation, I realised that I didn't really understand myself, and if I couldn't understand or accept myself, then they would never understand me. I wrote down my new beliefs in my journal.

- To feel understood I must be understanding and accepting of myself

- I am loved and I give love

- I'm not always responsible for what my eyes are seeing but I am responsible for how I perceive what I am seeing

- I trust myself

I thanked my mum for being the manifestation of the lesson that I needed to learn. As I began to feel the new energy anchoring into my body I started to notice a shift in my perception. I noticed all of the qualities from my family that supported my new beliefs of feeling understood and accepted. I felt like a child learning for the first time, I was seeing the world through the eyes of love.

How to master your ego

Set a timer for 5 minutes.

Sit crossed legged on a pillow with a straight spine, close down the eyes, palms faced up on the knees.

Start by taking a few deep breaths and sink into your body.

Start to witness what thoughts are coming to the forefront of your mind. Are you thinking about what you should be doing instead of mediating, what you will cook for dinner or making lists? Maybe there are toxic belief systems or stories that are coming up like, "You are not worthy", "You should be doing this or that", you may have guilt for spending this time on yourself.

Your ego might be very loud. Stay committed to moving past this phase. Face your ego head-on and be willing to feel it and heal it.

Journaling

Write down all of the negative dialog or toxic thoughts that came up after the 5 minutes of stillness. This is a great tool to implement. Acknowledge them as fear-based thoughts. It is very important to have no judgement towards yourself when you see them written down on paper. Just completely observe your ego. We must bring things to our conscious mind in order to release them.

Detach

Imagine in your mind's eye detaching from these words and state, "This belief system no longer serves me; I release it back into the universe to be recycled back into love". You may then take the bit of paper you have written on and burn it.

It is a great idea to remove all expectations of how long this stage should take you. Everyone is different and your journey is unique to you, so never compare the time it takes you. Don't think, "I've been doing all this work for so long now; I'm not getting anywhere." YES, YOU ARE!

The only thing you have control over is showing up for yourself and doing the work. The longer you sit with yourself in stillness and the more you will begin to hear and trust your intuition. Instead of running away from things that trigger you, lean into it. Will it be uncomfortable? YES! Of course it will. But you are strong and your future self will thank you for it.

You may notice even though you are doing this work your ego will still be very loud with your day to day. You might find after a while the only way you can hear your intuition is when you are in meditation. If you want to be in alignment with your intuition but find you're still making ego-based decisions which aren't leading you in the right direction, remember the ego projects our past experiences onto our future and it is why we end up doing much of the same or finding ourselves in the same situation. If you are not getting the answers through meditation there are many tools that you can use to help access your ego and shadow such as Timeline Therapy.

In Timeline Therapy we all have a way in which we store time in relation to our physical body meaning PAST, PRESENT, & FUTURE. In this process we are looking for the root cause of an emotion or limiting belief and for most that means PAST which could mean before, during or after your birth. Before your birth could mean the womb, past life or passed down generationally. If we look at birth and womb, when a mother feels a certain emotion, especially significant emotional events the baby also feels that emotion as well in the womb. Painful and significant emotional events can also travel in family lines until someone is brave enough to feel it and heal it!

If you want to connect with your intuition and create new opportunities and experiences you must look towards your future as unknown, be completely present, trust, surrender, have faith and be brave enough to feel it and heal it.

You know exactly who you are and why you came here at this time. In order for you to build a connection with your intuition, meditation might be something you need to do every single day. This takes dedication and a lot of willpower, but if you are ready to hear your intuition and follow the guidance, be committed to your inner journey.

The best gift you can give your children, your family and the people around you is the gift of your true spirit, of you being your higher self, living in joy and living in beautiful positive emotions. I was so inspired by my healing journey that I knew I had to share it. Teaching people how to heal themselves and giving them the tools to do that is my passion. I create an environment to hold space and feel safe being uncomfortable and feel nurtured, held and loved in the process. Be proud to say, "I'm uncomfortable but I'm willing to unlearn and relearn."

So, if you are feeling uncomfortable. Great! That means change is right around the corner. I am so proud of you. Thank you for reading this chapter and I hope it gives you a better understanding of the significance of your own trauma and how you can start your healing journey.

If you are feeling called to connect with me personally head over to my business Instagram account @wyldchyldhealing or check out my website www.wyldchyldhealing.com.au for your FREE Meditation to connect with your soul. Sending you so much love.

ABOUT THE AUTHOR

STACEY HOLLOWOOD

STACEY HOLLOWOOD is a multifaceted practitioner, facilitator, and guide to bring healing to your life across all levels. She is the founder of Wyld Chyld Healing and her work has been recognised and featured in Peninsula Essence Magazine August 2021. Stacey is a qualified Reiki Master, Timeline Therapist, and NLP Coach. She has a strong connection to her intuition and psychic empathic abilities which deepens her level of work encouraging and empowering her clients to release stored toxic emotions and belief systems that limit their expression and experience by guiding them back home to themselves.

Stacey offers a 6 Week Timeline Therapy Program for women who struggle with emotions and embodiment, guiding them to lean into what they are feeling without judgment and transforming the energy to create their best life.

Connect with Stacey here:

Website: https://linktr.ee/wyldchyldhealing

Free Meditation: www.wyldchyldhealing.com.au

Socials: https://linktr.ee/wyldchyldhealing

IRMA VARGAS

THE MAGIC OF SEEING AROUND CORNERS

A LESSON IN TRUST!

The Untruth

There are many untruths that we must unravel in life, and when we finally do, the trust that comes about is so incredibly warm and comforting. It brings about a joyfulness that nothing can dissuade us from. Imagine never giving anyone else the power to control how you react or feel about anything because you are so firmly in your own corner. That isn't ego or stubbornness, it is confidence in self.

In the year I was born, my mother had already birthed 10 children before me: three boys and seven girls. She was 44 years old and had daughters that were embarrassed by the fact that she was giving birth yet again. Some untruths are decidedly generational and so I was born into shame. My mother never shared with the family that she was pregnant with her 11th child until the day came for her to get to the hospital in short order. As the months of her pregnancy had passed, she lost weight instead of gaining, so her appearance never really changed.

As the story goes, she had to call a taxi and ask a neighbor to watch my two-year-old brother. She got to the hospital and within the hour I was born. When my father arrived home from his construction job, he was told my mother was in the hospital and he then told the family that my mother had birthed another child. There was an uproar, but not of joy and good cheer.

The older children who were in their 20's at the time were so upset they refused to go see me and my mother. It was not a time to celebrate in their eyes and they were even more upset that they had no clue it was happening.

Today, the story is comical and we laugh. The painful truth is that I listened to this story over the years and what I, in my innocence, received was that my mother was ashamed of me. I bought into the idea that she should not have been having so many children and not so late in life. I didn't understand why she would think it was a good idea, and there was no one to ask.

My mother, who as I write this is 105 years old and still a force to be reckoned with, tells me to this day that I was like a doll to the others; they loved and spoiled me. This was not what I believed growing up. I formed the opinion in my head that because I was not acknowledged in the womb that I should not be heard, not have an opinion, not subject to consideration, or participate in the family as an equal. I intentionally became virtually invisible!

Today I understand the untruths I learned as a child, and it is comforting to know that we can unravel them eventually.

The Discovery

When you look at your life and your upbringing it can be difficult, painful, and at the same time joyful. This is how life works. It is everything and nothing. We are what makes the difference. Our understanding, our perspectives and whether we are living these truths from within us or from the outside in.

You see I discovered through a failed marriage and the aftermath of divorce that I was born for a reason. I always had everything I needed, and it was up to me to name, claim and aim my talents to serve me. No one owed me anything and the discovery of this was so enlightening and so freeing. It created the space I needed to expand my true self, my desires, take on challenges and celebrate my successes.

It wasn't easy and the realization wasn't automatic. It was painful because I had to accept responsibility for my part. In high school, I joined the school choir and when it was time to attend a performance, I was the one who never mentioned it or asked for a ride. I sat knowing that I was not being responsible to my obligation but the fear of having to open my mouth and ask for what I needed was greater than turning my back on my obligation.

When I graduated high school, I received an educational scholarship to attend California State University at San Jose, CA and when I showed my father what I had accomplished he told me flat out I could not go. I was to stay home and go to work. No college for me.

In my dismay, I went to Mexico City to visit family and stayed for over a month. In my father's eyes this was acceptable because it was not out of the realm of what he would have wanted for me to do. When I returned, I informed the college that I would not be taking the grant and I would not be attending. The scholarship was only valid if I started in the Fall. Instead of fighting for my education, I turned my back on myself. To this day it brings tears to my eyes because I realize how ill-equipped I was to be my own advocate.

This is how far down the totem pole I had put myself. Have you ever let what you have heard others say become attached to you; then created a story around it without even verifying or confronting the idea or person? That is what I did for decades.

I went to work as was expected, I took courses at the local community college, and within three years quit school and married. I never thought it was the life I was supposed to be living. I imagined most days that it was the life others expected me to live. When this happened, it wasn't that I was miserable, or that life was bad. It was that in the final analysis it wasn't what I wanted or who I was meant to be.

Within six years of being married I was a single mother. As the single mother of three children, I began to use my voice for them, and it was the beginning of the change I had to make for myself. I began to ask myself questions that helped me unravel and understand that we all have an intuition, a sixth sense, and if we learn to trust it and claim it, we will be more valuable to ourselves and others. It is this process that led me to a most enlightening moment that changed my life.

You see, my children were four, three and one and a half, and on the weekdays my alarm was set to 5:30 a.m. so I could get up, get ready, then wake them up and get them ready to be taken to my mother's house so I could get to work. On this one particular morning, I woke up at 5:13 a.m. and I immediately cursed what I considered my bad luck, my miserable existence, tired body, and depressing situation. In that instant, my life felt heavy, dark, and futile and then I looked again, and I realized it was still 5:13 a.m., and in that next moment my heart flooded with the understanding of what the heavens wanted me to receive.

I was born on 5/13 and it hit me like a ton of bricks. I was born for a reason. I was awakened at that very moment so I could realize and acknowledge that I had three beautiful souls to watch over and help become the best people they were meant to be. They needed me and I needed them. I had a place to take them that was safe, and I had a job that I was blessed with to provide for them. I had so much to be grateful for. All I had to do was turn that kaleidoscope to see it. From that day forward to this day I celebrate my birthday every day in time at 5:13 a.m. or p.m. or both. Now I don't even set my alarm. The universe taps me on the shoulder, and I look at the clock and there in neon is my birthday moment.

This moment each day provides me with an intimate space of time to reflect on the blessings, to edify myself and to claim who I am and have always been. I am introspective, strategic, kind, generous, I have a spiritual gift of discernment. I never had taken the time to claim my intuitive self because I was wrapped up in who others thought I was. I accepted who others expected me to be without question. I discovered that I was wrong, and I came to understand that my family did not dictate how I felt or who I was in the world apart from them. Did they influence me? Yes undoubtedly, however, I always had the final say so.

How do you do that? How do you move into really accepting yourself with all the bumps and scars that come along with life? Begin by acknowledging yourself every day. Celebrating yourself is the best way for you to let your brilliance shine and begin to claim that intuitive self that was perfectly birthed when you were.

I invite you to participate in a Birthday Moment...EVERY DAY!

    1) When is your birthday? (Mine is 5/13)

    2) Set your phone or clock alarm to go off at the time which corresponds to your birthday a.m./p.m. or both.

    3) For 1 minute edify yourself with "I am" (I am kind, I am worthy, etc.) statements. Remember it can be those that you would like to manifest as well.

4) These are statements that are more than words, they are part of our being, your intuitive self, they are not casual or trite. They describe and are the core of your essence.'

The Trust

Birthday moments provide the power to deal with any issue or situation that presents itself. You want to give your input in a thoughtful way, coming from your strengths as opposed to reacting from a weakness. Find your voice in your strengths and they will not let you down. Will you be perfect? No, you will be better; you will be perfectly human.

This is where you move into trusting yourself, confident in who you are. It is how I can remember that young girl who thought she should be invisible with kindness and love. She was wrong and it is ok. We are all a constant work in progress and if you can see around corners like me, claim it.

In the process of working and going back to college to obtain my Bachelor of English Degree and subsequent master's degree in Public Administration, I discovered the 'Clifton StrengthsFinder Assessment'. It provided a formal view of the talents that I was born with. It provided me with a guideline to fortify what I had started with the birthday moments. I decided to help others do this very thing. It was so powerful and so life-changing.

As a StrengthsFinder Coach I provide that space for clients to peel back who they have always been by discovering, declaring, and developing their talents so they can more effectively communicate with others, in work and in play. They are more likely to stand up for themselves and others because they have taken control of who they really are. They no longer let what doesn't serve them dictate how they react. There is a certain stance that you see in others that goes beyond confidence when they are living and trusting themselves, they have everything that they need within them. This stand tall moment in me, and my clients is what propels me to get up and live life to its fullest. The joy that comes from being you and letting your light shine in ways that creates a rainbow is a most beautiful existence.

Imagine living every day in near perfection and alignment with what you value, authentically responding to situations and having them be harmonious rather than difficult. Does this mean that you won't have "bad" days or that challenges won't present themselves? Decidedly not, this means that the person who is your highest, most brilliant self will rise to the occasion more and you will trust when something isn't for you. You will have the strength to say no, to ask for what you need and be more productive, contribute more readily and be more fulfilled in what you participate in and ultimately be more appreciated by others. You will be the wonderful person you were put on this Earth to be without apologies or hesitation.

Today when I sit quietly, it isn't out of fear or self-doubt. It is because I am a thinker. I like to contemplate, and I will speak when I need to for myself or in defense of others. It is a wonderful life knowing that I can be me, love me and help others understand me so they can at least know where I am coming from. Ultimately, I don't need acceptance of others because I accept myself. My sincere wish is that the same will be true for you.

ABOUT THE AUTHOR

IRMA VARGAS

IRMA VARGAS, the Host and Producer of "Be Brilliant-Enjoy the Journey" Podcast is a Certified StrengthsFinder Coach. Her top five talents are: strategy, connectedness, learning, intellect and development; what does it mean? She sees around corners, loves connecting people to their needs through collaborations, is introspective and helps others see their own brilliance. Her work is centered around helping others Discover, Declare and Develop their talents into strengths and trusting who they are intuitively.

With a Master's in Public Administration, Irma has worked, trained and taught others to effectively communicate who they are, by using strength-based methodologies for over 25 years. She has always encouraged those she trains to enjoy a balanced, joyful life in work and play. She is the co-owner of Canterbury Business Center, V1H Consulting, LLC and Guacamole Greetings Designs.

Irma is a private coach with Emerging Sisterhood, a boutique Mastermind for women who desire to be part of a community as they rise in their entrepreneurial successes together.

Be served, listen in, and connect with Irma:

Website: https://IrmaVargas.com

Free gift: https://v1hconsulting.com/free-gift

All socials: https://linktr.ee/guacgreetings

PART IV

INTUITIVE PRINCIPLES OF ART, NATURE & EMBODIMENT

KELLY BOUCHER

RADICAL TRUST: ATTENDING AND ATTUNING TO THE WORLD

To the many...
The 18 month old standing between her daddy's legs beside a tropical creek
The 10 year old navigating friendship groups in a small town
The 17 year old intrepid traveller stepping out into the big, wide world
The 28 year old worthy of great love
The 35 year old scraping trauma from her bones
The 41 year old navigating deep, salty grief
The 44 year old coming back safely
They are the ones who travelled alongside...

That sweet little bush babe
The darling girl
The vibrant teenager
The unsure young woman
The bold and brassy one who started to fade
The worn out and depleted one, silvering around the edges
And the one who returns

The one...
Returning to her days through acts of kindness and self love
Tending to it all with gentle reverence

With radical trust and the simplicity of noticing
She is attending to it all
Cultivating
Tuning in

This chapter brings together multiple life stories told in sections. Through these pages I move away from the highly structured writing that has shaped my career in academia, and into a more artistic style where I rely on intuitive prose to shape the sections. Writing in this way through an artist's conceptual lens gives me an opportunity to write like I might create a painting. As an arts-based education scholar, my work focuses on coaching teachers to 'think education otherwise' and open up to radically different approaches to everyday practice. In these pages I tell my own story of embracing a deeper unconscious and intuitive process, and explain how I bring these together to serve in the education context.

Story(ship)

My story is like a ship. A majestic, creaky galleon wayfaring across oceans in full sail. This is my storyship. The art of telling and the vessel that holds this life unfolding. This vessel has kept me safe all these years and holds many tales. Chapters that form a great volume. This vessel has many shapes.

It's the magical glass-bottomed boat of a tropical reef childhood. It's the hulking ferry crossing to a Scottish island home. It's the small cup of leaves holding offerings of flowers and flames to the most sacred of rivers. It's the gasp of awe at the perfectly preserved Viking ship unearthed in a Norwegian field. It's the great eucalypt scarred with the shape of a canoe removed from its bark. Reverence. Ancestral memory. Multiple layers playing out together all at once. Memories that are non-chronological, yet remembered in a sequence of sorts.

This story unfolds in snippets, snippets of a life well lived and so much more to come. This is a tale of noticing. Of tuning into random memories, thoughts and ideas. Fleeting, yet lasting forever, and returned to. These moments catch our attention and become an everyday force that can create worlds. When attuned to, the noticing can offer a way to live our days in deep reverence for the now, and in gentle anticipation for what is to come. This story is multifaceted. These pieces of life are mosaiced together to form a whole.

The 'mosaic approach' is a data collection method used in educational research with young children. Developed by education scholars Peter Moss and Alison Clark[1], the mosaic approach gathers, collects up and brings together small pieces (individual tiles) of daily lived experience. Once gathered, the researcher's (or in this case, the reader's) task is to collate the pieces to form a larger picture or story. I'm using this technique to collect my own data. I'm gathering up pieces, snippets and memories, and arranging them here in these pages to form a greater whole. These pieces tangle together, knot up, unfurl in threads and propose multiple patterns to read.

Tell(ing)

My 17 year old intrepid traveller self now takes up the story. This is a telling of how she survived as a vibrant and independent young woman with the world before her. She was a nature girl who grew up in a tiny town in the deep, tropical north of Australia. She was practical, resilient and responsible. In her final year of high school, she saved enough money to buy a one way ticket on the overnight train to the big city. She wanted to explore the world, and when her final exams were completed, without hesitation she dived in. She described herself as an empty vessel ready to be filled with all that life had to give her.

Those early days of travel were a time of magic unfolding. She was deeply attuned to what felt good, and she made decisions based on being social and having fun. She was having the time of her life! This was also a time of spiritual experiences that opened her up to profound and unexplained phenomena. She walked through days where multiple synchronicities and coincidences unfolded. Like the time she randomly knocked on the door of a house because it looked like cool people lived there. It turned out they had ties to her good friends in another state, and they too became lifelong friends and collaborators. She also experienced what she described as 'dream recall'. A deja vu, 'been here/done this before' feeling, but experienced through the vivid recollection of dreams she'd had years before.

Her personal story is a lived example of radical trust and how intuition guided these early days. Maybe she was naive in her youthful exuberance, but she was bright-eyed and open to full-bodied and heartfelt experiences. This positivity, optimism and deep connection to nature navigated her through multiple and complex life-layers. Optimism, confidence, spirit and hope were her guiding force. This is the world she gave me. The unexplained experiences described

---

[1] Clark, A. (2017). *Listening to young children, expanded third edition: A guide to understanding and using the mosaic approach*. Jessica Kingsley Publishers.

above were mind-blowing to my younger self, and the awe and wonder at what unfolded for her was exhilarating. However, the older silver-toned woman I am now is well and truly grounded. The profound beauty of life still takes my breath away, but I've learnt to bring these experiences into my body, and allow that to be the force that nourishes my days. I have learnt to trust my life unfolding, and to maintain stability in a somewhat wobbling world.

We are all mosaics. We are a whole made up of individual moments. The more I come to know my adult self, the more I am grateful for my teenage worldliness. Looking back into her world, I see how she shaped me into who I am today. She was the spirited one who fiercely followed her intuition. She was the resilient one who taught the foundation life skills of independence, confidence and kindness that serve me so well now. She taught me intuitive knowing – to be comfortable that my logical mind wouldn't comprehend many things. She taught me that life was messy sometimes, and the knots and tangles were also beautiful phenomena to be experienced. I am so deeply grateful for her wisdom.

Reverie

I am a girl of about 10 years old. I am on an adventure with my friend and her mother. The tropical beach is white and the rainforest crawls down to meet the sea. We sit on milk crates and eat sandwiches, wiggling the warm sand between our toes. We walk through thick rainforest, our heads tilted up into the canopy. In shafts of sunlight, we are surrounded by fluffy seeds floating down from somewhere high above. Fairy umbrellas we're told. I am in awe, full body reverie. There is magic here suspended in the humid atmosphere.

The old open-topped Toyota landcruiser rumbles homeward along a bush track. We're later than expected returning and it's dark now. We follow parallel white sandy tyre tracks through the bush. Trunks of gum trees are luminous in the headlights. It's a rattly, and sleepy, yet mesmerising drive home. Home to a quiet family. My sister is sitting in the middle of her bed. I sneak in under the mosquito net canopy. She's absorbed in the task of untangling a huge mass of thick, red wool. I sit cross-legged facing her and reach over to pull at some threads too.

Greet(ing)

To greet is to offer a friendly acknowledgement to someone on meeting or parting. It's a welcome, a gesture of kindness when coming together with people. But what about the more-than-human? I've learnt from my friend and educator, Weilwan and Gamilaroi woman, Rachel Shields[2], to greet the bush like family – to acknowledge Country as your relation, and to be sincere in your gesture of love. Country is kin.

When performing a welcome to Country ceremony, Boon Wurrung senior elder, N'arweet Dr. Carolyn Briggs[3] explains the word Wominjeka (welcome in Woi-Wurrung language) is a welcome, but also a request to come with purpose. This means that by being welcomed onto Country, the visitor has a responsibility to care for Country and an obligation to come with respect. This obligation is also a 'doing', a gesture for non-indigenous visitors to show how we might activate authentic allyship towards First Nations people.

I greet Country every day because I'm learning to listen, to notice and be called into connection with place. I'm being shown that even though I'm led by what 'feels good', I also respond deeply with nature when I don't.

In Scots language (slang), the word 'greet' also means to cry. This word most likely evolved from gráta, an Old Norse word which means to weep or cry. When I am weeping I am also learning. Country teaches me because I listen. I am learning to come together in relation *with* place. For me this is reflected in my everyday moments of practice. These moments are my daily 'noticings'. These moments set something in motion. I am in relation with Country and I am learning to come 'together-with' the world. An example of coming 'together-with' is offered by composer Jarbas Agnelli[4] who, inspired by a photograph of birds sitting on electrical wires, wrote a music score based on the positions of the birds along the lines. Their bodies became notes for a melody. Through his own moment of deep noticing, Agnelli was called into connection with/in a melodic world, and offered the viewer/listener a moment of reverie.

Gather(ing)

All of this phenomenon –the recalling, the visual that makes up my aesthetic experience, has brought me to who/where I am now, and is my reason for what I do in the world. I'm holding my experiences and memories up to the light, like pieces of sea glass. I'm noticing. To me, these noticings are signals,

---

[2] https://knowinginnature.com/
[3] Port Phillip Council, (2020, November 8). NAIDOC Week 2020: Welcome to Country [Video]. YouTube. https://youtu.be/mDoMk-bkqiQ
[4] Agnelli, J. (2009, September 7). *Birds on The Wires* [Video]. YouTube. https://youtu.be/LoM4ZZJ2UrM

symbols and meaningful messages. They are narrated snippets and shiny moments that show me how I am coming to know the places I dwell. Attuning to these sensorial phenomena offer me different lenses to learn/look through, and in doing so I am 'thinking otherwise' with the world.

The Cambridge University Dictionary defines intuition as *'an ability to understand or know something without needing to think about it or use reason to discover it, or a feeling that shows this ability'*.[5] In other words, intuition is to understand something without using logic. In this way, noticing leads to being attentive, which offers us the capacity to attend and attune to/with the world. Noticing > Attending > Attuning (Tuning in) = Intuition.

For me, intuition means being called into connection/attention to/with the world. I've come to understand that being with the world in this way is my biological wiring and how/why/what I notice in the everyday. This coming together-with the world is what physicist Karen Barad explains as entanglement. *"To be entangled is not simply to be intertwined with another, as in the joining of separate entities, but to lack an independent, self-contained existence. Existence is not an individual affair; rather, individuals emerge through and as part of their entangled intra-relating."*[6]

In this way, I am part of the world, and the world is part of me. I am the (k)not, the knowing, the (un)knower, the learner and the (un)learning. I am the careful collector who gathers up, then scatters everything outward again. Each piece is multifaceted and newly configured. Ideas (re)form and are (re)gathered back together, and the mosaic continues to grow and (re)image itself. To me, noticings (everyday moments) are points of intuition –like pinholes in black fabric that illustrate patterns of the universe in a way I can understand.

Being called into connection like this is how I interpret scholar and theorist Donna Haraway's writing on 'string figuring (SF)'. Among other interpretations, the string figures that Haraway proposes are those of cat's cradles. Cat's cradles are a game played between two people using hands (or sometimes feet), where string figures or patterns are created. This is one of the oldest games known to humans, and is a storytelling tradition practiced

---

[5] Intuition. (n.d.). In *Cambridge University's online dictionary*. Retrieved from https://dictionary.cambridge.org/dictionary/english/intuition

[6] Barad, K. (2007). *Meeting the universe halfway: Quantum physics and the entanglement of matter and meaning*. Duke University Press, p. ix.

by multiple indigenous groups across the world for thousands of years. Haraway uses the act of string figuring as an idea or metaphor to think with. She writes that by string figuring, we are *"passing patterns back and forth, giving and receiving patterns, holding the unasked for patterns in your hands ..."* [7] To generate these stories/patterns also requires trust, trust that the other person/player/listener will receive the loops and threads, and in doing so, there is an active reciprocity in the holding out of hands. Without this relationship, the patterns would not emerge.

Learning to be Affected

In her essay, *A Naturalcultural Collection of Affections: Transdisciplinary Stories of Transmedia Ecologies Learning*, Katie King, Professor of Women's Studies at the University of Maryland, writes about the notion, 'learning to be affected.'[8] This notion explains that multiple bodies (and things) "attune themselves to one another: an interactive agency."[9] This interaction offers "a dynamic trajectory by which we learn to register and become sensitive to what the world is made of."[10] And in doing so, "bodies and things, processes and interactivities are all engaging together in the many possibilities..."[11] In other words, by tuning into multiplicity and complexity, we come to know the world as a dynamic, interconnected and continuously unfolding web of relations. Interconnectedness is a way to create new meaning out of the old structures (life/education).

Sometimes I experiment during the day. I might take a walk and get my directions by following the flight of birds, or by turning towards a certain tree in flower. In these moments, I always start by asking myself what am I noticing? How am I connecting with this day? This way of travel places me firmly within a radical trust and has many rewards. Like the experiences you might have along the way, or the response (feeling) to something you notice. To me, noticing *is* my intuition and how I am learning to be affected in/with

---

[7] Haraway, D. (2016). *Staying with the trouble. Making Kin in the Chthulucene*. Durham. Duke University Press. https://doi.org/10.1515/9780822373780, pp. 12
[8] Latour, B. (2004). How to talk about the body? The normative dimension of science studies. *Body & society, 10*(2-3), 205-229.
[9] King, K. (2012). A Naturalcultural collection of affections: Transdisciplinary stories of transmedia ecologies learning. *S&F Online, 10*(3).
[10] Latour, B. (2004). How to talk about the body? The normative dimension of science studies. *Body & society, 10*(2-3), 205-229.
[11] King, K. (2012). A Naturalcultural collection of affections: Transdisciplinary stories of transmedia ecologies learning. *S&F Online, 10*(3).

the world. What stories get produced when I intentionally tune into my day? To me this gathering together is the phenomenon of living, the calling on (the welcome *and* the greeting), that which is greater than ourselves or what we understand. What is at stake here? How do we create our tales for the telling? Or in the case of string figuring, what are the threads that loop around and in between held-out fingers and hands?

Earth(ing)

Today was magnificent. They spoke in scented sentences. They spoke in microbes.

Soil chemistry. Heritage varieties. Drought and smoke haze. There was an accent to their language. A glorious lilt of grief, made up into wild bouquets. Of family. Of home.

Today I tended my own heart garden. Inhaling d-e-e-p-l-y. Multiple scents from roses as big as my face! Nose and lips to petals. D-e-e-p diaphragmatic breathing. Paddock prana. Cinnamon, anise, clove, mango, lychee, jasmine, sunshine. Apricot, peach, blush, crimson, blood, caramel, dust, yellow, lilac.

The perfume has lodged deeply into my heart and lungs. The colours have entered my cells. My body is a microscopic, microbial paint-by-numbers landscape. Cellular attunement. Attending and tending to/with the world. Living well on a damaged planet. With rose kin, and the breath we still have left in our bodies of soil.

Sky(ing)

Eighteenth century romantic artists such as Turner & Constable had a preoccupation with documenting clouds plein air. This practice was termed 'skying'. They were also masters at painting light. I did a great deal of skying today. Absorbing that sun and big sky into me. I've been earthing too, rolling over and planting my face in the grass!

Today I'm like a black and white photo being re-coloured. Letting the world come in again, painting me with light and sound. Currawong's gulping rhythm. Willy Wagtail's titter tatter. Mother (she birthed me today all those years ago). Today I absorb colour and remember my first day on Earth.

(Re)Shaping

Noticing is the intuitive phenomenon that has shaped and (re)shaped me. Noticing is the phenomenon that (re)turns me towards radical trust. Noticing is the method I use to gather up and make sense of data. Noticing activates my curiosity of the world. This is the curiosity that cultivated during my childhood, and is the fuel to my desire to bring a deep connection to the world back into the current education system. What would happen if educators tuned into a deep and active intuitive knowing? How would education systems change if adults facilitated and supported children's own innate and embodied practices of noticing? How would teachers themselves shift perspectives if they too allowed deep noticing into their everyday practice? Where would these lines of deep inquiry take us?

A(lign)ing

Anthropologist Tim Ingold's book, 'The Life of Lines'[12] imagines that life is not lived in places, but along lines. Ingold proposes *"Nothing [in the world] can hold on unless it puts out a line, and unless that line can tangle with others. When everything tangles with everything else, the result is what I call a meshwork. To describe the meshwork is to start from the premise that every living being is a line or, better, a bundle of lines."*[13]

Lines create shapes. Lines cross over. Lines tangle and are tangled. The aesthetic ritual that is my life gets crafted along these lines. The memories, the cross-overs, the piecing together, and the letting go. Intuition is a coming together of all of the micro moments of life. Like neural pathways lighting up when new ideas are thought, and meaning is found. Meaning is a line that follows us, as we follow it.

Attun(ing)

How then do we 'do' intuition? How do we cultivate an attuned daily practice? Some may identify the act of attuning as slowing down, or 'being present'. Here, in the hum and vibrancy of the everyday, why do we notice certain things and not others? Attuning to the world orientates us and makes us aware of the noticing. Awareness is a precursor for change. In this place we stand with ourselves as an observer and a thinker simultaneously.

Claim(ing)

Most people come across my work because they are ready to shift. Whether it be as teachers in education settings, or individuals, my mission is to cultivate and nurture 'thought leadership' in the everyday. I support educators to claim thought leadership as everyday practice, and I guide individuals to shift into greater flow. By claiming this practice in their own contexts, these magnificent people learn to cultivate a life force that creates worlds.

---

[12] Ingold, T. (2015). *The life of lines*. Routledge.
[13] Ingold, T. (2015). *The life of lines*. Routledge. p. 3

This is a gloriously messy, and stunningly beautiful journey of coming back to the self. It's the Odyssey, the hero's path. So simple. So profound. So (in)significant! This is the most important decision one can make. To return. To return *is* to radically trust. To radically trust is to deeply surrender, and turn toward that which we might not have ever had the courage to face before, until now. As much as we are living in a turbulent world, this is also an incredibly exciting time. We are orientating, being present, and noticing. We are claiming and fiercely cultivating our inner power and intuitive wisdom. Let's keep going slowly, being present and attuning to that which shows us just how much courage we actually have.

Come, join me on the journey. I have some beautiful tools to support your growth and expansion.

ABOUT THE AUTHOR

KELLY BOUCHER

KELLY BOUCHER is an independent scholar, education consultant and personal breakthrough coach. She holds a Bachelor of Fine Arts, post graduate studies in education and is a qualified NLP, Time Line Therapy®, and hypnosis practitioner. Her current work supports teachers across the education sector by activating critical dialogue within theory and practice to 'think otherwise with the world'. Kelly presents at education conferences both nationally and internationally and her recent publications focus on place and materials as relational learning opportunities for children.

Kelly believes there needs to be more thought leaders in early childhood education. She serves early childhood organisations by providing coaching programs, masterclasses and online courses that help generate theory informed strategies to shift out of standardised practice and into pedagogical innovation.

In the personal coaching space, Kelly supports individuals (teachers or otherwise) via focused breakthrough programs to transform out of being stuck and unmotivated, and into alignment and flow. She thinks with concepts, lives slowly on Dja Dja Wurrung country and is cultivating her own inner ecology next to a huge eucalyptus tree.

Connect with Kelly here:

Website: https://www.kellyboucher.com.au

Freebie: https://www.kellyboucher.com.au/intuitiveliving

All Socials and more: https://linktr.ee/KellyBoucherArts

RIVKA WORTH

THE STORIES WE TELL OURSELVES

This isn't the sort of story that people really want to read. You might even be angry with me for writing it and exposing the shame. Some of you will prefer it to stay behind closed doors or under the covers from where it came. But I can't do that because it's bigger and more important than just you or I and I know I'm not the only one. It's about every woman who was sexually abused as a child. One in every four girls has statistically been so. I am not the first woman to be sexually violated by a family member or friend of the family either, as 60% of sexual abuse is reported to be by people that family trust. What I don't know is how many of us remember we have been sexually abused and cannot recall the details? There are no statistics for this yet. This is definitely not spoken about and lays silently in the far back netherlands of *that* closet. These dirty, shadowy and unspoken words get locked and stuck inside our skin. These stories become part of our fascia, our connective cellular tissue, and over time, imprint our entire system. These cells can hold our experience and memories as part of our beingness and, given long enough, have an ability to strangle our capacity to live freely and congruently.

I didn't always trust my body and rarely did I follow my intuitive guidance. My work, personally and professionally, has been uncovering what it means to be at home in one's own skin, to intuitively trust the wisdom of body intelligence. This mastery/mystery, I am not ashamed to share, has been developed through my exquisite f#cking up over and over again.

I spent most of my life in distrust of myself, in self-questioning, self-hatred, and self-harm. The embodied wisdom of my lived experience is what eventually led me to a place of self-forgiveness and, only now in my 50th year, to a place where I can reclaim, 'I trust myself'. What took me half a century to learn is that every time I don't trust my truth, I discard a potentially brilliant new future. The loyalty to my stories of the past become excuses for freedom. I would bet we all have that one voice in our head that will always rebel, sabotage and doubt what we know is good and true. Truth-choosing is a practice. Our bodies hold the instruction manual.

As a young child I remember spending lots of time on my own. I spent hours in the garden with the flowers and bees and my gazillion pets. I would chat to my plant and animal friends. What I didn't know then, was that I was apprenticing Nature. I was listening through my body. My body, the home of my biggest wound and trauma, the demolition site for my healing, and the temple for my soul. My body was the source of so many feelings, swaddled in blankets of numbness. Through the impact of sexual abuse my body became a bridge to both worlds, physical and energetic, seen and unseen. One of trauma's gifts is the ability to straddle the quantum and the linear. I now recognise this wound and power in others. The 'survival' split from our physical bodies creates a portal to the spiritual world, to the dark and the light, the seeing with eyes closed. This 'knowing' and 'feeling' our way through life becomes a path of embodied wisdom. For me, it has been a pathway to trusting truth.

It's very confusing when memories surface. I was twenty-one years old and had checked myself into a year-long residential drug rehabilitation program. I left the state, friends, family and work. I told myself I was letting go of everything. Truth was everything had already fallen apart. Addiction is the perfect truth mask. It works so well until it doesn't. How could I have been so successfully disconnected from my body to repress memories deep inside? I blamed myself for not knowing, as is common with many survivors. I blamed myself for burying my truth and carrying the damage. Shame carried in a person's body can hide and submerge many things. I realised as I thawed out, that even though I had spent my entire life up to that point as a dancer, intimately connected with my body, I felt the furthest from myself that I ever had. As I began to reclaim my home within my skin, I tapped into a deep curiosity of how my body was able to mask such an impactful experience. I lost trust in myself and in my ability to read my own physical cues. It was very shaky ground. Anyone who has uncovered or re-lived trauma knows this feeling of groundlessness. It's frightening, de-stabilizing and confusing.

During that time in recovery, I continued to dance. I had been studying Gabrielle Roth's 5Rhythms® and her book *Maps to Ecstasy*. Her cassette tapes were my medicine. Dance provided a route back to feeling centred and almost congruent with myself. Truth finds pathways through fascia, bones, breath and organs to release old and stuck memories. From this place of unravelling in my twenties I began a life-long soul search into the movement of trauma. Entwined in seeking my life's meaning and purpose was the uncovering of truth and trust through my moving body. The body knows, the body speaks and the body heals.

Experiencing trauma seems to be part of the human adventure. Just being born is a great initiation that imprints upon us in one way or another. Trauma is an embodied experience. It is our response to a particular event or series of events that can implant into our cellular body. The less we move our bodies the less opportunity we have to process trauma. No amount of talking will release the memory of the pain held in body tissue. Our highly-developed, screen-based realities encourage us to move less. Our houses and lifestyles, we tell ourselves, are designed for comfort. Even for an Embodiment Coach/Dance Facilitator, my work, communication and recreation add up hours of sitting or even lying down in front of a screen. You're probably doing this right now. In addition to this affecting our bone density, digestion, immune system and brain function, reduced movement means more stuck trauma. We became a society of 'trigger' bombs just waiting to explode.

How can we possibly know who we are in the world until we know who we are in ourselves? And how can we trust anything before we trust being in our own skin? Once we have allowed ourselves to dislodge, feel, integrate and heal past pain, we then have the capacity for embodied and generative intuitive living.

I don't want to hold the pain of past experience in my body any more. Do you? I choose to release the embodied trauma from my system. I plan to dance it all out and rinse it off in a delicious sweat. The thing is, it must be felt to be released. My mission is for all beings to find this freedom and safety in our bodies as home. The inner work of integrating the wounding, attachment and dis-ease is critical to feel fully alive. This journey takes time and what I have witnessed is our intelligent bodies know when and how much to share with us once we are ready to listen and follow. Our own embodiment is a coordinate to planetary embodiment. Collectively we are becoming more intuitive as a species. This excites me so much. This is why I do the work I do.

To trust ourselves is to know ourselves. I have found the quickest route to this through my body. Have you ever started stretching at a yoga class and wanted to cry, or maybe you did cry? I have many times. Have you ever had a peak physical experience like a massive run, a cold-water therapy immersion or an incredible orgasm, where emotion just bursts out of you seemingly from nowhere? These somatic release moments, through physical activation, are our clever bodies designing pathways to purge and express stored emotion. Some might even say this is our Soul moving through our body.

My daily practice is to stir this sh!t up. I work with movement, dance and somatics to know myself and I offer this work in collaboration with nature. I move my body to strengthen my connection with my animal primal self that always intuitively knows what's up before my mind has even woken up. It's a feeling thing. If we have been practising staying anaesthetised for a while It can take a while to regenerate feeling. Mixed messaging of old stories and past memories will continue to influence our path forward, clouding our intuitive discernment. We will repeatedly tell ourselves our past stories as a way to orient. The path to freedom requires discipline to authentically honour our past, feel it and let it go. Each time we do this we get to course-correct our future selves and design the life we dream about living.

Have you ever had an experience where you knew exactly what you needed to do for your highest self, for your truth and happiness but you didn't do it? That was me. I have abandoned myself way too many times. It has taken me many life lessons to learn how to live in faith.

One of my big lessons was staying too long in a relationship with domestic violence, drugs, dishonesty, you know all the 'hot' stuff we find ourselves attracted to for all the wrong reasons. I told myself "this is my family, the security that I have been longing for my entire life. They love me and it's going to be ok. It won't always be like this". I rationalise and convince myself to stay, and each time I do so I override my soul. And yes, I 'know' what I need but I am unwilling to see that I am replicating a version of my past. We all make mistakes, choose the not so ideal option, and then hopefully, eventually work it out. I denied my truth for fifteen years. It hurt to get honest with myself. Do you have the courage to tell yourself the truth?

I held on way past the use-by date because, to be really honest, I did not have the faith to leave. I took myself to the edge of that separation so many times but never jumped. I would pray for guidance and receive it loud and clear but then not be willing or brave enough to act. I didn't follow my own guidance and I paid the price.

One day I was walking home and out of the blue I just started shaking. I was flooded with dizziness and the world went sideways. I got home and lay down and didn't get up for the next three months. I had no idea what was wrong with me. I had tests for all the things, medical and alternative plus a few random diagnoses. I was bedridden with severe vertigo, migraines, and I just didn't want to speak to anyone any more. I woke in panic attacks almost every night and was too scared to go to sleep. It's very difficult to describe what a crisis of shutting down feels like. It was like a wave hit me and I was left tumbling, dumped and disoriented for months. I had no choice but to meet myself in my darkness. I began to dig deeply into my soul work, allowing myself this breakdown/breakthrough, death and eventual rebirth/awakening. One day I found my body moving gently under the covers and soon recognised I was dancing a 5Rhythms Wave. In this bedridden reality, the *Wave* moved through my body and began to heal me. I danced *Waves* daily, horizontally under the doona until I was ready to meet the vertical.

Besides hobbling to the bathroom and appointments, I hadn't been upright in months, let alone danced. I can still hear the Warlpiri 'old ladies' I had been working with, singing me up. This first dance on my feet is one that I will never forget. It initiated a four year journey to become a 5Rhythms teacher guiding others through fear, numbness and grief to whole their souls through their bodies. After my first post-recovery intensive, I returned home and left my partner. Gabrielle Roth's map is so profound. She says, "Intuition is intelligence at the speed of light". The dance clears things up and out every time. 5Rhythms is a dance to truth, a dance to power and a dance to freedom. Once again it saved my life. It took a spiritual emergency for me to end that 21-year relationship. I got there in the end, however I do imagine how my life might have been if I hadn't listened to the stories I told myself and instead acted on my intuitive guidance a decade earlier.

Fast forward and I find myself in another relationship that my soul knew was time to leave. Yes, here was another time I knew I needed to leave way before I actually did. Kept thinking it would change; it did - for the worse! After experiencing an incredibly destructive break up that almost killed me, I got really lost in the darkness. As part of my recovery I set myself a challenge. I bought one of those large 12-month planner boards and each morning I would ask myself 'What would love do?' then I would take the action immediately. It was challenging to love myself enough to believe that the little voice in me knew what I needed. I did this every single day, marking a little heart on the calendar for 365 days plus one for good luck! Not only did loving myself become easier, I developed a whole online program called radical self-love that allowed me to create income during lockdown and supported others to listen and follow through on their own inner loving wisdom. This process showed me that by practicing the action of intuition it got stronger. Intuition became cumulative.

Intuition is a practice. We all have it. How many times, though, do we need to keep learning the same lessons around following through? What I have discovered is that each time we don't act on intuition, we turn our back on ourselves and very often we don't like the outcome. Intuition is feeling based and doesn't always seem sensible, practical or realistic. You might even hear yourself say, 'that's crazy' or 'irrational'. The rebel in us can be so quick to protest and tell ourselves a conflicting story. During these times I have to knuckle down and remind myself that it is human to want to 'know' and have 'evidence' and 'understand'. I am like a toddler who incessantly asks, 'But why?' Logic tricks us into confidence. Faith leads us into freedom. Truth is for the brave.

So why must we talk about the painful topics that we prefer shall not be named? Can't we just move to the 'clearing the past' and 'transforming our lives' bit? Isn't it time we just felt good? And my favourite, 'When will it end?'. Unfortunately I can't answer any of these for you but I can tell you that the thousands of dances and ceremonies I've experienced as both a student and teacher have paradigm-shifted reality and redesigned life in spectacularly unimaginable, expansive unfoldings. 'The thing(s) that kept you safe as a child will be your greatest gift to the world," one of my mentors says. As an adult I have returned to Dance and Nature as these were my childhood saving grace. What are yours? There's a property out bush where I spend time with giant rocks, trees, moss and ferns. I've been coming here since I was a small kid and the land knows me well. Nature is where I attune my listening body and receive the answers every single time. My newest body of work *Eco-Soma* has birthed from my ongoing somatic practice in Nature. I have witnessed as clients accessed new parts of themselves through the integrative practice of eco somatics and ceremony. Ceremony, in collaboration with Nature, initiates deep healing and connects us to authenticity, purpose and belonging. What are you currently working with in your life? What skins are you shedding and who are you becoming?

I often use this Tree-Portal process to support me in alchemising transitions. You might find it serves you also. Take yourself to a private outdoor place and go for a walk to find your trees. You are looking for two trees with a gap between them and clear ground on either side. Ask the trees to show you. These trees hold the pillars of your gateway to pass through. You are about to create an intentional portal of change where you will exit one world and step into another. Choose the one thing you are working with right now that you are ready to leave behind. Might be a relationship, job, behaviour, identity. Whatever it is, you need to commit and step through without looking back. It is powerful to say out loud the thing you are leaving behind. You might even build a fire to sit and honour this part with before stepping through. As you step through, speak clearly what you are stepping into; immerse yourself in the words and the feeling of the new reality. Done properly with a rich foundation of preparation, this ceremony is incredibly transformative. You are designing a new existence. Remember to thank your trees when you close your ceremony. Do not look back from where you came until next time you visit this place where you can then reflect and honour the changes you have implemented. If you ever want some support and guidance around deepening your embodied relationship with nature or designing your transformational ceremony, it would be my honour to work with you. You can access details on my website for upcoming online and face to face programs to support you with somatic tools for aligning body & soul to expand your capacity as an ambassador on Earth.

The underlying methodology of all my practice is listening. The stillness, quiet and spaciousness of being in Nature, invites a receptivity within our nervous system that is ripe for attuning to the signals and sensations in our bodies and deep inward intuitive listening. Our First Nations people have been doing this for billions of years and are waiting for us to catch up and listen to 'Country', a word used to describe not simply Nature but a term encapsulating place, custom, language, spiritual belief, cultural practice, law, material sustenance, family and identity. Once we meet ourselves this way it can be an unforgettable awakening. By simply being present in our bodies we can access a quality of stillness that brings us to truth every single time. No matter what experience or relationship you have with your body, there are strategies to support you to befriend and trust yourself even more, to deepen your safety and comfort in your own skin and eventually feel the sanctuary of your body as home. Through moving your 'stories' you will begin to navigate and intuit your way harmoniously through decisions, confusion and discernment with embodied power and personal authority. It is time to claim yourself back. No one else can or will do this for you. There couldn't be a better time to reclaim yourself. The world needs you.

Your truth is shaping your reality. What is standing in the way of you trusting yourself? "We are managing the consciousness of our souls," says Carolyn Myss. Our stories matter. We need to tell them so that in our own way, we can let them go. They determine how we author our lives. What stories have you been telling yourself the last ten, twenty, fifty years? And what new story will you begin today?

ABOUT THE AUTHOR

RIVKA WORTH

RIVKA WORTH is a somatic, shamanic and sonic entrepreneur who grew up talking to trees, rocks and flowers. Her love of dance and nature come together in her work, *Eco Soma; devoted to re-building healthy relationships with nature through embodied practice*. Rivka offers Eco-Somatic practices of listening, presence and renewal through physical and sensory bonding with the natural world. She is one of Australia's leading exponents of Conscious Dance, facilitating diverse human embodiment in health, justice, education, arts and environmental settings. Her dance floors range from church halls, sandy lined shores, leafy green forests and red desert earth.

Rivka's qualifications include BA Dance, Eco-Somatic Educator, Certified 5Rhythms teacher, Certified Futuring Trainer and her job titles have spanned Artistic Director, Film Maker, Choreographer, Community Cultural Development Officer, Writer, Mother, Futurist, Healer, Visionary, DJ, Soul Guide, Embodiment Coach and Boss Lady. She thrives on bringing humans together in ceremonial dance, where freedom, connection and transformation are individually and collectively embodied. Rivka is an Earth Ambassador who is dedicated to connecting us back to nature through our own embodiment. She is a queer mother of two men, living in the tree fringes of Naarm (Melbourne).

Connect with Rivka here:

Website: https://www.rivkaworth.com

Freebie: https://www.rivkaworth.com

All socials: https://linktr.ee/RivkaWorth

KATE LIONIS

SITTING WITH IT

THE SEARCH FOR SUPPORT, SAFETY AND LOVE WITHIN

I remember seeing Uluru for the first time. I could feel the energy coming off of it in waves and an ancient wisdom that was being dampened by the footsteps of people climbing all over her. Fast forward 15 years; I heard that we were no longer allowed to climb on this magnificent rock, and this overwhelming sense of relief rushed over me in waves. It was as if the Earth was able to finally breathe again and in that first breath her first and only outcome was to heal. In that sense of relief, I felt a sense of change that the Earth was going to take back what was hers. And she did. Within the month, bush fires like we had never seen before emerged all over the country and eventually the world. The goal of fire was to clear away what no longer was needed, the deadwood. This smoke was a cleansing ritual, to remove old stagnant energy, a beginning of the healing process.

To heal, the first thing any of us can do is rest, and that is exactly what the Earth did. Through serendipity, or by design, a new virus emerged causing us as humans (as well as industry) to stop, allowing the Earth to quietly take back what was hers. In that time she flourished.

I felt every part of this process as it unfolded even if it didn't make sense until later. I have always had a sense of the energy around me on a personal and up to a global scale. I had an intuitive knowing of what was happening underneath the surface, the ability to see the intention or the 'why' beneath the facade. Little did I know that what was happening on a global scale would be reflected in my personal narrative.

My story is one of looking for love, support, and safety in all the wrong places from people who were not giving it. I learnt to heal by learning to sit with it, being uncomfortable and understanding my personal narrative and habits. By taking the wisdom of the Earth and communing with her I found all the love, support and safety I needed within myself. By finding the faith in this wisdom of myself, my intuition only flourished and grew stronger.

The Universe was giving me quiet prods to remind me that this is not where I needed to be, and I didn't listen. I allowed every method of not listening to my intuition to take hold: the to-do list, being busy, which is an easy thing to do as a mum, the social media and generally being a human pinball rushing from one place to the next, not understanding why I was never getting anywhere. In the background the Universe quietly continued to nudge, trying to guide and show me that there is another path, a better path. As the world, the Earth, began her transformation of healing, an opportunity the Universe would not let me pass up (this time) threw me onto my journey of transformation and ultimately, healing.

Through 2019 I was rushing from one place to the next, never allowing an opportunity for reprieve. Through the year I began to get a feeling that something was not quite right. I ignored it and pressed on. Then physical symptoms of bleeding and an irregular cycle manifested and still I pushed on. Slowly, very slowly, the symptoms became more pronounced and now it included pain and a general feeling of malaise. It was here, through the busyness, I began to ask myself what was going on? But I was too busy, and honestly too scared to learn the answer and so I pushed on.

Finally, in March 2020, I had the courage to ask what was happening to my body. My doctor sat me down and told me I had a bacterial infection. As I was diagnosed with this infection the world shut down in response to a new viral infection taking hold of the globe. As I learnt of the infection, I readied my body to shut down and go into shock, and it did.

You see, this was the second time I had been diagnosed with this infection and I pride myself as a person whose health is a priority for the benefit of my family and conduct myself with integrity. To become sick in this way was a metaphorical punch to the gut. It left me broken and with no bearing. All I could say at the time was, "Universe, I get it, I know what you need me to do."

Then the world shut down and the energy surrounding me was of uncertainty and fear. Every person withdrew to protect themselves and prepare for anything this scary new scenario was going to throw at us. So, I was alone, cut off physically and metaphorically from any potential support, unable to give myself space to heal because my children were home, and it was my primary function to protect them. I was scared, unsure and broken. The sentiment in my home was, "Get over it, get on with it." I no longer felt supported or safe. Love felt conditional.

Then the next punch came. The symptoms did not stop after treatment.

What a slap to the face by the Universe!!

Through the weeks in shut down, surrounded by the energy of the fear of the unknown, adjusting to isolation and homeschooling, the only reprieve was to go to the doctors and the hospitals trying to understand why this infection was not leaving my body. Each appointment, each procedure was another violation compounding on the initial trauma, leaving me asking the Universe why this was happening. Asking the Universe, "What are you wanting me to do?"

The Universe answered. It told me to stop and sit with it.

For a person who is programmed not to stop, who finds validation in being busy, this was a tough transition. It started by promising myself to go for a run every morning, to allow myself to have that time every day, to find stillness in the movement. Then I dedicated five minutes a day writing five things I am grateful for, to remind myself in that small window to be present and find the light in the darkness. Then the journey of meditation began. As my mind was consumed with trauma, I knew I needed the stillness meditation brings and I made a discipline of listening to one guided meditation every day. I already had a home-based daily yoga practise and very slowly my mind stopped twirling around and gradually became still, and in that stillness I was able to sit with the experience, to understand it and to allow my intuitive knowing to tell me what to do next.

There were days that I went through the motions of each of these practices with no heart in it as my mind was consumed. But the discipline of practising each day reaped rewards as stillness was attained more and more every day.

Eventually, we left that first shut down and it seemed like we were going back to normal. My physical symptoms had finished, but I never found out why my body had held on to the infection for so long.

Then it happened again! Intuitively, I knew it was the Universe becoming fed up and it was going to make me listen whether I wanted to or not! It was no longer a quiet push, but now a screaming punch... GET (BAM!) A (POW!) MOVE (WHACK!) ON (THUMP!) NOW (WHAM!)!!

So, I did. This time I decided to listen and act on what the Universe, my intuition, had to say, even if it did not make sense at the time, and the strangest circumstances began to happen. Universal doors opened and situations came to me with ease. It was as if the Earth herself was conspiring with me and my world began to shift.

What I didn't anticipate about these weeks following the first lockdown was the opportunity to be quiet and sit with it. The silence revealed so much. The quiet allowed me to make choices without input from outside sources, without distraction, allowing my intuition to become stronger and every choice that came from my intuitive self only benefited me and those around me.

After the initial lockdown ended I became a yoga teacher and an Ayurvedic lifestyle consultant with ease. My art, when I viewed it as a method of meditation, as an act of stillness, became undemanding. The product was one that came from my soul. I realise now that the creation of this art was a method to 'sit with it' and it was my method to purge the emotions that were bottled inside. To create something beautiful from the ashes of trauma. Each act of creation became a lesson into the self. Watercolour painting was a lesson in being prepared (have the right materials), then letting go of the outcome. Oil painting was a lesson to be deliberate in exercising patience and the result will reveal itself. Pencil drawing was a lesson of observation without distraction by your own perception of the subject. I allowed myself the opportunity to sit with it and slowly, ever so slowly, decisions and ideas began to reveal themselves.

As I meandered on the journey of healing I processed and documented the different facets and feelings brought forth through photography. I explored the connection of my purging and healing with that of Mother Earth, who, concurrently, was undergoing the same process. Each photo I took described my connection and surrender to the Earth, allowing transformation and healing to take place. As the Earth and I underwent each stage of healing, I created imagery that reflected the transformation, allowing it to integrate into my body and embody the change. By observing this journey of healing in myself and the Earth allowed perspective on how far we have both come. Documenting this journey became an art of healing.

I began to support this healing physically by cooking nourishing food and establishing and maintaining boundaries with people who drained my time and energy. I learned to become mindful in each action I took, by sitting with it. Each supported my mental, emotional, and physical body and my intuitive knowing followed suit.

The learning gained during this time allowed me to understand what I intuitively knew to be true. The most important step in setting an intention is to let go, to lose expectation of an outcome. Every single time I held onto any expectation to an outcome the outcome NEVER happened. As I learnt to sit with it, I found methods to keep the mind quiet, to not let it whirl and catastrophize, through creating art and yoga. As these were practiced over time, the intuitive muscle was flexed. As it became stronger, my emotional and mental health improved.

I was able to access this place most easily by "sitting with it". By "sitting with it" the intuitive knowing was able to emerge and give quiet guidance on what to do next, to show the next step on the path. The more I listened and flexed that muscle, the easier the intuition could emerge.

As 2020 came to close there were many changes that had happened on the Earth and in myself. 2020 may not have been an easeful year for humankind, but Mother Earth flourished. If you don't believe me, watch the documentary "The Year the Earth Changed" by David Attenborough. In my own life the greatest change was an increased connection to my intuitive compass and that led to a quiet, grounded self-assurance and I was slowly learning that love, support, and safety comes from this place within. And this place is unlimited.

However, I had another feeling, another knowing. We were not done with resting yet. There was more that needed to be learned, to be embodied, if I was willing and brave enough to take it on. And didn't 2021 deliver on that! If 2020 was the year of fear, 2021 was the year of frustration.

All over the Earth, at various times in 2021 people were again shutdown, this time for a much longer period than the first time. It felt that the first shut down was a taste, a practice run to be ready for the second, where the real work began. Mother Earth continued to purge, to remove what was no longer needed and to rest and in this year again she flourished even more.

By this point the daily practices to cultivate my intuitive knowing were stronger and I was gaining more confidence. Now the next lessons in intuition were ready to be learnt and the Universe was ready to slap me in the face with it again.

The next shutdown proved to be longer and more arduous, and as it began I suffered a financial trauma. I was forced to sign a financial document my intuition did not want me to sign. This trauma reinforced a lesson that the Universe had been teaching me since the beginning: do not find love, support, and safety outside of yourself, it starts from within. Again, I was metaphorically punched in the gut and again the sentiment of my surroundings was, "Get on with it, get over it." Again, I was the support for my family in a global time of fear and confusion. And again it was during a time I needed to heal.

On this occasion I was grateful for the space from the distraction of people and life to be able to concentrate completely on healing. To embody the idea that true love, support, and safety comes from inside and to do this the Universe told me, "You have not finished. Stop and sit with it." And I did. In a climate that reeked of frustration, polarisation, and confusion, I continued my journey. While Mother Earth continued to rest and clear what no longer served her, I continued to do the same in my own microcosm.

This financial trauma released me from any notion that true support is found outside of myself and that I needed to start within to find and build on that foundation. During this time opportunities arose, and with an attitude of curiosity and play I explored them. I was given the gift of isolation and quiet. It was here that I knew a habit I had previously embodied of working to distraction was no longer going to serve, so I made a concerted effort to have a project and be mindful to not allow it to take up all my attention. People emerged in this time who assisted me on this healing journey. As the healing progressed, I learnt that the choices I used to make and the people I used to attract no longer served me. I discovered that they were detrimental for my emotional and mental health and they were cleared away, like the dead wood of a bushfire. And just like that, my intuitive knowing became stronger and more grounded.

It was here that I discovered my pattern and how I had gotten myself into this situation. It was here that I was finally capable of taking full responsibility of my life and more importantly how to change these patterns of behaviours.

I harnessed the idea that self-doubt had blocked my intuition and that self-doubt comes from the ego and fear of stories we tell ourselves to keep ourselves 'safe'. One of my teachers introduced the term 'interference', which I much prefer. The terms self-doubt or lack of self-confidence are ideas that we can embody and become. Terms like interference or obstacles are outside entities that block the path of our knowing and intuition. We cannot embody these ideas and it is much easier for us to separate ourselves from them, see them for what they are and easily walk around the obstacle to continue along the path. The moment I began to see self-doubt, fear, resentment and other ego-based sensations as interference or obstacles, it became much easier to disassociate, identify and remove them from my path. The more I practised this the better I got. This was the single most important lesson I learned in fostering the growth of my intuition.

I became aware of the decision to choose between intuition and any obstacle that came into my path. I could choose to identify and embody the self-doubt allowing it to become louder than my intuition, so that I would run, freeze, or overcompensate, which I have done many times. Or I could stop and observe and sit with it. Not to react, not to embody the situation, but to step back and see it for what it is. If there is an obstacle or an interference blocking the way to my intuition this method allows me to identify it and then eventually understand why. Is there a habit or perception of myself that I held and did the obstacle reinforce this idea? I was truly able to achieve this when I slowed my mind down and stepped out of my own way.

Sitting with it can last for seconds, minutes, days, months or maybe even years. This could be a process that lasts for the rest of my life, but like life, it is a process. When I am sitting with it, I cannot identify with the problem or obstacle because the problem does not exist in the present, only in the past or in the future.

Sitting with it stopped me from catastrophizing or embodying my self doubt and allowed me to understand how life is, how it truly is at present, and any outside perceptions and projections slowly fell away. Over the quiet months of shutdown I learnt to catch myself with these ideas before I could embody them.

To understand and identify people and situations that throw me off kilter and raise red flags, and do so quickly, and I now had the tools to deal with it effectively. Like a bushfire I was able to clear the deadwood by clearing situations or people that no longer served, or, as I was learning, were no longer in alignment. I honed my techniques to access the quiet, the process of making art, moving meditation of yoga, tapping, and removing myself from many sources of self-doubt. As these obstacles were moved my intuitive knowing became strong and a wonderful by-product, I became emotionally and mentally strong, grounded in the faith of my own intuition. I found my own endless well of support, safety, and love in myself.

As I am writing this, I am still undergoing this process and little by little, every day my intuition becomes stronger and more refined. The faith I have in my intuitive knowing has become secure and, in that assurance, I have found the everlasting well of support, safety and love within myself. I still have days that I falter, and I fall, and I lose faith, or my ego wins with resentment, fear, and anger, but I can now identify these feelings much more efficiently.

The world is emerging from her forced rest and like Mother Earth we have all changed just a little or maybe even a lot. It will be interesting to see what the next phase brings to the Earth's evolution and understand how that is reflected within my own.

I invite you to go and find that thing, whatever it is, that allows you to come to stillness. Allow your mind to become quiet, so you can 'sit with it'. Have patience and your intuitive knowing will emerge and show itself to you. Allow whatever is happening in your life, at this moment, to come up and when it does, let it. Do not judge or shame whatever emerges, just sit with it and when you do, watch the miracles unfold.

ABOUT THE AUTHOR

KATE LIONIS

KATE LIONIS is a yoga teacher, artist, and mother of two. After completing two degrees in the Medical Sciences, Kate went on to explore more alternate healing modalities of art, yoga, meditation, ayurveda, and reiki to find a sustainable healing practise for herself and to share with others. Kate's art is a visual manifestation of the healing process she has undertaken. Using different mediums allows freedom of expression and different types of healing to take place. Kate shares her techniques of healing through art to allow the artist to discover their own healing practice.

Kate's photographs have been featured in multiple editions of House and Garden UK and Art Edit Magazine. She has been a finalist in many competitions including Australian Photographer Magazine Photographer of the year and Capture Magazine Emerging Photographer. Kate's images have been shown in galleries in Sydney and the world.

Her goal is to inspire and give the tools to empower women to intuitively heal themselves.

Connect with Kate here:

Website: http://www.artimageyoga.com

Photographic website: www.katelionisphoto.com

Freebie: Sitting yoga pose, watercolour picture and "sit with it" Meditation

Linktree: https://linktr.ee/katelionis

BIANCA DE REUS

LOVING WHISPERS OF A FURRY KIND

USE INTUITION TO TUNE INTO SOUL LANGUAGE AND THE ANIMALS AROUND US SO THAT WE COLLABORATE AT A HIGH VIBRATIONAL LEVEL

Have you ever wondered what goes on behind the beautiful eyes of animals? What they are thinking, and how they are experiencing life?

I know that every animal has a story to tell, wanting to express how they feel, and share their wisdom with the world.

How do we know they can do this? How can we hear them? What can we learn from them so that we have a better experience and understanding of ourselves?

When I am out and about in nature and around animals, they often just start talking to me. It doesn't matter whether I'm wandering amongst them or I see a picture in front of me; animals' need to communicate with me is ever-present.

Whether they have a specific message or just want a chat, I find that communicating with our animal friends is a fun, healing, loving, and therapeutic experience.

Over the years, I have learned that many people are curious about what their beloved pets are thinking. What goes on in their mind? Am I doing enough?

What can we do together? Dogs, cats, guinea pigs, birds, sheep, cows, lizards. All animals can communicate with us, and we with them.

We simply need to be quiet and listen.

It is the people who are open to listening to the animals that can help them share their stories and wisdom with us humans, so that we can learn, be inspired and create a positive change in ourselves and in the world.

I am writing this chapter not just for you but also on behalf of the animals so you can be inspired to connect with your true self and your pets at a deeply spiritual and high vibrational level. You may be amazed by the wisdom the animals will share with you. So that you trust and feel confident in your ability to help them, and more importantly, help yourself to expand and grow, and live from a place of intuition, love and harmony.

Animals are sentient, just like you and me. They are Soul Beings, living with genuine love, absolute passion, and a desire to serve the planet and all beings on it.

Communicating with all animals, from companions at home, to those on the farm and out in the wild, is the beginning of a new and peaceful world.

Are you ready to be inspired? Take a breath, and open up to the possibility that you too can practice talking and collaborating with animals around you.

Let's enjoy this journey *together*.

A Glimpse into Connecting with Self and the Animals

Let me start by sharing how communicating with animals became part of my life, after I discovered some of my spiritual abilities.

I'd love this to be an insight for you, an assurance that you are not alone and that you can learn to connect with yourself and your pet, or any other animal around you (and even spirit guides).

I was born into a loving family, with inspirational parents and a cheeky, fun-loving and hard-working brother. We were raised with love and we learned to make our own choices around what we wanted to do with our lives.

Throughout my life I've always had a knowing and could sense things. I never really knew what that was or how I could do it. People have always, and continue to, come to me for guidance, advice and support. They say, *"Bianca knows everything. She will make it right."*

"Bianca will help you feel better."

"Bianca will be able to guide you in the right direction or help you with clarity."

"When I am around you, you always make me feel happy, at peace and light."

Up until recently I denied knowing everything, but on many occasions, it was made clear to me that I did know a lot! I feel what is right and what is wrong; I know which direction to go or where to guide a person. But I never knew how, or why.

Not knowing drove me into a spin and depression for a long time. I felt alone and different. Especially in my younger years, I felt I didn't belong, and that feeling lasted well into my adult life.

I see myself as a practical, down-to-Earth woman, who certainly doesn't tap into the "woo-woo" of life. To me, it has to be tangible and analysed. I love to find out why things happen, and because I couldn't figure out the WHY, it drove me nuts! Why did I know so much? Why did I feel what I felt and why couldn't I describe it? Why didn't I know where it was coming from? And WHY did it feel like such a heavy responsibility?

Then, around 2007, things started to change on a physical level. My hands and the space between my eyebrows had sensations of tingles, heat and chills. Sounds became too loud to bear. I had no idea what was going on!

I was afraid to talk to anyone. Even my wife, Lana, didn't understand half of what I was going through, and I was too scared to tell her. What would she think?

Finally, my mum came to the rescue! She explained what was going on and guided me to work with my hands. As a Reiki Master and universal energy healer, she could see that I was holding too much energy in my body that I subconsciously received from the Universe. She taught me how to move and use this energy for good. Since then the physical challenges have disappeared.

From that day onwards I studied to be a Reiki Master, and worked with people and animals to practise. I also researched and studied more about spirituality, healing and metaphysical abilities. I learned from teachers and mentors, and implemented all my learning.

My depression, coupled with not really knowing how to apply this knowledge, was a struggle every day until I learned to actually have more fun with the connections I experienced and to have boundaries in place so I was in control.

I can now happily say I am who I am, and I can do what I do, because it is part of me.

In 2011 I was introduced to animal communication by a wild snake. During a bush walk the snake started talking to me out of the blue and told me, *"Go out into the world and do your job. You are to reconnect the animals with the humans again so they live side-by-side in harmony."* This became my purpose in life and changed everything for me. There is a lot more to this story that we can talk about over a cuppa!

Now that I have animal communication as another layer in my abilities on this Earth plane, I am living fully from my heart, being who I truly am. And I know you can do this too.

Before I learned animal communication, I always wondered what was going on behind animals' gorgeous eyes, especially my dogs'. They would sometimes stare at me as if to say, "Don't you know what we mean, Mum?" My boy Toby (RIP) especially could stare at me all day! Until I *could* hear him. That changed everything for our relationship.

Are you experiencing your pets looking at you, staring as if they are telling you something or asking questions, but you just can't hear them?

Tuning in to Animal Language

Talking with animals is an intuitive process, and usually happens via telepathy initially. Of course they can hear our voice, but don't necessarily understand our language. What's important is what we project to them, including our energy. That is how they understand what we are saying. They can send us a picture, a smell, a colour, or words via telepathy. We receive this only when we are tuned in to them.

Animals live from their hearts. They are connected to Spirit at a higher vibrational level and give absolute and complete unconditional love. It gives us such a great feeling to see our own beloved animal approach us, wanting us to receive their love.

Whether you have a pet in your family, have animals on your farm, or rescue animals from misery and abuse, everyone can learn this wonderful and important skill.

Over the years, I have spoken with birds, dogs, cats, goannas, horses, guinea pigs, cows, sheep, koalas, kangaroos, and certain insects. I feel so honoured to be able to communicate with animals. It feels great to hear the different voices and feel the different energies. I am loving it, and I am sure you will too!

I always speak with animals with gratitude, love, and respect. Whether animals have a specific message for us or just want to have a conversation, communicating with our animal friends is an enjoyable and therapeutic experience.

Animals are able to teach us a lot about the environment we live in. They also teach us about ourselves as human beings, as Soul Beings, and as Spirit in this human form.

For example, I had a client whose neighbour's cat pooped on her doorstep one morning. Aware of the fact that animals communicate, she asked me to tune into the cat. I learned my client's issue was boundaries and the cat was showing this in the form of trespassing.

Most importantly, they teach us about why and how we are all connected to each other.

Each one of us has a soul, and is connected to Source energy and hence we are all connected to each other. We are all sentient beings, both humans and animals. I know from experience that plants and trees hold energy the same way we do, and can provide us with healing and wisdom. It is this healing and wisdom that animals show and provide us through the same Universal energy.

Animals want nothing more for us than to connect to our true self, our higher self, our inner voice. We can only do this when we sit or walk in stillness, tune in and listen. Truly listen, with an open heart. When we do this we increase our energy, lift our vibration and are able to align with a frequency that allows us to hear, feel and sense who we are, what we say and learn from our wisdom. We follow a similar process when we tune into the animals. I will share an exercise with you later.

But before I take you through that exercise, I must tell you that nine times out of ten, when I work with an animal, they have something to say about the human guardians around them or the family they live with. Sometimes it's not easy to hear what the animal has to say about us, as it may not be all positive. I have learned that a particular animal can manifest my working with them in such a way that the human guardian actually finds me and engages with me. And one of these ways is through behaviour. Behaviour can change for an animal as we need to pay attention to something that is not working in our own lives.

Let me share a couple of examples:

Audrey the Cat

A few years ago, I worked with a friend's cat, Audrey. This beautiful cat formed part of a loving family. She was mature, and usually very friendly, yet kept to herself. She had her favourite spots around the house, and was living out her life in a gentle way.

However, one day this suddenly changed. Audrey became quite aggressive towards people, something she would otherwise never do. In particular, she showed aggression towards one member of the household. They couldn't figure out what was going on with her, and asked if I could help.

I connected with Audrey, and my, what a fussy eater she is! The main issue though, was that one particular family member was drinking alcohol at night, and she didn't relate to that very well. She didn't feel that it was good for that person, because it had a negative effect on them. Being aggressive was her way of letting them know, "I don't like what you are doing, it's not good for you, you need to stop this."

The family member listened to Audrey's request and Audrey returned to her normal self once the drinking eased.

Rami, the Cat with the Keyboard Fetish

Rami was an eight-year-old cat who lived for cuddles and belly rubs. His normally docile behaviour changed over the course of a few weeks, when he began sitting on his guardian's computer keyboard. If she moved him, he would either jump straight back up, or turn and bite her. This was very uncharacteristic behaviour for him.

Rami's guardian, Mem, tried all the tricks in the book to distract him, but he insisted on sitting on the keyboard or pushing it off the desk.

As Mem worked from home, it was important to her that Rami's behaviour stopped. At her wits' end, she called me for help.

Rami was finally able to explain that the work Mem was doing was actually not suited to her, and she was doing herself a disservice by continuing. This was confusing and alarming for her, as she was working three different roles from home, and was uncertain which one he meant!

I was able to clarify this, and she began to pay attention to when Rami was particularly persistent (and annoying!)

Within a month, Mem reduced her workload significantly, and Rami returned to his usual docile, snuggly self. He still lets her know when she is being distracted from what he sees as her 'true work', but for the most part he picks a cushion near her desk and snores while she types.

This is yet another of my many examples of how our pets really do know what's best for us, and will do anything to try and let us know!

When you have a dog suffering anxiety, a cat who is shying away from humans, or a bird plucking feathers from their body, then we need to address this with and for our pet, and also look at ourselves and ask:

"What am I doing that might create this behaviour?"

"What is happening in our direct environment to create this behaviour?"

"What can we do to change that?"

Once we recognise this, and trust me, it's sometimes not easy to acknowledge, we can implement the right changes for ourselves and our animals.

Our animals are our guides, our teachers, and our mirrors. When we tune into them, we learn what we need to focus on to shift, expand and be more of who we are. They want us to be happy, fulfilled and at peace.

Connect Through Your Heart and Raise your Vibration

Communicating with animals allows us to share words, images, feelings, emotions, and colours with them. They will in turn share these titbits of information with you too.

The connection comes from a place of unconditional love via telepathy and intuition, once we have *permission* to connect with the animal. They too have boundaries!

We go through the steps to raise our vibration and get onto the same frequency as the animal. It's like tuning into a radio station; you keep turning the dial until you are at the desired number of the radio station, so that you can hear the music coming through. When we work with our energy to raise the vibration, it will tune into the frequency of the animal. Then the communication line is open.

Following are the steps to help you connect in a very practical way, and includes a beautiful meditation to connect with your inner self[14].

Are you ready?

In doing this exercise, you will raise your energetic vibration, and open you up to Universal love and energy, to be able to:

- let go, relax and trust
- connect with your heart and your inner self
- connect with your spirit guide(s)
- connect with whom you want to connect (both humans and animals)

I suggest you find a comfortable, private area, where you will not be interrupted and can take all the time you need. Have some water with you, as well as a pen and a notebook (or an audio recording device) so you can take notes of the conversation and experience.

1. Place your hand over your heart.
2. Close your eyes.
3. Breathe deeply into your heart, 5 breaths in, 5 breaths out.
4. Stay still for a moment after the last out-breath, allowing the energy to surge through your body.
5. Ground yourself, by visualising roots coming out of your feet, directly into the Earth.
6. Visualise yellow/golden light coming through your feet into your heart.
7. Visualise a green light circling around you, emanating directly from your heart, and white light coming from above, through your crown chakra (the top of your head) into your heart.
8. Think of a person or animal you love absolutely and unconditionally, and allow that feeling of love to enter your heart.
9. Send love to them and be in that energy for a while, so you become more familiar with how this feels.

---

[14] Self = Soul Eternal Love Flame

10. You are now raising your vibration.

11. As you have raised your vibration and you are ready, invite your pet to connect with you by visualising them in front of you.

12. Send them the green light from your heart and ask permission to connect. Tell them you come with love and wish to have a chat.

13. Once you have permission, you are on their frequency and the communication line is open, ask anything you want.

After the conversation, give thanks, and come back slowly. Feel yourself physically present, and open your eyes. Make your notes and drink lots of water to refresh yourself.

Congratulations! You have connected with your inner self and your pet! Well done.

There are so many layers to communicating with animals. Delving into the world of Spirit means we listen to our own intuition, and possibly our spirit guides, before we can effectively chat with animals.

Following the steps in this chapter is a wonderful place to start; keep practising!

I am thrilled that you are open to connecting with the animal kingdom, the spirit realms, and more importantly, helping yourself in a loving and compassionate way. I can't wait to hear some of your stories and experiences.

My wish is that you are inspired to move deeper into the world of spirit abilities with the help of the animals, for the benefit of yourself and everyone around you. That you feel empowered to follow your heart, and enter a world of animal wisdom, where you can also be their voice.

That you feel loved, knowing that when you tap into your heart and listen to your voice, you can live a life filled with joy, love and happiness.

I bring animal communication to the world with compassion, love and joy. To help others become skilled animal communicators and voices for the animals, so we can help them, ourselves, and others around us. I do this through one-to-one and group coaching programs. I warmly invite you to join so that together we can collaborate at a high vibrational level for us and the animals around us.

When we tune into Universal language, we can help humankind and the animals, from a place of unconditional love. We can all make a difference in the world for the animals, for ourselves and live connected, compassionate lives, together in joy, freedom, harmony and love.

"Thank you for taking the time to read and learn, and thank you for being a part of this! To download my free guide "Six steps to talk to your pet" go to: https://www.biancadereus.com/6steps/

Say 'hi' to your pet from me and stay connected with love & grace.

And so, it is.

Bianca de Reus

ABOUT THE AUTHOR

BIANCA DE REUS

BIANCA DE REUS is an inspiring, passionate and award winning soul coach and animal communicator, helping pet parents connect with their inner self, enabling them to align and live from a place of pure love, harmony, and joy.

Bianca is a warm, engaging, and inspirational speaker and a published author, spirit channel, intuitive mentor, and Reiki Master.

She is The Soul Connector™ and founder of Connecting Soul Beings® community, programs and podcast. In 2018 Bianca published her first book called: *Hello? Can you hear me?*

Originally from the Netherlands, Bianca lives her life in Australia with passion and enthusiasm. From the lessons learned during her life, she steps into her heart and is guided by her soul voice.

Bianca is a harmonious human being who enjoys her work, travel, photography, music, nature, and spending quality time with her wife, dogs, and family and friends.

Connect with Bianca here:

Website: https://www.biancadereus.com

Book a Clarity Call: https://biancadereus.as.me/alignmentclaritycall

LinkBio: https://lnk.bio/biancadereus

KATE GARDNER

THE COURAGE TO CLEANSE AND CONNECT

ALCHEMISING OUR INTUITION AND EROTIC INTELLIGENCE

*I*n this moment, I knew it would take all of my courage to cleanse, to connect to what I knew to be true – I could not, and I would not fall apart, my young children needed me. I had to get up and breathe life into all the things that gave us balance, rhythm and consistency. This was not going to take me hostage. In all honesty, I was doing a good job of it, myself, and I was my own worst enemy at present. I already knew this, I'd intuitively known for a while, I just didn't know how to stop the fully loaded freight train from spiralling out of control on route down the mountain - It felt like hell was pumping through my veins and I was burning from the inside out. All I wanted to do was slip away.

My life before children was very different. I spent most of my time outdoors in nature, although out of my body, to be honest. I had been living a life of disconnection and abuse through strenuous exercise, alcohol and social drugs. A shift worker in mining for 17 years, I held various roles in production, mine planning, emergency management, and later held a supervisory role. I thrived on high levels of stress. It's what I'd come to know well and known for most of my life. I was intuitively aware this had to change, and change it did, very rapidly.

Two months short of turning 39, I birthed our darling girl, Ruby T, and 15 months later our beautiful boy, Leroy B. I recall a whole new world began, I'd become used to the busyness of life, living on adrenaline, looking for the next quick dopamine hit, now I was to learn to access it from within. Like the land coming alive after drought, a life force was springing from me.

Weeks after Leroy turned one, my husband Danner was diagnosed with colorectal cancer. I intuitively knew and trusted that he would make it through, and with a lot of disruption to our lives, he did. The process of chemo, radiation and surgery was barbaric. Eventually, life returned to what would now become our new normal and only twelve months later we had news it had metastasized to his liver.

We chose not to return to the allopathic and western way of treatment and today we are both grateful we didn't. We dived deep into alternative healing which included various modalities of mind body medicine, weaving nature and elements to assist in cellular regeneration. Danner's journey opened a vault within me that has become my life's work and new levels of resilience and courage unfolded.

Here I was years down the track, ignoring my own screams within. You see all disease begins from unspoken emotions and disconnection from self and nature and I was doing both of these. I'd become a prisoner in my own body and life, lost in my own thoughts and darkness.

I'd lost my mojo and definitely my fire. What had happened to me? How did I end up here? Have you ever felt like this?

My hair had been falling out and my health was deteriorating. I'd been losing the capacity to hold and remember conversations. My deteriorating cognitive function and memory was now causing concern for my family. I had zero energy or excitement for anything. I couldn't continue to ignore all the signs, especially when my beautiful caring dad, a man of very few words, pulled me up one visit to ask how I was and with my usual reply, "I'm ok, I'm just tired". He gently grabbed my wrist, locked eyes with me and said, "Don't give me that bullsh*t. You're not well and you need help". The truth of his words resonated in every cell of my body, and still do as I write this today. Standing there, fully seen and witnessed, not wanting to feel the pain and enormity of what was to unfold. He was solid and always had been present in my life. My intuition spoke loudly in this moment and I knew it was time. I could no longer run and hide from myself, and looking back, in all honesty why would I? It was time, permission to trust and surrender within.

My dad and I always had a special relationship, and growing up on the land, my soul was free. It's where magic happened. Truth be known, I had always flourished in nature and wide-open spaces, breathing in her beauty since I was a small child. I was craving to be back in her arms, back to what I knew was home. I knew from this place my soul would sing, it was time to cleanse and reclaim my life and my body.

I remember the doctors wanting to do a heap of tests and I had already done a handful. I swore I was not getting on that merry-go-round. I had experienced this with my husband's cancer journey and took this as my wakeup call. His journey with cancer definitely took me to the edge twice. It was a catalyst which allowed me to grow and expand. I will be forever grateful to him for this and our wonderful children, it was now time to find my way home. I had fallen prey to the busyness of life and that of my business, forgetting me and the stillness I once knew within. Moving away from the country and off the land had brought me into a faster paced energy, and I could no longer keep up.

After Danner's cancer journey, we had decided to leave our beautiful country home in Queensland and moved over 3000km back to our family in South Australia. Having lived away for 24 years, both overseas and in remote places, I now found myself back home on the Fleurieu Peninsula south of Adelaide. It is here we opened a colon hydrotherapy business, which largely contributed to saving Danner's life through cancer, and ultimately mine in the aftermath. We had a dream (and no business plan, might I add) of creating change in the world. It felt strange returning. I found everything to be super, super busy, including my mind and body. This is where I was to learn and experience and embody stillness and calm in the chaos. It was from this place that I would discover true connection to self. I couldn't fold now, although to be honest at times I really wanted to turn out the lights.

I trusted myself and knew that my intuition would guide me. Life brings magic and miracles if we listen. I believe we are always gifted with what we need, not necessarily what we want. So accepting this, I leant into learning unconditional self-belief and worth, self care, self love, emotional expression, expansion and awareness, and that of community and social support.

It was like a magnet was pulling me along, and with my intuition gaining strength I knew I needed to connect back with nature, to live with her in everything I did. I had to be a part of her and her a part of me. This took me on a beautiful deep journey of meeting the plant spirit kingdom and many other magical kingdoms would come. A huge lesson in learning the true meaning of the "art of giving and receiving". The spirits began to weave into my world and I was meeting my own wonderland.

The Healing Begins

The courage to lean in, to look within and be brave enough to meet the landscapes of the soulful warrior, was going to take all the strength I could muster. Despite being tired, exhausted, and burnt out, I honoured my path, lived fearlessly and claimed my uniqueness through multidimensional cleansing. Allowing my mind and body to rest, my heart to connect and my soul to align, I began to let go of attachment and expectations, and I started reclaiming and creating spaciousness.

When we are able to identify our programming and beliefs we can then begin to shift our perception and create our own reality, consciously choosing how we respond not react and from this place we live intuitively. Just like Mother Nature - in flow.

I immersed myself into healing, replenishing my body with the therapeutic use of herbs, bringing balance. Allowing this would engage the heart, soul and spirit, supporting me to nourish my body. I returned to both my inner and outer ecology, and from this into a deeper communion and connection, each creating communication through light, sound and vibration. Plants have the capacity to raise consciousness where true healing can take place, and offer us a guide to our spiritual growth and evolution. I had not known this before, this place of what I would come to know as my sacred temple and ultimately reclaim my life force, and my freedom.

As my healing journey unfolded, I found myself studying a diverse range of indigenous and ancient shamanic practises with renowned teachers and mentors, culminating in the art of feminine embodiment. Learning and having the capacity to trust yourself, to be in touch with your own body, implement healthy boundaries, know your values and know your pleasure potential allows for diving deeper into feeling and meeting your sexual energy and erotic intelligence. This is a game changer. It brought orgasmic bliss into my everyday world of whole food plants, nature, flowers, anointing, and so much more. It was meeting my own inner divine feminine and masculine in this space that was ultimately life-changing for me and allowed me to set healthy boundaries. The effect was very wide reaching, and the way I go about my life now is so far from where I was that day. Not only have I flourished, so has my business.

I am not and will not ever be the wounded healer

I am a self-governed, self-empowered, intuitive, wild-hearted mother, daughter, sister and feminine leader, who leads and supports others to naturally nourish and flourish, upgrade and embody radical feminine self-love and care. I teach embodiment for a new and intuitive high-vibe way of living, growing and evolving. I support clients to reconnect to nature's elements and to their souls path, through meeting their erotic intelligence and awakening and enhancing intuition through nutrition. I educate on the art of cleansing and the art of arousal, amplifying our intuition and influence in the world. We are vessels for feeling, being seen, being heard and being understood. Real raw expression allows us to be all that we are created to be, I now make no apologies for who I am.

Meeting my spirit allies and my erotic intellignence was a huge part of my healing journey which allowed me to unearth parts of my intuition and deep trust of self to heal, connecting and weaving this back to nature's cycle and our elements heightened my intuition and my ability to trust even deeper.

By cleansing and detoxing across multi-dimensional landscapes which we have both in our inner world and outer worlds, we connect to core inner radiance. Incorporating and embracing the elements of life - air, fire, water and earth, we cultivate trust to know our deep inner wisdom. From this deep place of being, we know what is true for us - that our soul dances and our resilience meets our own magnificence and blueprint, opening to unlimited potential. It is here that we create and manifest our miracles, it's a place beyond our human comprehension, but accessible to our consciousness in meditation.

From a sacred place that we have often never met until we need to meet it, where there is nothing left to do but surrender into the void, the knowing we access from here is to let yourself drop into intuitively living every moment. Allowing every breath to take away the human attachment and expectation of getting it right or being enough. From this place we live with moments of pure joy and abundance.

Health is our greatest asset, it is our well-th, because our body is our temple. It is so important to know and care for all parts of self. Ultimately the four basic processes in our bodies are digestion, absorption, utilisation, and elimination. This can be applied across all areas in life, relationships, finances, business etc.

How do we digest life?

How do we absorb the information, utilise what we receive and eliminate, cleanse or release that which isn't serving us? Like our bodies, it's important to notice how we digest life. When we become a clear channel / vessel, our intuition is able to be at a greater capacity. Nutrition and environments support our intuition and enable us to enhance our light from within. Our energy anatomy is multidimensional and it functions on many different levels.

The conversations will never be enough – you must find the peace from within – the answers will not be found on the external. You are your greatest guide, allowing a multi dimensional cleanse and detox to create a connection that you have never known will be the greatest gift and your ultimate freedom. A multi-dimensional detox works with clearing toxicity emotionally, psychologically, physically, energetically and spiritually, incorporating all worlds which opens up opportunities to receive divine guidance from the other realms and kingdoms.

We are miracles living in human form

We are able to facilitate complete cellular regeneration. When we connect back to self, we connect to God/ source/ divine and all the living and ascended, from this place is the purest form of healing power available. The first step to reach this place is stillness, which relaxes and restores our nervous system. When we drop into our breath the parasympathetic system will come in and the body will drop into homeostasis. Intuition is heightened from this place of health. Never shy away from yourself. When we begin to see ourselves, in the light and dark we embrace our wholeness. It is safe to be you, don't be afraid to change the story that you have been in. You are worthy, loveable and enough. Changing your story will for sure change your life. Trust the journey home.

Upon waking, take a moment to drop into and notice your thoughts and how your body is feeling, let it speak through feeling - finding stillness, notice the scents that are around you, the sounds of birds, wind, water and those within, letting your thoughts go as you tune into the felt sensations on your skin, the way nature is presenting to you, how do you present to her?

The more we eliminate the toxins and noise from our mind, body, relationships and environments the easier it is to connect. I regularly have clients who say they are numb and yet when we take them on a journey and facilitate multidimensional cellular cleansing and regeneration the life force and connection that returns is life giving. Hydrating our cells is imperative for wellbeing on a daily basis, kicking off with lemon water is a great way to start the day. Melons and berries are great to support the body to hydrate and cleanse too. Daily and regular bowel movements are imperative for optimum health, well-being and vitality. Supporting the lymphatic system is also important as it's the body's sewer system. Just as we eliminate our waste, the cells eliminate their waste into the lymphatic system. Moving our lymphatic system is vital to assist our body to detoxify. Sweating is another way and the skin is the largest eliminative organ, also known as the third kidney.

How do you do this?

Do I really have to go through this journey of pain and destruction? NO you do not. Generally most of us will, as this is where we experience our shero's/hero's journey. This is why I feel so grateful to share with you what I have learnt from my journey.

I know that my journey has brought many gifts:

One of them was finding my way home through multidimensional cellular care and cleansing, connecting and accessing spirit and that of my erotic intelligence. Another was igniting a fire from deep within the inner landscapes of beyond time and space, and releasing attachment to those I love the most. Another was accessing a deeper love for all, letting go of what I had previously known life to be, and following that deep inner knowing of what I knew to be true for me. I also learnt to trust the energy and guidance all around me every day, as well as accessing and being in partnership with spirits.

With all these gifts, I was not only able to reconnect and light up my lifeforce energy, it also lit up my sexual energy and increased my libido. As a result, my spirit and soul energy became alive again, awake to breathe the magic and joy of each moment, yet this time it was different. This time it was an embodied experience from the well of plenty, from the well-ness that was flowing from within, a place I had not known prior to this and at this depth.

Whole, healthy and like a beautiful piece of art, I was able to let go and surrender into the beauty of what the cleanse was allowing me to experience, dismantling my programs and beliefs. You see I had changed. I had grown and evolved, although I was still trying to fit into someone that no longer fitted me.

The birth of our children and Danner's cancer journey radically changed me. They allowed me to find my way within – from this place I was home, I was free, I embodied my intuitive self and with that, intuitive living became a part of my everyday life. I began to flourish and embody my radiance from within, which I now share with the world. The courage to cleanse and connect deeply is a gift every human deserves to experience. It is from this place I became a 'know thyself' specialist, knowing it is from this place of be-ing you find home.

YES YOU CAN HAVE THIS TOO, I am no different than you. What you see in me lives within you.

ABOUT THE AUTHOR

KATE GARDNER

Kate Gardner is an Adelaide based Wellness leader who is a powerful and compassionate modern-day medicine woman, healer, educator, transformational guide, and a sacred soul mentor.

With strong feminine leadership skills, Kate inspires women and others to become more enlivened, fully connected and expressed in their inner ecology, radiance, and femininity. She believes that by tuning into ancient healing wisdom, we will discover contemporary ways to heal ourselves, our families, and our planet.

After the birth of her children and her husband's multiple cancers a decade ago, Kate was confronted with her own spirituality and health journey. As a result, she became a certified therapeutic Colon Hydrotherapist, ISOD Detox Specialist, Integrative Nutrition Health Coach, along with other alternative healing modalities.

Kate has completed a rigorous 500+ hours training and mentorship with Shamanic Energy Training® to be certified as a Sacred Space Weaver and Spirit Weaver Practitioner Training + on-going mentoring with Sharon Bolt. She also completed an internationally recognised 500-hour professional women's holistic sexuality and feminine embodiment training which certifies and insures her as a Fembodiment Method™ facilitator.

Connect with Kate here:

Website: www.kategardner.com.au

Freebie: 7 Healthy Habits for Raw Radiance

Socials: https://linktr.ee/radicalrawradiance

JOANNE MAKAS

EMBODIED AWARENESS

BECOME THE CREATOR OF YOUR LIFE

*I*t is freezing cold. Bright. I am shivering. Alone, but not afraid. I slowly start to become more aware of my surroundings. Remembering, with haziness, that I am waking up from an operation. I start to feel the heavy warm blankets on me, weighing me down, preventing movement. I feel as though I'm tucked into a strait-jacket, but I can wiggle my toes. I don't want to move because my head feels dense and groggy. This post-operating room is like a freezer. Sterile. I can taste gas in my throat and smell cleaning solution. I want to sleep but this shivering is out of control. It's too hard to keep my eye open so I close it and focus on the warmth of my breath in my nostrils. It feels familiar and comforting. Soft. I can barely hear my breath, but it is there. Reminding me that I am alive. I am awake. I have survived.

This is not the first time I have been here. I have had a few operations and even though I am only seven I know this is a few too many. I start to hum and feel the vibration caressing my heart and soothing my heaving chest. I visualise and feel a golden light flowing with my breath through my body. Warming me up. Relaxing my trembling limbs. Eventually the shivering stops and I fall asleep.

Trauma, stress, undigested emotions, anxiety, memories and experiences are all held in the body. Fortunately, the body knows how to release them through movement, sound and breath. Something my body intuitively knew how to do at that young age. The body will naturally want to tremble and shake, cry and scream as a release mechanism. If we don't let this happen the sensation will remain trapped and frozen in our nervous system.

This chapter is about feeling, trusting, and cultivating an embodied awareness of our feelings, so our bodies don't hold onto past traumas.

Why is this important?

Because feelings are the language of the body and when unprocessed sensation and experience are held in the body we become numb and disconnected, making it difficult to connect to our intuition.

Through a weaving of science, alchemy, and creativity I reveal how the equilibrium of the nervous system is interconnected with our innate essence, the intrinsic creative nature within us.

This chapter is about how an awareness of your deepest, most intuitive and embodied self anchors you into the safety of your body so that you can become the creator of your life.

The Felt Senses

So, what got me onto that operating table? I was born with a birthmark on my right eye and as a result have monocular vision. This means that my depth perception, or the ability to judge spatial distance from one object to another is impaired. Colour, light and shadow, brightness and texture, are vital for how I judge depth. I believe this way of navigating the world heightened my external and internal felt senses. I developed deep awareness and intuitive focus, leading me to work in the creative industry all my adult life.

In my twenties and thirties I worked in the fashion industry. As I started getting more experience, production was where I found my niche and by thirty-two I was the production manager for Australian label Zimmermann. I was in an innovative and inspiring environment and found my role to be extremely creative and fulfilling. After a few years of leadership and management I began to crave the tactile and sensory act of making with my hands. A deep intuitive creative longing was bubbling away, and at thirty-seven, without an agenda, I nervously left the world of fashion.

Have you felt that deep intuitive feeling of melancholy? How does it feel? Where do you feel it? It is a feeling of fragmentation for me. A disconnect between my womb and my heart. The space between stares back like a shattered mirror. That was me when I turned forty. The same year I began my degree in fine art, majoring in painting. I was feeding my creativity, which meant my intuitive awareness could thrive. Encompassing colour, texture and surface, my art practice emerged. Traversing memory, place and experience, my work is about how we perceive, how we see and how we feel. It is about all the fragments of life interconnecting and becoming whole.

Most of my childhood memories are of reconstructive surgery and being in and out of hospital. But I also have colourful memories of my upbringing. I grew up in suburban Sydney with Greek migrant parents. I remember running around in the garden with my two sisters doing cartwheels and handstands. I can smell the lemon tree, feel the smouldering Australian summer heat, the sun kissing my skin and the water from the sprinkler cooling us down. The sky is bright, expansive and limitless, evoking these emotions, thoughts and feelings. I feel alive, full of vitality, connected to my body, to my sisters and to nature. I can smell the food Mum is cooking and my tummy rumbles, eager to eat her delicious dinner.

My mother loves to cook, and she gracefully surrenders her creative flair into this passion. We eat colour. My favourite is a Greek dish of vegetables cooked in the oven. Warm and nourishing, soothing the tummy and the soul. Simple yet sumptuous. We eat this with BBQ lamb cutlets, drizzled with oil, oregano and lemon. Sour, pungent, sweet and salty, caressing my taste buds, warming my body and filling my heart with love and joy.

Creativity is how I sense the world. My mother showed me that we are born to create through providing, beautifying, and connecting. You may not consider yourself artistic or creative, but creativity is everywhere and everything. We inherently have so much creativity within us. It is the way we live everyday life and it can appear in the most unassuming ways. The way you dress, how you decorate your home or office, what you cook, how you plan your holidays, your to-do list, or how you solve problems in your own unique way. The way you learn or heal in an embodied way intricately connects you to your creative life force.

Sometimes my creative life force is overshadowed by external consumption. This desire for stuff emerges from deep feelings of not belonging. I try to fix my melancholy by accumulating things. It is a pattern I fall into when I don't feel safe or secure. Through consciously returning to my internal creativeness, I feel grounded and connected to myself, to others and to the universe, and stop relying on those material things to fill the gap. I'm sure you know the feeling.

Creative Life Force

What got me past my trauma, past my coping mechanisms? What gets us all through it? My creative life force that I was intuitively connected to as a young girl gave me a uniquely sensitive way of rendering the world. Seeing beauty in everything, I cultivated the ability to experience life with subtle awareness. But, as I grew older I became disembodied due to the multitude of operations I underwent. Some operations were very much needed and others I believe were not. My parents desperately wanted to help me. They wanted me to have a happy and somewhat normal life. My birthmark became *the problem to be fixed*. This made me feel unworthy, resulting in numbness and a frozen nervous system.

Have you experienced a situation where the need to "fix yourself" is seen as the solution? Chances are the answer is yes because these days, social media is feeding this more than ever. Research continues to reveal the negative impact of social media on our mental health. Women and girls in particular feel that their bodies are not good enough as people add filters and edit their pictures to look "perfect." We see women being mothers, lovers and career women, while at the same time living a life of luxury and ease. So many of the grids are highly curated, showcasing a glamourous life.

I have fallen into the trap of following the same "type" of feed, creating a narrow worldview and making me feel "not good enough." Obsessed with perfection, I never celebrated my achievements and only focused on what I still needed to accomplish. Focused on all the things I needed to fix in my life.

Before Instagram, it was fashion, lifestyle and wellbeing magazines, movies and TV that made us feel 'less than'. As a young mum with many dreams of a successful life I worked hard, exercised excessively and tried to be the perfect wife. In my twenties and thirties I became more disconnected from my body and my intuition. I subconsciously was internalizing the impossibly high standards of physical fitness, beauty and sexual expression, falling prey to the Superwoman Syndrome.

Can you feel the pressure of juggling family, career and the general demands of life? Quickly fixing, doing and making sure that life is running smoothly for everyone else? The go-to person for support and help? Writing this, my chest is tightening up and I am clenching my jaw. I can feel my breath shorten and my heart beating fast. My leg is starting to shake. I don't feel great. A subtle reminder of how stress lives in our body and can be activated through thoughts. I intuitively stop writing and accept the energy of this stress, allowing my body to shake it out.

A *problem-fixing* attitude is inherently disempowering, contributing to a state of disassociation that many of us feel. I never realised how I was operating within this belief system until recently. In 2014 at the age of forty-five I was diagnosed with Spinocerebellar Ataxia Type 7, an inherited disease of the central nervous system that leads to neural degeneration. Initially, I ignored the changes my body was going through due to the condition and did not slow down. Four years later I was suffering from chronic fatigue and burnout. Oblivious to the perimenopausal symptoms that had started to appear, I accused my body of letting me down. I felt disempowered and angry. My passion for art was diminishing. My creative life force was burning down like a candle. It had almost blown out.

Watching my father, who also has the condition, slowly degenerate and become completely dependent on others for his daily existence was overwhelming. My initial reaction was to fix my burnout and fix my body so that I could continue to support everyone else. My identity and feelings of self-worth were deeply rooted in the ability to rescue. Who would I be if I wasn't this person? What would my life look like in ten or twenty years? Imagining myself with a walking stick at 60 instead of hiking with my husband felt surreal.

We are part of an interconnected web made up of all the relations around us, and healing modalities are often passed down through these relationships. Through my husband I found a positive way to move forward. Manuel has an autoimmune condition that led him to the Wim Hof Method, which includes breathwork, cold exposure and mindset. Inspired by Manuel I decided to commit daily to this method, to help me understand my ataxic perimenopausal body. I was learning how the autonomic nervous system, the brain and the body function, and how they are all connected. The interconnection of the universe, living beings and matter was something I was exploring in my art practice, yet I didn't think of applying this lens to myself.

Until now, I had put so much emphasis on feeling good and being in the parasympathetic state that I missed the importance of the sympathetic branch of the nervous system. The one that initiates the fight-or-flight response and is needed for going into inspired action. I was starting to understand how the two branches of the autonomic nervous system are equally important.

We are so busy labelling things that we get pulled away from the complexity and truth of nature and listening to our biology. This labelling of 'bad' and 'good' pushed me into thinking that I needed to be relaxed to feel better. I stayed in that state for too long which made it difficult to become motivated and productive. The ability to flexibly move between states is imperative for our optimal functioning. This flow between states is a sign of well-being and resilience.

This newfound knowledge and experience helped me with the chronic fatigue brought on by the Ataxia. I enrolled into Shakti School, in 2018, to study Feminine Form Ayurveda and learn a holistic feminine approach to healing and looking after my body. My masculine energy of *fixing* was starting to melt like a large cube of ice left on the kitchen bench. Slowly, the liquid spreads out, taking form, shape shifting and changing direction without warning. My learning was like this slow watery liquid, contained and then flowing out into the world.

My creative life force was re-ignited and I felt the urge to paint again. The teachings opened me up to elemental alchemy, the energetics of the moon phases, the intricacies of the female body and her reproductive system, hormonal health, food as medicine, herbalism and so much more. I felt deeply nourished and nurtured in this interconnected world of ancient wisdom and modern science.

But most importantly Shakti School gently guided me back to my spirituality. This internal deepening sparked memories of my grandmother (or Yiayia, as I called her) and the Greek cultural traditions embedded in my DNA, in my cells, and in my blood. Yiayia taught me how to be with myself. How to feel safe within myself. It was not what she said, but what she did. She was comfortable in her skin and she was able to be herself. I continue to carry her essence within me.

I am once again that skinny awkward seven year old, in recovery now after my operation. I feel Yiayia's large, warm body next to mine. Hand gently resting on my thigh, ready to tap me if I fidget too much, or lovingly caress me if I stay quiet. I feel content and happy, but also bored. I quickly look around to see if I can escape. I try to get up, but she grabs my leg and shakes her head. Not now.

At least we are sitting at the front and I can see everything. This church is so majestic. The opulence of the paintings, the artifacts and the priest's robes are so enchanting. The sounds and the smells are intoxicating. I close my eyes and start to feel warm sensations move through my body. Yiayia and I are breathing together. Slow inhale and slow exhale together. Count of five in and a count of five out. How does she keep this rhythm going while saying her prayers? I stop counting and start dreaming. Playing in a magnificently green forest. Swimming in a crisp flowing river. Sleeping on luscious soft grass. Moon bathing.

Yiayia taps me. The service is over.

Embodied Awareness

I no longer feel I need to fix myself, or anyone else for that matter. My journey to this point has given me the courage to look deeper within and past the ataxia. Embodiment practices have become integral to staying deeply anchored in my body, with the intention to ensure my nervous system is balanced, flexible and resilient. As I enter my wise woman phase I remember my grandmother and the ancestral lineage of creative, intuitive women who reside within me. With this knowing, my desire is to help guide women back to the wisdom of their body.

Awareness is one of the embodiment gateways to bring you into your feeling body. *Embodied Awareness* is having consciousness of all your bodies: physical, emotional, energetic, spiritual, and mind. It is a way back home to your essence. From this place you can make choices to shift patterns and bring your body, mind and soul into equilibrium. For me, embodied awareness is what many artists call being "in the zone". It is when I am deeply absorbed while painting or drawing. It is a dance between focus and relaxation, when mark making becomes gracefully effortless. Once I enter a thinking and critiquing mindset, I am no longer engaging with embodied awareness.

A way to develop embodied awareness is through the practice of noticing and naming:

Check in right now as you are reading this. How are the muscles in your face? Your shoulders? Your neck? Your collarbone? Close your eyes and focus your attention where there may be some frozen tension. Does it have a texture? A taste? Take your time with this. What is its quality? Name this sensation. Is it fuzzy or brooding? Cold or hot? Slimy or opaque? Don't analyse it too much. Keep feeling the feeling.

You may want to softly breathe into it. Hum to it. Tell this frozen tension that you love it, feel it, acknowledge its pain. Sigh with it. Allowing this tension to relax and feel safe.

When expressing focus and relaxation simultaneously, we meet experience more fully. Once you can trust being in your body and being aware of your shifting thoughts, feelings and sensations you encounter a positive feedback loop that you can integrate to become the creator of your life.

This is the gift of Embodied Awareness.

ABOUT THE AUTHOR

JOANNE MAKAS

JOANNE MAKAS is a visual artist, mindset mentor, feminine embodiment coach, and sound healer. As a modern mystic, she is a passionate space holder for soul-centred visionary women who align with her mission to consciously create life so they can live with courage, calm and clarity.

Through a combination of creative practices, the alchemy of breath, sound, and self-care rituals, Joanne's desire is that all humans are connected to their intrinsic creative nature, feel safe in their body, and expand into their most authentic self.

Joanne holds a certificate as an Ayurvedic Wellness Coach, Feminine Embodiment Coach and Facilitator, Sound Healer and Modern Mystic. With 30 years in the creative field, across fashion, colour design, and visual art, Joanne has a Master of Fine Art from National Art School, Sydney and was the managing director and program producer at STACKS Projects, 2015-2020. She has exhibited at Articulate project space, George Paton Gallery Melbourne, Artereal Gallery, Floating Goose Gallery Adelaide. Joanne has been an artist-in-residence at Packsaddle, New England Regional Art Museum (NERAM) Armidale, and École Supérieure des Beaux-Arts (ESBAMA), Montpellier, France.

Born in Australia, Joanne lives on Bidjigal Country in Sydney's East with her husband and cavoodle. Having adult children, she can spend four months of the year living in her family home in Athens.

Connect with Joanne here

Website: Joanne Makas

Free Video: Embodied Awareness Practice

Socials: Joanne Makas | Linktree

ABOUT HILLE HOUSE PUBLISHING

KRYSTAL HILLE founded Hille House Publishing in early 2021 in answer to the call of collaborating with thought leaders so that collectively, we can bring human consciousness to a tipping point of personal power and sovereignty.

With this third anthology, we have now helped over 60 thought leaders become international bestselling authors to share their stories and expertise and position themselves as leading experts on a global stage.

We will continue producing books that awaken, inspire and empower humanity into deeper sovereignty and connection and applications for our next book, *Inspired Living*, are now open.

Krystal is also a Soul Leadership Coach, Embodiment Teacher. She helps change makers and conscious creatives to step into their zone of flow and discover the essence of soulful leadership so their passion can ignite global change.

With 30 years in leadership, a background in theatre directing and female empowerment, Krystal is a multiple international #1 bestselling author, winner of the CREA Brainz Global Business Award 2021 and host of the Soul Leadership Podcast.

Aware of her multidimensional self, pre-Covid, Krystal facilitated spiritual retreats to Egypt and ran the Temple Nights across Australia.

She holds a BA in English Literature & Theatre Studies, a diploma in Life Coaching and TimeLine Therapy and is a certified Tantra Teacher and Reiki Master. She is a popular contributor to international festivals, summits and podcasts and has written two solo books and contributed to a further four anthologies.

Originally from Germany, Krystal lives with her two children in county Victoria, Australia.

If you would like to join future multi-author books or write your solo book through Hille House Publishing, connect with Krystal here:

Website: https://krystalhille.com

Email: krystal@krystalhille.com

Socials and more: https://linktr.ee/krystalhille

Made in the USA
Las Vegas, NV
26 July 2023